AN INDIAN AFFAIR

COTTONS SUCH AS THIS PAINTED PALAMPORE
REVOLUTIONISED WESTERN FASHION AND KEPT EUROPEAN
TRADERS COMING BACK FOR MORE.

First published 2001 by Channel 4 Books
an imprint of Pan Macmillan Ltd
Pan Macmillan, 20 New Wharf Road,
London, N1 9RR
Basingstoke and Oxford
Associated companies throughout the world
www.panmacmillan.com

ISBN 07522 6160 6

1 3 5 7 9 8 6 4 2

A CIP catalogue record for this book is
available from
the British Library.

Designed by Jane Coney

Printed and bound in Italy by New Interlitho

This book accompanies the television series
An Indian Affair made by
Takeaway Media for Channel 4

TAKEAWAY MEDIA

An
Indian
Affair

ARCHIE BARON

DEDICATION

TO MONICA, HANNAH AND ELLA

Contents

INTRODUCTION

Deep in the humbling vastness of the Indian countryside, you are liable to stumble across a crumbling building that seems to have been incongruously transplanted there from Cheltenham. You'll do a similar double-take whenever you encounter a marooned gothic church, a set of bagpipes in the expert hands of a spruce bandsman, or even a purple-wrapped bar of Cadbury's Dairy Milk on a tiny stall a day's walk from the nearest road. Regardless of how prepared you are by history for these sights, they may well affect you more than any number of books, films or family stories touching in their various ways on the extraordinary love–hate relationship of Britain and India. Perhaps that is because they all dramatically beg the same basic question, the question at the heart of this book: how did Britain, a small island in the north Atlantic, leave such a mark on India, a subcontinent of Asia as large and varied as Europe, home to over a billion people, professing many faiths and speaking something like 700 different languages?

RURAL INDIA SCARCELY NOTICES THE STRANDED REMAINS OF BRITISH DOMINATION. A WATER-CARRIER IN FRONT OF THE FORMER BRITISH RESIDENCY IN SRIRANGAPATNAM.

Most people think they know the answer: the Raj. The images immediately come flooding in: an atlas with vast swathes of the Earth's surface tinted the imperial pink; Victoria, the Queen Empress, thrilled at a distance with India, her Jewel in the Crown; armies brilliantly but brutally scything down their foes; a punkah-wallah with a cord looped round his big toe fanning the stuffed shirts passing the port in the dining-room; Gandhi and Mountbatten, an unlikely couple, one near naked, the other with medals running halfway across his chest, ending the anachronism of Empire but not its aftershock for the people of India.

Yet the Raj did not even officially start until 1858, when the British Crown and State first acquired formal sovereignty over much of India. By then Britain and India had been closely involved together for 250 years, for most of that time in ways that bear no relation to the imperial clichés. Nevertheless, these clichés have taken root with such force on both sides of the globe that the extraordinary prism of the Raj has largely distorted popular perceptions of the British–Indian story. In particular, whatever their personal feelings about the Raj, most Britons and Indians have tended to look at history backwards. It is all too easy to assume that what happened, happened with intent; that conquest, colonization, domination and racism, roads, railways, law courts and churches were all part of the project; that there was one broad road to the Raj.

The hope here is to focus on the pre-Raj era, to expose some myths and to tell a rather different story. At this distance we can map out a road, albeit one poorly marked, full of twists and turns, blind alleys and steep inclines. But nobody setting off on this road knew they were on one, let alone where it was going. Most Britons in India had a sense of purpose, but for most of the time this had little to do with Empire. Those Indians who met Britons along the road saw they were strangers. But the subcontinent was an ancient and advanced civilization accustomed to strangers and inclined to absorb them with confidence and tolerance. For most of the time, most of the people would not have regarded the British as enemies or even threats.

There was an empire in India in the eighteenth century, but it was not British. Most of India still owed official allegiance to the Mughal Empire whose Emperor sat in Delhi. But in practice this meant next to nothing, since the Mughals had lost most of their effective power early in the century. Instead India was a complex patchwork of successor states and principalities, many of them up for grabs. There were few fixed borders or well-entrenched dynasties. Regional and local power switched with bewildering rapidity as a result of frequent wars, coup d'états, alliances and deals. Many of the new rulers were almost as foreign to the populations they taxed as the British, French or other European traders and adventurers on the Indian scene.

The heart of this story is the heyday of the East India Company, the remarkable private corporation that traded with and then – almost despite itself – came to rule most of India, a full hundred years before Victoria claimed it as her own. The Company's directors were hardly being immodest when they described themselves as 'the Grandest Society of Merchants in the Universe'. At its height, this multinational had cornered half the world's international trade and had a commercial presence not just in India but in virtually every entrepôt and port in Asia, from Canton to Singapore, the Philippines to Burma. Their business was business, not empire. But in the turbulent arena of eighteenth-century India, just like in post-Soviet Russia or post-colonial Africa, business was not conducted in suits. To protect your business, you needed to keep ahead of the competition and keep an eye on local politics. You needed guards, just in case… Temptation or necessity sometimes turned the guards into fighting soldiers, which put up your costs, which meant you needed to increase your income, which you could only do by renting out your army, carving a bigger slice of the market or diversifying into the tax-setting business (a.k.a. ruling). But you genuinely did not want to do any of this. What you really, really wanted was quiet trade.

And while you were doing that, you did what all ex-pat businessmen tend to do: you relaxed a little and tried to make yourself comfortable. For some that meant sticking to the ex-pat bars and dreaming of Surrey over yet one more drink. But for many that meant genuinely getting to grips with the local culture, the local people, the local women. You were as likely to shed prejudice as to gain it. You might even have kids, put down roots and think of it as home. Meanwhile, your Indian neighbours would have little reason to resent your presence. Some of them were friends and lovers. Others were business partners, clients or suppliers. You were all in this together.

This original fusion culture when Britain met India has been all but forgotten because it was deliberately erased by what came afterwards, the self-satisfied Victorian rigidity of the Raj. What follows is the story of how Britain and India were, and might well have remained, had not this mutual exploration helped to arouse a conservative backlash that ushered in an age of reciprocal incomprehension, contempt and something like apartheid.

Books need heroes and villains — even though history is of course right to conclude that it isn't that simple. The hero of this book, warts and all, is Warren Hastings, the East India Company's Governor-General in India for more than a decade in the 1770s and 80s. Hastings is usually cast as such a villain that a 1995 BBC radio programme nominated him the sleaziest Brit of all time. Its mistake was to swallow whole the prosecution case in 'the trial of the century', Warren Hastings's seven-year impeachment by the British Parliament. As we'll see, Hastings should rather be remembered for being chief patron to an extraordinary period of enthusiasm for India, far removed from any blueprint to impose British values on a civilization that he grew to love.

As for villains, there are candidates aplenty. Certainly not Tipu Sultan, the Tiger King of Mysore, who was shoe-horned by the British into that role as they finally set their minds on empire. To the British public, Tipu became the original 'black bogeyman'. His main sin seems to have been to come closest to standing up to the British. Robert Clive – 'Clive of India' as he came to be known – looms large on any short-list of villains. He was undeniably a rogue, but then so was almost everyone he came up against. In such circumstances, villainy can be almost attractive, particularly when it pays off against the odds. Yet as we'll see, for all his schemes and escapades, imperialists and Indian nationalists alike give him far too much credit for launching the empire on the battlefield of Plassey. A better candidate for bad guy is Richard Wellesley, elder brother of the Duke of Wellington. At the turn of the nineteenth century, Wellesley was the one who decided to conquer India as quickly as possible, mainly because he thought that would look good on his resumé. Wellesley, though,

would probably blame Napoleon. And though it's typically British to blame the French, perhaps he's got a point. Without Napoleon, there might well never have been a Raj.

The fallout from the Raj is such that, more than fifty years after independence, it still crops up from time to time, both in Britain and India. When it does there is usually a debate, in some form or other, between the apologists and the apologizers. Whatever its ills, the apologists argue, the Raj was a stupendous achievement and left India the world's largest democracy, its citizens protected by the rule of law and united by the English language. At this point it is customary for them to mention the awesome Indian railway network, the roads, irrigation and bridges, and to highlight the selfless and able administrators of the Indian Civil Service who put their all, and often gave their lives, into making India a better place. India, the apologists conclude, would have been a lot worse off without the British Empire, whether left to its own devices or fallen into the clutches of another imperial power. It should be grateful.

The apologizers reply that nothing can excuse the subjugation of millions of people, the repeated instances of abominable treatment, the constant culture of racial disdain, the exploitation of a land whose economy was skewed towards imperial wants rather than local needs. The real legacy of the Raj, the apologizers maintain as they hit their stride, was Partition, the bloody dismemberment of ancient, multi-faith Hindostan into India and Pakistan, a tragic consequence of Britain's divide-and-rule tactics. This left India an artificially divided nation, which was also hopelessly stratified, obsessed with hierarchy and ground down by bureaucracy, still trying to shed its in-built inferiority complex, the consequence of centuries of servility and abuse. Forget gratitude. India's owed a very big apology.

In a sense this debate is sterile. Partly it's sustained by myths bound up with the Raj but actually untrue. But more importantly, by pushing the focus back we might move the discussion on.

For a start, Britain didn't civilize India. It was civilized long before the Company arrived there. What British traders and adventurers discovered in India was that it was in many ways a richer and more sophisticated land than their own. That's why they kept on coming back. Secondly, it is entirely wrong to assume that Britons went to India with the intention of turning that bit of the map pink. In fact, neither Britain nor the East India Company wanted to acquire territory or rule India. So the Raj came into being more by accident than design. Thirdly, when the Company did begin to take over regions of India, most people assume that they were considered alien conquerors. But actually, the Company had the active and indispensable support of powerful Indian partners. It was they who invited the British to help them mount coups against their unpopular rulers. The arrangement emphatically profited both sides. It was often difficult to tell who was using whom. Fourthly, contradicting popular misconceptions again, the

British did not always see themselves as a race apart. There was little racism for the first 150 years of the encounter and not much evidence that Indians were considered inferior. Far from it – to begin with, the Company actively encouraged mixed-race relationships. Moreover, some fell in love with India as well as Indians. Orientalists like William Jones believed Indian civilization was on a par with Ancient Greece and Rome and directly linked to both. In a classically inspired world, that now made East and West inseparable and on the brink of a new Renaissance. Meanwhile, within their jurisdiction, the Company banned missionaries and preserved and enforced Hindu and Muslim rather than British law. So it is not surprising that some Britons, like the remarkable Charles 'Hindoo' Stuart, 'went native', converting to Hinduism or Islam and fully adopting Indian customs and traditions.

Moreover, this wasn't all one-way traffic. As Britons went East, the first Indian tourists and settlers came to Britain. These included men of substance as well as poor sailors, servants and mistresses. They were shocked in several respects by how backward Britain was. The lack of personal hygiene in Britain was what first hit them. They also worried about the low status of women in British society.

If the milieu seems familiar it may be because the eighteenth century, unlike the Victorian Age that followed, was a period in Britain in many ways strikingly like the present. Then, as now, metropolitan society was buzzing with enterprise and ideas. It was tolerant, liberal, unstuffy, sexually adventurous and hedonistic. It was also sleaze-ridden, pitiless, under-regulated and vulgar. Politics was largely about personalities – ideology did not get a look in. The press was vicious and celebrity-obsessed. Everybody liked a gossip. You could also, as we'll see, call it multicultural. Thousands of Asians were now living in Britain. Meanwhile, all things Indian were briefly the height of fashion. London had its first curry houses. The in-crowd lapped up a version of Indian fashion, music, design and even health fads.

In all these ways then, there's room to challenge received wisdom about the British–Indian encounter – which is that a dynamic western society meets a stagnant eastern society and fulfils its mission to shake it up. Instead, this is the story of the meeting of two sophisticated cultures in the eighteenth century, of their mutual love affair, and of the souring of that affair in the early nineteenth century as British respect for India turned to rapidly enforced change, scorn, distrust and domination. Only then was the old instinct to live-and-let-live supplanted by a new lust for territorial conquest and overall political supremacy. Unlike their predecessors just a generation earlier, imperialists like Richard Wellesley wanted to be Caesar, building a new Rome in India. Legislation was passed officially discriminating against Indians and 'half castes'. Evangelicals began to demonize Hinduism for its idolatry and attempted to convert India to Christianity. Modernizers simultaneously declared India's past was of so little value that it was even said they were proposing to demolish the Taj Mahal. The noble cause of progress fuelled the dream of creating in India a new utopian liberal society of 'Brown Englishmen' free at last from backwardness and vice.

The problem with all these plans was, of course, that they reflected what influential Britons thought India should want, not what most Indians did want. So it's no wonder the long relationship quickly unravelled in the first half of the nineteenth century, paving the way for the cataclysmic confrontation of 1857, variously described as the Indian Mutiny or the First War of Indian Independence. In fact the only surprise is that by now the British were so out of touch with Indian opinion, and so arrogant about their own invincibility, that they did not see the Mutiny coming. With it came the end of Company Rule and the birth of the Raj.

Perhaps today, finally, the British–Indian relationship is coming full circle after the 150-year cul-de-sac of Empire and post-colonial trauma. Take today's fusion Britain, twenty-first-century India's dynamic and diverse regional powerhouses, or even our globalized world economy, dominated by business rather than ideology, and you get more than a momentary sense of déjà-vu.

CHAPTER ONE

ROGUE TRADERS AND SPICE GIRLS

The surf in Madras is awesome or off-putting, depending on your take on big breakers. All year round, huge waves roll in at frequent intervals, tossing the fishing vessels about dismissively as they head for shore. The spray flies, the pomfret, lobster and king prawns slide around the bottom of the catamaran (from the Tamil for 'tied logs'), and even the most experienced Coromandel seafarer holds on or ends up in the Bay of Bengal.

Today you're spared such an arrival, and ease into India's fourth largest city via its (for India) ultra-sleek International Air Terminal. But for the adventurers and chancers aboard an eighteenth-century East Indiaman, this was the hazardous, sometimes fatal, entry-point to India. So on 1 June 1744 the passengers leaving *The Winchester* clambered down onto small boats to complete the last and most perilous few hundred yards of their 15,000-mile journey from London. It had been a tedious and unfortunate passage, fifteen months rather than the normal six, after poor weather forced a diversion to Brazil, where the ship ran aground and suffered damage that took months to repair.

FOR THOSE WHO LASTED THE JOURNEY, THE FINAL FEW YARDS TO THE BEACH AT MADRAS WERE OFTEN THE MOST HAZARDOUS.

Now, all that remained were a few stomach-churning moments in the surf. Finally, when even the catamarans could go no further, there was a welcome, if undignified piggyback ride from a sure-footed local, who ignored the fierce backwash and heaved the bizarrely over-dressed Europeans onto dry sand. The eighteen-year-old Robert Clive had met his first Indian. Not a bad metaphor, the piggyback, for his future relations with India and the Indians.

Even in his own lifetime, this son of a hard-up Shropshire gentleman-farmer would become known simply as 'Clive of India'. Before long, as the British Empire grew, the rhetoric swelled with it. He was 'the heaven-born general' of whom the nineteenth-century historian Macaulay wrote, 'our island has scarcely ever produced a man more truly great either in arms or in council'. Yet when the man deemed by imperial history to be the Raj's founder arrived that day in Madras, he joined no more than a few hundred British colleagues at the white-walled enclave of Fort St George, the oldest sovereign British settlement in India. Though ordered and elegant, this East India Company outpost comprised little more than a few warehouses and barracks-houses, the Town Hall, St Mary's Church and the Governor's lodgings. The new arrival would have been reassured by the compound's impressively sturdy gates, its familiar classical architecture and the understated reminders of home such as a duck pond and bowling green. Nevertheless, it must have been immediately apparent that the real life and action, in terms of business or adventure, took place over the fort wall in the City of Madrasspatam, built by the Company for its Indian partners, agents and servants and known to the English simply as Black Town.

Isolated and entirely independent of the three other small Company settlements in India at Calcutta, Bombay and Surat, the aims and activities of the British in Madras were routine, specific and mercantile. To the British, the Company was already a vital economic force, accounting for over 10 per cent of British public revenue. But the trading activities of these coastal stations, far from the centres of Indian power and wealth inland, were still largely marginal, even insignificant, to the life of the subcontinent.

Richard Clive, the Market Drayton farmer, had simply hoped India might sort out his impulsive, mildly delinquent son. With a lot of luck it might help feather the family's nest. The ambition was money. No one was even dreaming of empire.

———————————

Despite its antiquity and history, the startling fact is that India never really existed until independence in 1947. Even then, at the moment of its birth, Partition deprived India of its integrity. The founder of Pakistan, Muhammad Ali Jinnah, had promised to 'have India divided, or India destroyed' – at least one part of that promise was fulfilled, and arguably both. Certainly before modern times, India was never a unitary state. At the height of the

British Raj, the Queen Empress Victoria recognized over 560 Princely States within India, autocratic enclaves whose independence was sometimes, but not always, a charade. Before the British, India scarcely existed even as a concept or vision, let alone a single entity.

Even the subcontinent's greatest and most glorious rulers had been engaged in perpetual conflict with external and internal enemies. India's favourite hero, Asoka (273–232 BC), managed to extend the territory of the Aryan Maurya dynasty from the Himalayas as far south as Mysore. After his epic victory at Kalinga in 261BC, at the cost it is said of 100,000 men, he also won control of the North East including Bengal. The carnage so appalled him that he renounced violence, turned to Buddhism and preached peace through proclamations carved in stone throughout his lands. This was no way to run an empire and within a century it had evaporated. India had returned to normal, invaded (on this occasion by the Greeks and the Scythian Kushans) and broken up into a tangle of warring regional strongholds.

Five hundred years later, the golden age of the great Hindu monarchs, the Guptas (AD 300–647), saw renewed peace and stability within an effective empire throughout Northern India from Sind to Bengal. At the height of its glory, Gupta sculpture and Sanskrit literature contributed to a classical civilization to match or outmatch Rome's. Yet Gupta power only extended as far south as the northern fringes of the Deccan. The Southern Kingdoms, and in particular the Tamil dynasty of the Pandyas, based in Madurai, looked for trade and contact as much to Rome and the Far East as they did further north. Meanwhile, the Gupta Empire disintegrated and for the next thousand years, India's history pits Hindu rajas and warlords against each other and invading Mongols, Rajputs, Afghans, Turks and Persians.

Though a Muslim and a foreigner, Akbar, the greatest of the Great Moghuls, came closest to forging a single nation of Hindustan (which Europeans were beginning to call India). During his reign (1556–1605), Akbar managed not only extensive conquest but to unite Hindus and Muslims within a common national culture, framed by uniform legal, administrative and taxation systems. Akbar's direct contemporary Elizabeth I couldn't even manage that for Scotland. Akbar's less attractive successors, Jehangir, Shah Jahan and Aurangzeb, held sway over even more territory. They retained Kashmir, Kabul, Bengal and Sind, and gained Assam briefly while pushing Delhi's writ far south. But their religious intolerance, fratricidal conflict and extraordinary brutality ultimately provoked opposition that sent the Mughal Empire into its long tail-spin. By the last quarter of the seventeenth century, Sikhs, Jats, Rajputs and above all Hindu Marathas, inspired by their legendary warrior-leader Shivaji, were stretching Aurangzeb's empire at its seams. Within decades of his death in 1707, the fabled Peacock Throne of the Mughals had been carted off to Persia (present-day Iran). Though Mughal emperors thereafter still possessed a full harem and impressive cohorts of eunuchs, often their powers extended no more than a few miles

beyond Delhi. Macaulay sized them up sniffily: a 'succession of nominal sovereigns, sunk in indolence and debauchery, wasted away life in secluded palaces chewing *bhang*, fondling concubines, and listening to buffoons'.

So by the mid-eighteenth century, India had reverted to norm: a weak centre, continual intrigue and conflict, and frequent wars and power struggles. Paradoxically, this did not mean that it was in a state of anarchy or even much disorder. On the contrary, strong, autonomous regional administration led in most places to better leadership and economic growth.

That's not how the story was told later from the clubhouse veranda. It's a key British imperial myth that Mughal weakness plunged a once great empire into poverty and chaos. Britain then supposedly stepped in through its vigour and courage to fill some sort of power vacuum. It then realized the latent potential of the slumbering subcontinent by enforcing stability and security and gradually modernizing, the necessary preconditions for growth and prosperity. In reality, much of this is nonsense. India was not some blank slate awaiting new emperors. Many regions boasted highly sophisticated, fully functioning market economies. They flourished thanks to India's natural resources and its ancient, hybrid, cosmopolitan civilization. It had looked outwards as well as inwards since the days of the Greeks, Persians and Romans. In addition to its obvious artistic, architectural and literary achievements, it had excelled in science, mathematics, astronomy and metallurgy – giving the world, for example, zero and algebra. But it wasn't just an ancient treasure chest stuffed with knowledge and loot, ripe for plundering. In the eighteenth century it possessed a modern banking system, adroitly spreading huge amounts of capital around the country, supporting buoyant internal trade and providing ready finance and credit. This supported, for example, the world's largest and most dynamic textile industry in both silks and cottons. India also took advantage of a remarkably advanced and monetized cash economy, where even the peasants paid their taxes using common currency rather than in kind. With such a solid financial framework, producers, artisans and merchants were in a position to link up and develop some of the world's most valuable and sophisticated pre-industrial production of commodities and manufactured goods.

Of course that was the attraction all along to the British and other Europeans. The consensus in the seventeenth and early eighteenth centuries was that India was, after inaccessible China, the richest place on earth. To Europeans, any piece of the action was welcome, however small. The ideal was a coastal toehold that didn't get them sucked in beyond the strictly commercial. The East India Company had a phrase for it that came to define their mission: they wanted to pursue 'a quiet trade'. India tended to humble Europeans and make them feel small. Beyond almost every traveller's habitual obsession with the weather, the state of his bowels and the perils of getting ripped-off, their journals resonate with jaws hitting the floor. Alexander Dow summed it up in his *History of Hindostan*, published in 1768: it was 'one of the richest, most populous and best cultivated kingdoms in the world'.

THE GREAT MOGHUL, AKBAR, SHOWN HUNTING IN THIS MINIATURE, DATED C. 1590, CAME CLOSEST TO UNITING HINDUSTAN AS A SINGLE COUNTRY.

The first Europeans to settle in India had been the Portuguese centuries earlier. Ironically, they were also the last to leave, not relinquishing their colony at Goa until 1961 when the Indian army forced the issue. On 20 May 1498, in search of Marco Polo's fabled Indies, Vasco da Gama dropped anchor at Calicut on the lush south-west coast. This is a moment that panoramic historian Felipe Fernandez-Armesto chose to dub 'the most important single event in history'. Its significance was what it started. Vasco loaded his three ships with spices, silks, sandalwood and ivories and returned to Lisbon, where his cargo paid for his voyage sixty times over. Spices did not just pander to the European fad for flavour or a tiny taste of the exotic. Cloves, pepper and nutmeg helped preserve meat through the winter in an age that had not cracked winter fodder, still less refrigeration. That's why the search for spices was the motor of the Age of Exploration, fundamentally changing the world's history, culture and political geography, worth all the risks as well as the adventures. Ten pounds of nutmeg could be bought out East in 1600 for less than half a penny. In Europe it would sell for £1.60 – a 32,000 per cent mark-up and the equivalent of around £250 today.

It took a hundred years for the Portuguese to face European commercial rivals in the East. First the Dutch sailed, then shortly afterwards the British and the Danes, bound not for India but what they called the Spice Islands, mostly corresponding to the modern Indonesian archipelago.

The British traders represented 'The Company of Merchants of London trading into the East Indies', later known as the East India Company. This private trading company, run by its directors on behalf of its shareholders and investors, came into being on 31 December 1600, when Elizabeth I granted it by Royal Charter a monopoly of British trade to the East Indies. The Company's first two voyages ignored India, and its first permanent 'factory', or trading station, was at Bantam in Java. But in 1608, hoping to pick up Indian cottons to sell on to the Javanese in exchange for spices, the first British ship to reach India landed at Surat, north of Bombay. Its captain, William Hawkins, fell foul of the Portuguese and spectacularly failed to achieve his simple trading objectives. In frustration, he set off on a remarkable journey to Agra in search of 'The Great Moghul' himself. Diplomacy at Jehangir's court moved at a snail's pace. Hawkins became a trusted confidante of the Emperor, receiving a salary, a title (khan or duke) and even a wife plucked from the Imperial Harem, who, being an Armenian Christian, did not offend Hawkins's religious scruples. But after nearly two years, Hawkins returned to Surat without the precious *firman*, the imperial licence needed to establish a factory.

Those who swiftly followed were more successful, larding their diplomacy with presents for Jehangir, including a set of harpsichords and some raunchy pictures depicting 'Venus and Cupid's actes'. In January 1613 the *firman* from Agra finally arrived, permitting trade to and from Surat. A proud letter conveying this news to the Directors in London

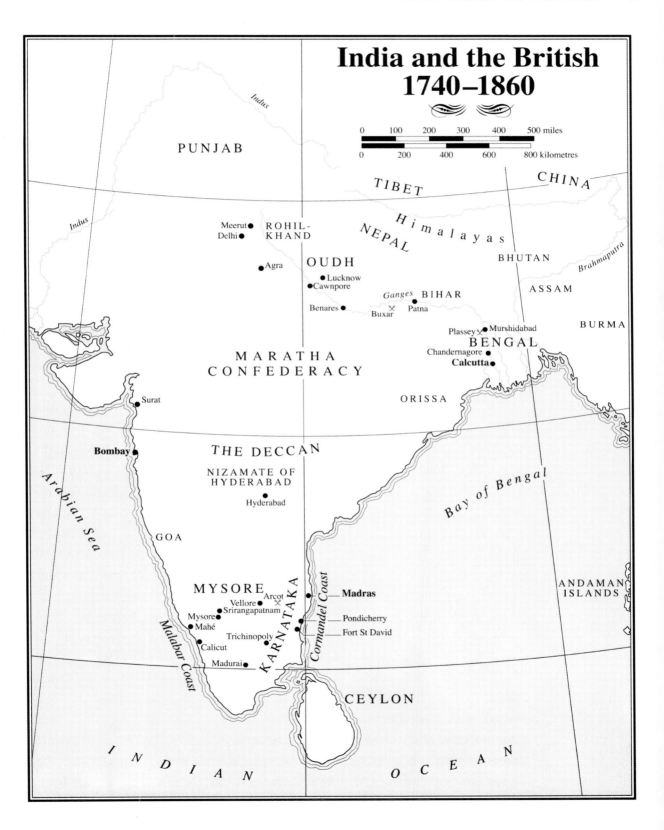

India and the British 1740–1860

| 0 | 100 | 200 | 300 | 400 | 500 miles |

| 0 | 200 | 400 | 600 | 800 kilometres |

Indus

PUNJAB

TIBET   CHINA

Indus

H i m a l a y a s

Meerut   ROHIL-
Delhi   KHAND   NEPAL

BHUTAN   *Brahmaputra*

Agra   OUDH

ASSAM

Lucknow
Cawnpore

Ganges   BIHAR

BURMA

Benares   Buxar   Patna

Plassey   Murshidabad

BENGAL

MARATHA
CONFEDERACY

Chandernagore
Calcutta

Surat

ORISSA

THE DECCAN

Arabian Sea

Bombay

NIZAMATE OF
HYDERABAD

Hyderabad

GOA

Bay of Bengal

ANDAMAN
ISLANDS

MYSORE   Arcot   Madras
      Vellore
Mysore   Srirangapatnam
Mahé   Pondicherry
Trichinopoly   Fort St David
Calicut

Madurai

Malabar Coast

KARNATAKA

Cormandel Coast

CEYLON

I N D I A N   O C E A N

explained that the Company now possessed 'the fountainhead from which we may draw all the trade of the East Indies, for we find here merchandise we can take and sell in nearly all parts of the Indies and in England' . The emphasis would remain trade alone. Sir Thomas Roe, sent in 1615 as ambassador to the Mughal Court, warned, 'It is an error to affect garrisons and land wars in India.' That would lead to the British being sucked into expensive politics and making the same mistakes as the Portuguese, whose 'many rich residences and territories' were the 'beggaring' of their trade. Roe famously concluded 'let this be received as a rule, that if you will profit, seek it at sea and in quiet trade'.

Throughout the seventeenth century, the Company's trade remained focused further east than the subcontinent. So it's not surprising that the next Indian foothold was Madras, leased from the local ruler in 1640 and a handy staging-post to the Spice Islands. Bombay followed in 1661 – a present to King Charles II from new friends Portugal on his marriage to Catherine of Braganza. Like many wedding presents, it seemed nice at the time but soon enough Charles didn't know what to do with it. His solution was to rent it to the Company for a tenner a year. The letters patent fixing the deal charmingly describe Bombay as 'pertaining to the Manor of East Greenwich in the County of Kent'. Finally, in 1690, the Company, which had been trading in prosperous Bengal for several decades, erected its first tents and huts at Calcutta, on the banks of the Hooghly River. One early visitor recorded that the site was chosen 'for the sake of a large shady tree'. In every other respect this malarial swamp, reeking of putrefying fish, was so close to hell-on-earth that British sailors nicknamed it Golgotha. 'Yet on this bog the British created their capital in India,' wrote Geoffrey Moorhouse, author of perhaps the best book on Calcutta. 'Nothing but commercial greed could possibly have led to such an idiotic decision.'

The next fifty years certainly justified the effort. India became a kind of magnet for the get-rich-quick tendency. In the south they traded not just in pepper and spices but in sugar for export as far as Japan and Persia. In the west the warehouses were stocked with indigo dye extracted from a local plant. In Bengal, one great prize was saltpetre, to be used in Europe for gunpowder and as a preservative. But increasingly it was India's textiles, its silks and cottons, which drove demand back in Europe. English woollens, its greatest historic trading asset, had failed to wow the subcontinent. But the Indian fruits of the loom had a revolutionary effect on European taste, fashion and lifestyle. Indian cottons were a kind of new wonder fabric, outperforming expensive, home-produced linen and scratchy, sweaty wool. Cottons were colour-fast, soft, easily washed and highly adaptable. Homes were transformed by tablecloths and napkins, affordable trousseaux of cotton bedsheets and a vast new range of choices in curtains and soft furnishings. Cheap, easily laundered cotton underwear must have been one of the most welcome innovations, doing its bit to stop Europe itching and stinking. Meanwhile the wardrobe and the dictionary suddenly burst

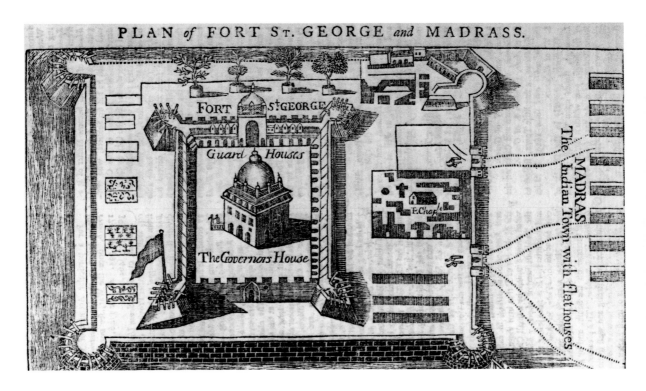

PLAN *of* FORT ST. GEORGE *and* MADRASS.

with new Indian varieties. Calico, taffeta, gingham, muslin, chintz, cashmere and silk were all products of the most advanced textile economy in the world.

The European appetite was insatiable for raw yarn and cloth and the bewildering array of finished handloom products. In the first half of the eighteenth century this helped ensure that East India Company stock, which had originally been a highly speculative risk, was solid blue-chip. Often the Company was so flush it could lend the British Government the odd million. Year on year, shareholders received an 8 per cent dividend from profits on up to twenty annual sailings. Meanwhile, Indian producers and traders were doing equally good business with the Dutch, Danes and Portuguese as well as with the newcomers, the French. The 'Compagnie des Indes', founded in 1719, may have been arrivistes yielding a century of experience to their competitors. But they were soon matching the British *godown* (warehouse) for *godown*, factory for factory, settlement for settlement right up the east coast from Pondicherry, within spitting distance of Madras, to Chandernagar on the Hooghly upriver from Calcutta.

Not surprisingly, other European nations wanted to get in on the act, as did individuals who lacked an entrée to one of the existing companies. The Swiss and the Swedish briefly dabbled. Meanwhile, the East India Company frequently fretted about British 'interlopers' acting privately and independently. A number of them teamed up with a group of enterprising freelancers claiming protection from the Hapsburg monarchy to constitute the 'Ostenders', some of whom just might have been Flemish. When the British and Dutch complained that the upstart company had no right to trade in Bengal, its nawab (ruler) replied that 'he did not care what nation they were, so that they did but bring money'. Back in Europe, the Emperor in Vienna was heavily leant on and eventually suspended the Ostenders' Charter. It mattered little. The same team switched allegiance to the King of Poland, justifying their flag of convenience by asking on what grounds anyone could question 'His Majesty of Poland's right to send ships with his passport to India'. Meanwhile, the shareholders in London knew but couldn't rein in the real rogue traders, the Company men themselves, almost all of whom were engaged in 'country trade', working for themselves rather more than the Company. Certainly, most East Indiamen arriving at East India Docks in London were as laden with private profit as official company cargo.

You could call it eighteenth-century-style globalization – the Wild East in mid gold rush attracting adventurers and fortune seekers from throughout India and around the world. There were the big corporations with their eye for the bottom line, operating under licence, richer than nations, a law unto themselves, and fiercely competitive. There were also the jack-the-lads operating first and foremost for themselves, nominally their companies, rarely if ever with any sense of national mission. India was the perfect arena for these young, ambitious, entrepreneurial types to make it big. If they survived the journey, the climate, the culture-shock and the diseases, huge fortunes might be made relatively quickly. A gentleman who actually succeeded in making it back from the East Indies would certainly be a man to be reckoned with.

More often than not, however, would-be adventurers were hugely disappointed. Life as a human xerox-machine in the Writers' Office, the lowest rung of Company service, was oppressive and dull. Day after day, the young writers sat in their shirt-sleeves hunched over ledgers, copying out orders and totting up bills. The salary of £5 a year, plus £3 living expenses, was pitiful. Promotion, and with it better access to private trading opportunities, could take five years. With a rigid hierarchy, stultifying ceremonial, communal dining and compulsory chapel twice a day, the atmosphere in these small Company enclaves must have resembled the claustrophobia of public school, with no end of term in sight. No wonder so many turned to drink. No wonder too the tedium nearly drove the young Robert Clive, newly arrived in Madras, to suicide. He'd had much more fun back in Market Drayton.

Robert Clive, according to legend, had been an unruly and rebellious child. On one occasion he supposedly responded to a dare by climbing right up the spire of the local church. He then perched himself at the summit on top of the dragon's head spout until promised enough money to come down. Another story has him leading a local gang who operated a kind of protection racket, threatening shopkeepers with broken windows unless they were paid off. Such juvenile recklessness and rapacity delighted, or was the invention of, his early biographers. The only hard evidence we have to his character is that, when Robert was seven, his uncle wrote with some concern that the boy 'is out of measure addicted to fighting'. Though relatives think that of many small boys… However hard people have searched, nothing in Clive's youth really prefigures founding an empire.

Maybe Clive was a born adventurer in search of scrapes? But in all likelihood his passage to India was more the journey of an economic migrant. He had done so badly at school that no real career opportunities presented themselves. His father's small and somewhat mortgaged estate would certainly not supply his son with a living. So it was good news indeed that Richard Clive knew one of the directors of the East India Company, based in Leadenhall Street in London. Like so many before and since, Robert Clive was abandoning limited prospects at home to seek his fortune in more economically promising lands overseas.

The young writer's letters home reveal just how miserable life in Madras was. To his father, filial piety demanded he put on something of a brave face. But far from making money, he was clearly short of cash. The unexpectedly long journey left him on arrival already in debt to the ship's captain. Rather pathetically, he requested money for extra clothes because the 'intolerable heat' forced him to change twice a day and the *dhobis* beat all his outfits to a useless pulp within a few washes. He also apologized to his father for the wine bill. But one needed variety and the only alternative drink was punch (from the Marathi word for 'five' after its five ingredients: arrack, lime-juice, sugar, water and spices). In letters to his uncle, Clive did not bother to hide his abject homesickness: 'If I should be so far blest as to revisit again my own country, but more especially Manchester (the centre of all my wishes), all that I could hope or desire for would be presented before me in one view.' In a letter to his cousin, he was positively overwhelmed with self-pity: 'I have not enjoyed one happy day since I left my native country.' Apparently he had not made a single friend and his only solace came in receiving mail, all of it of course at least six months old: 'Letters were surely first invented for the comfort of such solitary wretches as myself.' Soon it all seems to have got too much for him. One night, according to an early biographer, he put his pistol to his head and pulled the trigger. The gun failed. He tried again, only to get the same result. Conveniently for the biographer in search of the prophetic moment, he is said to have exclaimed, 'I have been spared for some purpose.'

India did not spare many Europeans. The saying at the time was 'two monsoons are the age of a man'. The handsome monuments in St Mary's and St George's churches at Madras and the tombs in Park Street cemetery in Calcutta show this was hardly an exaggeration. The epitaphs hint at the horror and pain even as their elegant prose does its best to console the survivors who fear they're next. Thus Josiah Webbe 'fell a martyr to an ungenial climate in the prime of life' and Captain Samuel Best succumbed to 'jungle fever contracted during a few hours passed on the Yailegherry hills', while John Jollie simply collapsed into 'premature and sudden dissolution in a distant clime'. As for Rose Aylmer:

> *What was her fate? Long, long before her hour,*
> *Death called her tender soul, by break of bliss,*
> *From the first blossoms, from the buds of joy,*
> *Those few our noxious fate unblasted leaves,*
> *In this inclement clime of human life.*

She was fresh off the ship, had just turned twenty and stood little chance against cholera.

Reliable calculations suggest that 57 per cent of Europeans died of sickness in Bengal between 1707 and 1775, rising to 74 per cent in the worst decade mid-century. One of the earliest visitors, Captain Alexander Hamilton, noted 1,200 Englishmen living in Calcutta at the beginning of the eighteenth century, of whom 460 were buried in one single season. With those kinds of odds, it is not surprising these were men in a hurry in search of big profits. It was said even the surgeons spent most of their time chasing private trade.

This was an era with little or no understanding of tropical medicine, or even of the advantages of basic hygiene. The heat and humidity helped the healthy swiftly into their coffins, even when their ailments initially seemed trivial. The swamps around Calcutta and the channels and sewers of Madras bred malaria and every other major tropical disease. But a significant proportion of the deaths can be attributed simply to excess.

Apparently, locals never ceased to marvel at just how much the English ate and drank. The main meal in Calcutta, served at noon in the heat of the day, consisted of fifteen courses. Dishes included 'Kishmishes, Bengall Goats, Sugar Candy, Almonds, Brahminy Bull, Soyce, Turkeys, Geese, Sheep, Rabbits and Lime'. Supper was only slightly more modest. At Surat, the new chaplain recorded the menus in amazement. On weekdays there was pulao, 'cabob' (kebab), 'dumpoked fowl' boiled in butter and stuffed with raisins and almonds, and mango pickle. On Sundays they lived a little with 'Deer and Antelopes, Peacocks, hares and partridges, and all kinds of Persian Fruits, Pistachoes, Plums, Apricots, Cherries etc'. Depending on rank, it was all washed down with a lot of

punch and a little wine, or a lot of wine and less punch. It is reckoned one in ten deaths were from alcohol poisoning. Later in the century communal meals gave way to domestic eating, but the tables groaned as before. Eliza Fay recorded she would typically serve for supper: soup, roast fowl, curry and rice, mutton pie, a forequarter of lamb, rice pudding, tarts, cheese, butter, bread and Madeira. The British in India much admired Mughal cooling techniques and later became ingenious architects of ice houses. But it is probable much of this food much of the time was past its best.

Although Fort St George and the other Company enclaves were islands of rather rigid Britishness, the young servants of the company seem from the start to have been far less insular. This first wave of wide boys and rogue traders hardly stand out for their intellectual curiosity. But if they did not get to grips with India's culture and civilization, they were drawn to more superficial Indian lifestyles and customs. They took readily to smoking the hookah (water pipe) and chewing betel nuts. They relaxed by getting out of their western clothes, donning turbans and looser native robes and lolling on cushions. A party wasn't a party without its nautch (dancing) girls. No one yet disapproved.

Perhaps it is only the distorted prism of the Raj that makes us expect disapproval. Yet search as we might, the evidence is not there. Indeed, what is striking about the relationship between Britons and Indians until the last decades of the eighteenth century is the relative absence of racism. Later, the Raj was buttressed by ideological conviction of innate British superiority. Its success literally went to its head. Under Victoria, Britons congratulated themselves on their global hegemony and attributed it in part to the unique qualities of their 'race'. The abilities and potential of all other 'races', particularly subject ones, were naturally constrained by their limitations. Even before Darwin, spurious science seemed to validate this dogma and convert prejudice into Natural Law.

This would have seemed absurd for most of the eighteenth century, when Company merchants were only too aware of how modest their achievements were in comparison to the wealth, sophistication and refinement of Indian civilization. That they lived apart was a sign of insecurity rather than prejudice. They did indeed relish the familiarity of their surroundings in the small coastal Presidencies, reassuring themselves with neo-classical porticoes and processions of mace-carrying aldermen in gowns that probably looked ridiculous outside Northampton. But far from discouraging communication with Indians, the Company did much to nurture it. This was of course pragmatism rather than multicultural idealism. Nevertheless, unlike Empire, commerce was of its essence colour-blind. As a result, the vast majority of Britons in India naturally formed close relationships with Indian business partners and Indian women. These continued long into the nineteenth century, by when they had been stigmatized as dissolute and demeaning. Until then the rogue traders happily tried to live up to the lusty old Company cry of 'a *lakh* [a hundred thousand rupees] and a lass a day'.

India was thought no place for an Englishwoman. The expense and the danger largely kept the memsahib away until the invention of the steamship. Though they needed little encouragement, for most of the eighteenth century the Company actively sponsored marriages between Englishmen and local women by subsidizing the weddings. The children of these unions were enthusiastically marshalled into service within the Company. In fact, religious differences made weddings comparatively unusual. But all the evidence suggests that mature, long-lasting, monogamous relationships were normal, accepted and rooted in far more than sexual satisfaction. As far as the Company was concerned, wedlock was optional. The only taboo was against the Portuguese. After all, it wouldn't do for a Company servant to take up with a Catholic!

Indian women were called 'sleeping dictionaries', an acknowledgement of their essential role in teaching the British far more than the erotic arts. The mistresses were known as *bibis*, and frequently lived with Company men as effective common-law wives. Even churchmen were known to keep them openly. Conveniently for the British, in accordance with the norm for both high-caste Hindu and Muslim practice, they tended to live in separate quarters. It was common for Company bungalows and lodgings to include a *zenana* within its compound.

Hard facts about these women are frustratingly elusive. It is thought the majority were Muslim but we know little about their educational background, whether they were raised in the palace, market or gutter. Despite their ubiquity, it is true that, although they were condoned, even encouraged, they were never themselves entirely accepted. Princess or pauper, casual floozie or life-long companion, no *bibi* was ever welcome at an official Company function. Prejudice worked both ways. The act of taking up with an Englishman would have cut many *bibis* off from their families. Any Hindu woman would henceforth have been an outcast – literally out of caste.

Yet the evidence suggests that genuine loving relationships emerged despite this unpromising context. Captain Thomas Williamson spent twenty years in India towards the end of the eighteenth century and decided to put his experience to good use by writing his *East India Vade Mecum*, effectively the original English Guide Book to India. The first edition, published in 1810, includes extensive advice about keeping a *bibi*. However, in a later edition fifteen years on, all references to inter-racial relationships have been bowdlerized.

Heading out for India, the new writer or cadet whiling away endless months aboard ship would have turned with sweaty palms to this well-thumbed section of his *Vade Mecum*: 'it is a very general practise for Englishmen in India to entertain a *cara amica* of the country'. Of course this was partly because to do so was so much more economical than keeping an English wife, who Williamson calculated could set you back annually a prohibitive £300. Nevertheless, 'the attachment of many European gentlemen to their native mistresses, is not to be described! An infatuation, beyond all comparison, often prevails, causing every confidence, of whatever description, to be reposed in the sable queen of the harem! In return, many of these women have conducted themselves invariably in the most decorous manner and evinced the utmost fidelity, in every particular way, to their keepers'. The new recruit would already have been aware of the fabled sexual allure of the Orient. So he would have been positively palpitating by the time he read that these women were themselves incredibly fastidious about cleanliness, washing themselves carefully 'after contact'. Wary perhaps that this

was forbidden fruit, he would have been reassured to read 'a woman under the protection of a European gentleman, is counted not only among the natives, but even by his countrymen to be equally sacred, as though she were married to him – some are said to have passed twenty years or more, without the possibility for scandal to attach to their conduct'.

Other writers directly compared white and native femininity. Innes Munro's journal records British men rejecting their compatriots for the 'upright, supple and slender well-rounded limbs' of Indian girls. Another Company official, Samuel Brown, is even more honest about the age-old male fantasy: 'the native women were so amusingly playful, so anxious to please, that a person, accustomed to their society, shrinks from the idea of encountering the whim, or yielding to the furies of an Englishwoman'.

Of course, these fevered tributes hardly measure up to today's benchmarks for a modern relationship. Given the disparities of wealth and power, it is not surprising that feminist historians are sceptical about whether such unequal partnerships should be held up as multicultural role-models. What can be said, however, is that the period of open intimacy between Britons and Indians, however unequal the relationship, made for better relations than the buttoned-up hypocrisy that followed, when inter-racial sexual contact was considered anathema to right-thinking Englishmen. As Ronald Hyam puts it in *Empire and Sexuality: The British Experience*: 'There is no reason why sex cannot be an act of racial conciliation. Though sex cannot of itself enable men to transcend racial barriers, it generates some admiration and affection across them, which is healthy and which cannot always be dismissed as merely self-interested and prudential… sexual interaction between the British and non-Europeans probably did more long-term good than harm to race-relations.'

Though their names rarely appear, contemporary official documents do prove that living with a *bibi* was standard right up until the end of the eighteenth century. One in three wills filed in Calcutta between 1780 and 1785 includes a reference, almost always a legacy, to a native concubine. Frequently, they are the beneficiaries of the entire estate. *Bibis* are described variously and euphemistically as 'my girl', 'my housekeeper', 'my companion', or 'a woman under my protection'. The baptismal register for the same period demonstrates that they were more than this. Church regulations meant that, because these women were neither Christian nor married, they were simply listed as 'native', or else the 'mother' column was left blank. Half the children baptized fall into this category, demonstrating that having a European father and an Indian mother was pretty much the accepted norm. Within twenty years a moral backlash reduces to 10 per cent the proportion of mixed-race baptized children. Legacies to *bibis* fall away too, but by far less, confirming these 'country-born' children remained common, even if racism deprived many of the sacrament of baptism. Working from these documents, it has been estimated that half the British men in Bengal were seriously involved with a local woman.

INDIAN *BIBIS* FORMED RELATIONSHIPS WITH EUROPEANS THAT LASTED DECADES. THIS IS THOUGHT TO BE JEMDANEE. THE ADORED MISTRESS OF DIARIST WILLIAM HICKEY.

By 1810, a third of Bengal's Europeans were 'country-born'. By then too, legislation had curtailed their prospects. But the first generations of Anglo-Indian offspring enjoyed full equality of opportunity. Many boys were sent to school in England where they constituted, along with mixed-race children from the West Indies, perhaps 10 percent of the public school population. Most went on to serve the emerging Company Raj. Many, like Sir Eyre Coote, Commander-in-Chief of the Company's forces, reached its highest rank. Some went on to found great dynasties at the heart of the British establishment. Lord Roberts, supreme commander in the Boer War, had a Rajput princess for a grandmother. Lord Liverpool, Britain's longest-serving prime minister (1812–27), was the grandson of the remarkable 'Begum' Johnson, of mixed-race descent, who saw off four British husbands and was hostess of Calcutta's most eagerly attended whist drives. Job Charnock himself, the legendary founder of the city, had rescued a Hindu widow from committing suttee on her husband's funeral pyre. The couple had four children, and every year after her death Charnock is said to have sacrificed a cock at her tomb.

Company men in India would invariably depend on a different but equally fundamental close Indian relationship – with their agent. Known as a *banian* in Bengal and a *dubash* in Madras, the agent was the essential interface between India and the foreign merchants. Without him, trade would have been impossible. In time, *banian* fortunes would match those of their 'masters' (see Chapter 3). But already in the mid-eighteenth century, *banians* were described as acting as 'interpreter, head book-keeper, head secretary, head broker, the supplier of cash and cash keeper and in general also secret keeper' to their British partners. In particular, they played the key role in accessing the finance that made private trade and a comfortable lifestyle possible. Without capital, Europeans could do little. *Banians* were expected to arrange the loans and themselves often supplied the credit. Interest rates of 9–12 per cent were lower than Indian borrowers paid. But with a high death rate among young Europeans, *banians* knew some of their loans would turn into bad debt. Company servants who scuttled back home without settling their dues were sometimes met with court writs from London lawyers hired by their *banians*.

For acting as effective CEOs, *banians* were paid a salary. More substantial reward came on commission – 10 per cent of all their master's business was the norm. But the real money came with the opportunity to profit on the side in almost every arena of their master's life and business. In addition, *banians* were able themselves to take personal advantage of the Mughal Emperor's grant of 'duty-free' status to Company trade and the private trade of its servants. *Banians* might also be well placed to become official suppliers of silk or other produce to the Company warehouses.

Indian nationalist history has tended to characterize *banians* as collaborators, in the pejorative sense of the word. But *banians* would have found nothing unusual about working with the

Company – after all, the subcontinent had been a cosmopolitan trading region for over a thousand years. Of course, to the distaste of so many later commentators, whether British imperialist, Indian nationalist, or Marxist, the whole business of business as practised by the Company and its servants was exploitative. But it's worth reminding ourselves that much of the profit much of the time was being made by and for Indians. Military muscle had not yet undermined the basic rules of fair trade. In essence, British silver bullion was being exchanged for a variety of goods for which the traders paid handsomely, even if the mark-up in London was colossal. Politically and economically, India very much still held the upper hand.

The Company had no territorial ambitions, no imperial strategy – quite the opposite: it wanted low costs, high profits and an easy life. But to safeguard this in the cut-and-thrust world of eighteenth-century India, Company armies were necessary, and were also effectively available to the highest bidders. The Company was competing with the French to impress the local rulers and get the trading concessions. They were increasingly scheming with Indian bankers and merchants to further their joint interests by interfering in local politics. And they began to find that in one area, warfare, they had much to offer. By accident, not design, the battlefield was to be the making of Robert Clive and of British India.

Chapter Two

Accidental Empire

The GPO in Calcutta is without doubt the mother of all post offices. Built in 1868 when mid-Victorian confidence was at its highest, it is designed as a temple to communication, modelled on Greece and Rome, and with a scale and self-importance to match either vanished imperium. Two massive Corinthian porticoes, inside each of which it seems you could run the hundred metres, beckon you into vast halls. The entire gargantuan hulk is topped by a large silver dome. Today, Calcutta's habitual grime and decay make the place much less pompous than it must once have been and, though it is still grand, the human activity beneath the arcades does much to humanize the space. Passers-by shelter from a sudden downpour. Letter-writers sit taking dictation from those who need help with their correspondence. Public sector job application forms are spread out on the floor, and for a small sum a man will help you apply for a post in the Border Security Force or steer you through the triplicate demands of the Railway Recruitment Board. The amazing freelance parcel force take any bulky or misshaped item

Possibly the world's grandest Post Office, the GPO in Calcutta was built on the site of the Black Hole of Calcutta.

you're hoping to mail home, box it up neatly and wrap it in white cloth, which they then secure against tampering by stitching it up with strong yarn and melting red sealing-wax over the seams.

A small plaque on the wall informs you that the building occupies the south-east corner of the old Fort William, the Company's original citadel at the centre of the city founded by Job Charnock in 1690. But there's absolutely no indication anywhere that it occupies the site of the most notorious incident in the history of British India, one that so entered imperial mythology that for a time at least 'every schoolboy' really did know its story: a prison cell, a hot night, a cruel despot, British bodies pressed together cheek-by-jowl, disaster. The Black Hole of Calcutta is now the Post Office's 'V-Sat Centre', a tiny high-tech outpost where you can send money orders by satellite anywhere around India. But of course it is not at all, as the saying goes, 'like the Black Hole of Calcutta'.

It is perhaps appropriate that modern India has obscured this past. The Black Hole was one of a handful of events in the 1740s and 1750s that contributed to the defining mythology of the Raj. With hindsight, imperialists connected these events – Clive's soldiery in the south, the humiliating tragedy of the Black Hole and Clive's victory at the Battle of Plassey – into one grand Road to the Raj. The reality was much more piecemeal and haphazard, the beginnings of the British Empire largely accidental and certainly not understood, still less planned at the time. Like the equally unprepossessing eroded river valley on the site of the battlefield of Plassey, the lack of a memorial to the Black Hole at the GPO is fitting because these were at most minor incidents, even non-events. And yet within these twenty years a group of British traders did indeed become the paramount power in India.

––––––––––––––

As ever with British history, what really mattered was stopping the French. Indeed, arguably the British ended up with the Raj not because they particularly wanted an empire, but because it seemed the only way to prevent the French from getting one by carving up the subcontinent, monopolizing its trade and going on perhaps to corner the global market.

Of course the Company Directors in both London and Paris agreed that conflict was an extremely costly diversion and to be avoided if at all possible. In Leadenhall Street they still held fast to their 'quiet trade' mission, which reminded their servants in the field that 'all war is so contrary to our interest that we cannot too often inculcate to you our aversion thereunto'. Echoing London's warnings against local adventurism, the French Controller-General warned, 'We want only some outposts to protect our commerce: no victories, no conquests, only parity of merchandise and some augmentation of dividends.' Neither HQ would get its way.

Global politics and local greed were what scuppered the pragmatists. Later, the full ideology of empire had to be invented to justify the deeper engagement brought on by war and territorial responsibilities. Yet it was basically irrational and unnecessary that the world's fate was empire, rather than the alternative trading vision of what Daniel Defoe dubbed 'the unbounded Ocean of Business'. From now on, all the conquering, protecting and ruling took a heavy toll on profits. The view from the balance sheet is that the British Empire looks a poor investment in comparison to British trade with, say, independent South America in the nineteenth century, conducted vigorously without the hassle and expense of conquest, still less its moral burden.

Bizarrely, the British and French first came to blows in India because of the mightily irrelevant War of the Austrian Succession. This had in turn evolved out of the still more arcane conflict known as the War of Jenkins' Ear that had erupted between Britain and Spain in 1739 following a spat in Cuba (for which the casus belli was indeed an infamous Spanish cutlass swipe and the removal of an Englishman's ear). Of course no one in Madras or the French station at Pondicherry cared two hoots about Jenkins' organs or who sat on the throne in Vienna. The news that the two countries were at war had taken six months even to reach southern India. Meanwhile, the first instincts of both the British and French Companies there was for business as usual, facilitated by a swiftly organized local truce. However, an understanding ashore could not prevent engagements at sea, where the war offered spectacular opportunity for prize-money. In 1745 the Royal Navy overwhelmed a Compagnie fleet off the Malaysian coast which was heavily laden with goods from China to the value of £92,000, much of it 'private trade' belonging to the leading French officials in India. Poorly defended Madras must have rued the cavalier actions of the navy. Like the British, the French could ignore European war. But they were not prepared to overlook this assault on their own and their company's wallets. As soon as the British fleet left the region, the French bore down on Madras. It was hopelessly unprepared for real action.

Although small units had always protected the Company's outposts, these were token forces, mustered and kitted-out as cheaply as possible. The defence of Fort St George rested with a garrison of some 400 European troops under the command of a Swedish lieutenant who was already well into his seventies. By 6 September 1746, when the French bombardment began, a hundred of these soldiers were already AWOL or had admitted themselves to hospital. The rest appear to have been drunk, taking advantage of the extra rations supplied in the hope it would help summon up the blood. A counter-attack by hastily hired locals failed when they sallied straight down the ramparts and home to their villages. Meanwhile, the British cannon had proved near useless, the force of firing a few rounds destroying their mountings. The constant noise prevented the Company's merchants from getting their beauty-sleep and the servants had run off, forcing them to do their own cooking. No wonder the Swedish commander abandoned his post 'unable to bear the fatigue'.

Cometh the hour, cometh the man – yet there is no evidence that the young writer Robert Clive, holed up with his colleagues inside the fort, did anything to help with the defence. The surrender came quickly and involved much squabbling about ransoms, not least between the French naval commander La Bourdonnais and the Governor of Pondicherry, Joseph Dupleix, as to who pocketed the lion's share. Meanwhile, the French ransacked the Company's warehouses and those of its Indian business partners. The remaining British were given the choice between pledging allegiance to the French monarch or imprisonment. This experience must have left a deep impression on the homesick and bookish Clive, still described as 'a very quiet person'. One night in October he 'blacked' himself up, disguised himself as a dubash and slipped out of the fort. He made his way down the coast to the Company's surviving southern station at Fort St David (Cuddalore), which was now facing repeated French attacks. The officials there rather reluctantly offered him and other English refugees a monthly writers' contract. But he rejected this, being 'of opinion that acting in a military sphere (tho' then at a very low ebb) was the most honourable of the two and most conducive to the Company's interest'. He took to uniform immediately. In May 1747 a despatch was sent to the Company's Directors in London informing them that 'Mr Robert Clive, Writer in the Service, being of a martial disposition and having acted as a volunteer in our late engagements we have granted him an Ensign's Commission upon his application for the same'. Being a soldier was more exciting than being a tally clerk. In volatile times, it also had the potential to be far more profitable.

British naval superiority eventually reversed the Company's setbacks. Clive even joined an unsuccessful counter-attack on Dupleix's stronghold at Pondicherry. Meanwhile, the war between Britain and France was officially over, with Madras restored to the British in 1749 in exchange for a bit of North America. But this minor tussle heralded a new phase in the south, opening everyone's eyes to entirely new commercial and strategic circumstances.

First, the Company determined not to repeat its complacency, ending its former parsimonious neglect of military affairs that had led to undermanned and ill-equipped garrisons capable of little more than guard duty. Instead, as Clive was discovering, military careers were full of opportunity. The British and French began to reinforce in the south in an arms race that saw thousands more European and sepoy (local) recruits, increasingly transformed from ill-disciplined misfits into efficient and feared units. Of course, these mercenary armies were costly and needed to be kept busy if they weren't to get restive. Frequent action and rich spoils were now needed to defray the expense. From this point onwards, the Company's overheads were on the rise.

Secondly, these forces were seen for the first time to be spectacularly successful against far larger Indian armies. The British had in the past tended to be overawed by India's martial arts — much was made of the supposedly fanatical hordes, armed to the teeth with scary-looking weapons, their elite corps mounted on supposedly invulnerable elephants. But, outraged by this foreign war on his patch, the Nawab of Karnataka had sent a 10,000-strong army to relieve Madras. It met a French force of just 230 Europeans and 700 sepoys at San Thome just south of the city. The French won in spectacular fashion, their two guns and the infantry's musket volleys shocking the Indian troops into an immediate rout, terror-crazed elephants and all. It took several minutes to reload an Indian gun. The French could recharge up to twenty times a minute. At that moment, suddenly and immediately, the Mughal lost his invincibility. The lesson wasn't lost on the imprisoned English watching from nearby Fort St George. According to Robert Orme, who observed these actions and went on to become the Company's military historian, 'The French at once broke through the charm of this timorous opinion by defeating a whole army with a single battalion.' From then onwards, the British too became convinced that Indian troops, tactics and technology were no match for their own.

Despite their bravado, the French were in a pickle. The Compagnie's share-price had fallen by 90 per cent. To restore its trading position (and of course his own), Dupleix had to ignore both the international peace deal and the constant tickings-off he received from his supposed masters in Paris, who were rightly worried that he was a loose cannon. He lacked both French capital and sufficient ships to compete effectively with the British. Instead he embarked on a risky but brilliant new strategy which both rattled and impressed the East India Company. Abandoning the doctrine of quiet trade and limited engagement inland, Dupleix gambled on using French military skills to win him territory. In future, he hoped trading returns would constitute only one arm of the business. Instead he aimed to make his fortune and the Compagnie's, by profiting directly from the revenues and taxes paid by the peasantry. He would do this by intervening in regional politics, effectively hiring himself out as king-maker. The coffers would start filling once he had helped his grateful proxies on to their thrones. Later he put it very simply. His mission, he claimed, was nothing less than 'la domination française dans l'Inde'. So though war was undesirable to Britain, France and both companies, the entire region was plunged with far-reaching consequences into what has been called Dupleix's private war.

The new tactics were spectacularly successful. This officially being peace-time, Dupleix could not lay a direct blow on the British. But in little more than a year he managed to use his military muscle to oust the incumbents and get his pretenders installed as both the Nawab of Karnataka and the Nizam of Hyderabad. Suddenly the French were lords of much of central and southern India right up to the fringes of Bengal, enjoying its revenues and heavily influencing, via their puppets, its political destiny. Dupleix himself was said to have pocketed £200,000. The British, who were habituated to kowtowing cautiously to the existing powers and avoiding getting drawn into their endless power struggles, were utterly winded. The lessons, however, were clear. Usurping power was so much easier and more profitable than pandering to it.

The Company had little choice but to fight back in Karnataka. This was ostensibly in support of Muhammad Ali, son of its Nawab, who had died in battle at the hands of the French. The Carnatic Wars were bizarre and confusing, fought on an occasional basis by small units of European auxiliaries in the employ of their rival Indian princes, despite the fact that the companies were officially at peace. The decisive intervention came from Robert Clive. It turned him almost overnight from an obscure Company servant into a national hero, and from one of many men-on-the-make to a gentleman of such stature that he could afford to head home to England and buy himself a seat at Westminster, courtesy of the rottenest of rotten boroughs.

On 26 August 1751, Clive set out in command of a small force of just 200 Europeans, 600 sepoys and three field guns for a campaign that no one could have predicted would prove a decisive turning point in British, French and Indian history. He was still just twenty-six years old and a mere junior captain. Muhammad Ali, the British aspirant to the Karnataka throne, was besieged in Trichinopoly, the ancient temple city 200 miles inland, by his rival Chanda Sahib, the new Nawab, whose superior forces were aided by the French. Muhammad Ali's dispatches to the Company's Governor in Madras betray his increasing desperation: 'I must tell you that my whole dependence is upon your troops. I undertook the government of the Deccan country by the advice of the English… Don't let the French and Chanda seize me. I depend upon God and you… What can I say more!' Clive's mission was to draw the enemy's attentions away from Trichinopoly by staging a daring attack on Chanda Sahib's capital, Arcot.

That turned out to be the easy bit. The city of 100,000 people surrendered immediately and without a struggle. Clive's truly remarkable achievement was to withstand against all the odds the ferocious siege that followed. The capture of Arcot had indeed given Chanda Sahib the desired diversion from harrying Muhammad Ali at Trichinopoly. His army retook the city quickly, leaving Clive and his small force stranded in the fortress at the top of the town. For fifty days and despite heavy casualties, their unit resisted the pressure from an army of 10,000. On many occasions Clive prevailed by deciding attack was the best form of defence, making dangerous but morale-boosting sallies over the perimeter wall to demonstrate the Company troops' resolve. As his frustration mounted, the enemy commander promised to execute all prisoners if they did not instantly surrender. Fearless, or maybe reckless in the face of danger (remember his childhood steeple-climbing), Clive succeeded in rallying his troops through his own example. On one occasion an officer spied a sepoy marksman taking aim from a nearby building. He quickly stood in the line of fire and took the bullet destined for Clive.

Eventually, on 14 November, the final assault came. By this time, Clive had just 240 troops to hand, defending battlements a mile long. The next morning, when even this had failed, the enemy simply abandoned the siege and marched off. An English sergeant described the feeling to an early biographer of Clive: 'Thus did providence disappoint our fears, and relieve us from the dread necessity of starving or submitting to the terms of the merciless barbarians… We fully and unmolested enjoyed the fruits of the earth so long denied us, tho' every day in our sight, and solaced ourselves with the pleasing reflection of having maintained the character of Britons in a clime so remote from our own.'

It hadn't been a display of military genius, more a heady combination of courage and luck. Nevertheless, it's with good reason that the defence of Arcot has been described by Clive's biographer Nirad Chaudhuri as 'one of the most memorable military feats of the British in India'. Without doubt, it was the first real military success the Company had enjoyed on the subcontinent. Up till then they had impressed no one much on the battlefield. As such, Arcot was the launch-pad for a military reputation that was designed to protect the Company's commerce in India, but ended up doing that through conquest.

Without pausing to rest, Clive made good his temporary advantage by immediately giving chase to the enemy and their French allies. Recognizing the prevailing wind, many of the best troops switched over to his side. Within a year, the French strategy was in tatters. Indeed, they were never quite the same threat again. Not long afterwards the Compagnie summarily relieved Dupleix of his post and recalled him to Paris. Though he was in something akin to disgrace, Dupleix's vast fortune no doubt helped console him. He went home with 181 crates including two million livres of jewels and precious stones, five monkeys, two camels and an entire trunk of handkerchiefs.

Clive, who in so many respects was the mirror of his rival, reaped the immediate rewards of victory. The suddenly changed British prospects were instantly recognized as a personal achievement. A grateful Muhammad Ali rather tactlessly insisted that though Clive was still a captain, he 'deserves to be chief'. Ali showered Clive with tokens of his appreci- ation. He was granted the distinguished Mughal title of *Bahadur* ('the Brave'), got to sit on a *masnad* (a ceremonial cushion reserved for Mughal rulers) and, best of all, was given a very large *jaghir* (annuity). In a letter to the Governor at Madras, Ali insisted 'whatever advantages you may reap from this are entirely owing to the valour of Captain Clive'. The Company knew this. Though their presents were more modest, they too fêted the new hero. A despatch came from the directors in London acknowledging 'the great regard they had for the merit of Captain Clive, to whose courage and conduct the late turn of our affairs has been mainly due'. Ironically, thanks to Dupleix's example and Clive's retort, the

OVERLEAF:

THE SUCCESS OF THE

BRITISH IN INDIA WAS

LARGELY A RESULT OF ITS

SEPOY TROOPS, WHO WERE

HIGHLY TRAINED AND

WORE WESTERN UNIFORMS.

unambitious trading outfit in Madras now found itself pulling the political strings and harvesting significant revenues from much of South India.

From this point onwards the Company's strategy was partly territorial. As we have seen, this was not the pursuit of some grand imperial vision. It was simply found to be good business. And far from inventing this new cash-cow, the Company were simply acting in a manner traditional to India, where the purpose of political power was generally thought to be to enhance personal wealth. In the past they had fought shy of the perpetual conflict between rival regional powers, each bent on conquest to enable it to exact more tax from more people. Now, thanks to their support for Muhammad Ali, they took their first steps to wading in. The Company's revenues tripled in little more than a decade – Muhammad Ali alone paying up an annual 64,000 pagodas (approximately £30,000), the equivalent of the entire Madras revenues before the outbreak of war.

Imperialist and Indian nationalist historians tell the story very differently, but agree that Arcot was the turning-point. They are right that this was the first step on the road to the Raj. But this was far from being the plan. Indeed, more sanguine observers, such as the Company's recent historian John Keay, point out that the Company were scarcely aware of the political consequences, still less the administrative and moral obligations, of this emerging accidental empire. Moreover, there is little to suggest that the Indian inhabitants of Madras or Karnataka noticed much, if any, change. There is certainly no evidence of any sense of national humiliation. Hindu Tamils would have been hard-pressed to see any categorical difference between their domination by the English and their former subjugation by equally foreign, Persian-speaking Muslim Mughal warlords and their mercenary armies of Marathas, Pathans and Punjabis. Indeed, Keay goes so far as to venture, 'given a choice, it could well be, as the Company's men maintained, that the native population preferred the rule of Christian foreigners to that of Muslim foreigners, that of European factors to that of Asian imperialists, and that of a mercantile bourgeoisie to that of a militaristic aristocracy'.

The dramatic turn of events in the south was extensively reported in Bengal. Yet initially its lessons were lost on Calcutta, already by far the richest and largest of the Company's three Indian presidencies. If anything, Calcutta's defences were even less adequate than Madras's had been in 1746. This was a city turned in on itself, motivated by commerce and otherwise preoccupied only by its own internal squabbles. The old Fort William on the Hooghly River was too small, poorly maintained and undermanned to offer any refuge in an emergency. Merchants' houses clustered around its deficient ramparts, providing perfect cover for any enemy forces attempting to take the city. The Calcutta Council had approved no end of schemes to rectify the situation, urged on by the Company's Court of Directors in London. But for all the talk, the only action was a belated attempt, largely at the behest of nervous Indian merchants, to clear out the rubbish from an old defensive ditch marking out the boundaries of the city. This paltry action nonetheless aggravated the Company's effective landlord, the Nawab of Bengal, who had taken better note than the British in Calcutta of the implications of recent events. 'You are merchants,' he pointed out. 'What need have you of a fortress? Being under my protection you have nothing to fear.' In April 1756 the Nawab died, bequeathing the throne to his impetuous young grandson Siraj-ud-Daula. His dying words to his successor were: 'Keep in view the power the Europeans have in this country. On pretence of private contests between their kings they seize and divide the Empire – the power of the English is great, reduce them first.'

Few enemies of the British have been dealt a worse press than Siraj. A 1910 edition of *History of the British Nation* dubs him 'half mad, blood-crazed… the most evil despot since the Roman Emperor Caligula'. Yet his grievances were legitimate, his anxieties more than justified and his actions reckless and indecisive rather than especially wicked, given the norms of the time. Siraj was not only alarmed by the efforts, however half-hearted, to strengthen Calcutta's defences. He also rightly objected to the Company's widespread abuse of the *dastak*, the customs-free status granted Company trade by the old Mughal *firman* (imperial decree) from Delhi which deprived him of revenue. In its complacency, the Company thought they could buy Siraj off in the traditional way. Instead, in June 1756 only weeks after he inherited the throne, Siraj set out for Calcutta with 30,000 infantry, 20,000 cavalry, 400 elephants and 80 cannon. Even then, when the small Company force charged with defending the city advocated demolishing European houses close to the fort to afford them a better field of fire, the buildings' owners successfully objected to the plan, 'not knowing whether the Company would reimburse them the money they cost'.

The restored ditch proved no obstacle to such a vast army. In panic, some 2,500 Europeans retreated into the small fort. All semblance of discipline vanished and an all-night council session ended when a cannonball tore through the chamber, causing 'the utmost clamour, confusion, tumult and perplexity… leaving every member to imagine his proposals would be followed and put into execution'. The best that could be hoped for was an orderly evacuation of the city by river, with a dozen or so ships standing by for that purpose. Instead the next morning there was a mad stampede at the quayside, capsizing some of the boats so that a number of people drowned. The boats slipped away, some of them half-full. Among the most eager refugees were the president, the majority of the council and the military top brass. Of the commanding officer, Colonel Minchin, a council member later wrote: 'Touching the military capacity of our Commandant, I am a stranger. I can only say that we were unhappy in his keeping it to himself if he had any, as neither I, nor I believe anyone else, was witness to any part of his conduct that spoke or bore the

appearance of his being the commanding military officer in the garrison.'

The acerbic author was John Zephaniah Holwell, whose account of subsequent events unsurprisingly casts him in the role of hero. Holwell now took command, though he had been one of the first to advocate retreat and it was said only stayed because his own boat had left him behind. Within hours, Siraj successfully stormed the fort and the remaining Europeans were taken prisoner. It's worth noting that this in itself was an act of unusual mercy. Under prevailing European rules of war at the time, a fort that did not surrender but resisted an assault after a breach had been made could expect no quarter. The conquering troops were entitled to put all those who had resisted to the sword. Siraj, for all his alleged blood-lust, chose to forgo his rights. Instead the remaining European soldiers and civilians were locked up for the night in the fort's existing punishment cell. Unfortunately, 20 June 1756 was the hottest night of the year, the cell was far too small for its inmates, and by morning, ten hours later, a large number were dead. Most of the survivors were immediately released and allowed to head downriver to join their compatriots. As far as undisputed bald facts go, that in essence is the entire tale of the Black Hole.

Much of the rest of the Black Hole mythology is unreliable, being almost wholly dependent on Holwell's melodramatic, self-serving best-seller *A Genuine Narrative of the Deplorable Deaths of the English Gentlemen and Others who were suffocated in the Black Hole in Fort William, at Calcutta, in the Kingdom of Bengal*. Holwell felt compelled to put pen to paper on the boat home because 'there are some scenes in real life, so full of misery and horror, that the boldest imagination would not dare to feign them for fear of shocking credibility'.

According to Holwell, 'one hundred and forty six wretches, exhausted by continual fatigue and action' were crammed into the cell, which he described as an 18-foot cube of 'dead walls'. To the west there was a narrow, raised sleeping area and two small, barred windows, the only source of fresh air. Holwell is quick to point out he had earlier spurned the chance to escape when a colleague showed him a secret passage out of the fort because

he 'was resolved to share their fate'. Now, as the cell's occupants panicked, Holwell took command, appealed for silence and made a moving speech in which he 'urged to them that the only chance we had left for sustaining this misfortune, and surviving the night, was the preserving a calm mind and quiet resignation to our fate; intreating them to curb, as much as possible, every agitation of mind and body, as raving and giving a loose to their passions could answer no purpose but that of hastening their destruction'.

Despite the presence of one woman, a Mrs Carey, every man bar Holwell soon stripped. Those who collapsed to the floor were 'instantly trod to death or suffocated'. In desperation, many made futile efforts to force the door, while others insulted the guards through the windows in the hope they would start shooting and thus put the prisoners out of their misery. Holwell had the advantage of being pressed up against a window: 'I obtained air enough to give my lungs easy play, though my perspiration was excessive, and thirst commencing. At this period, so strong a urinous volatile effluvia came from the prison, that I was not able to turn my head that way for more than a few seconds at a time.'

'Water, water,' soon became the general cry, and a guard kindly brought some, 'little dreaming, I believe, of its fatal effects'. The far-sighted Holwell begged the guard to desist, but to no avail. 'Words cannot paint to you the universal agitation and raving the sight of it threw us into.' Holwell and those near the bars used their hats to pass the water to their colleagues, but 'there ensued such violent struggles, and frequent contests to get at it, that before it reached the lips of any one, there would be scarcely a small tea-cup full left in them'. The guards so enjoyed the spectacle of watching the prisoners trample each other to death over the water, that they kept up the supply. Holwell's two neighbours were now pressed to death and other senior officers were 'dead at my feet and were now trampled upon by every corporal or common soldier'. Holwell managed to abandon the crush and move into the middle of the cell where 'the throng was less by the many dead… Here my poor friend Mr Edward Eyre came staggering over the dead to me, and with his usual coolness and good nature, asked me how I did? but fell and expired before I had time to make him a reply.' Now thirst hit Holwell too with a desperate intensity. He tried drinking his own urine but it was too bitter to stomach. He did find some relief however 'by sucking the perspiration out of my shirt-sleeves'. But his neighbour, Mr Lushington, seized on the same sleeve 'and robbed me… of a considerable part of my store'. Lushington also survived the night and 'since paid me the compliment of assuring me, he believed he owed his life to the many comfortable drafts he had from my sleeves'.

By 2 a.m. Holwell was ready to give up, and got out a penknife from his pocket 'with which I determined instantly to open my arteries'. Holding back at the last minute, he instead lost all consciousness and was given up for dead. But so many had now died that there was proportionately greater air remaining per survivor. At day-break his colleagues

JOHN ZEPHANIAH HOLWELL WROTE THE FAMOUS AND CONTROVERSIAL ACCOUNT THAT IMMORTALISED THE BLACK HOLE OF CALCUTTA.

found signs of life in him and carried him to the window, By six, their ordeal was over and they were released from the Black Hole. Holwell counted only twenty-three survivors (including Mrs Carey) of the original 146.

Holwell's account has been tediously disputed ever since, first by British contemporaries who suspected him of embroidery and self-aggrandisement, later by historians, some of whom even doubt whether the incident actually happened. Holwell's statistics have been especially disbelieved, with one recent account suggesting that perhaps as many as forty-three survived of only sixty-four inmates, many of whom were probably carrying battle wounds before their imprisonment. To be fair to Holwell, other evidence is so scant that there is no more reason to disbelieve his account than to treat it as gospel. It should also be pointed out that he explicitly confirms the Black Hole debacle was accidental negligence on Siraj-ud-Daula's part, not a case of deliberate murder. Holwell says Siraj ordered the incarceration of the British prisoners in Fort William's existing prison, already known as the Black Hole, without knowing its dimensions. Then he went to bed, and as the prisoners started dying, no lowly guard dared rouse the Nawab to double-check his intentions. History reveals several cases where prisoners of the British died of suffocation in similar circumstances.

It took more than fifty years for the Black Hole story to loom large in imperial iconography. But by the end of the nineteenth century, cheap, lurid engravings and racy accounts tended to suggest that avenging this outrage was one of the main reasons Britain felt compelled to conquer India. At the time, of course, it was the loss of Calcutta that grieved the Company. There was no question but that they would immediately attempt to take it back.

The man charged with the task was Robert Clive, who had returned to Madras in search of further wealth after his dubious Westminster election victory had been quashed by the House of Commons. On 15 December 1756, Clive reached the Calcutta refugees at their pitiful anchorage at Fulta. A legendary 200 days later they had not only recovered the city but defeated and ousted Siraj, imposed a puppet nawab and become effective masters of the whole of Bengal. Immediately the business was done, Clive wrote breathlessly to Orme: 'I am possessed of volumes of materials for the continuance of your History, in which will appear fighting, tricks, chicanery, intrigues, politics and the Lord knows what. In short there will be a fine field for you to display your genius in.'

Of this list, 'fighting' was by far the least important. And as for the 'tricks' etc, the honours should be granted as much to powerful Indian factions as to Clive and the Company. As we shall see, behind the myth, the true story of the conquest of Bengal is that it was (mostly Indian) private enterprise attempting to throw off the shackles of public control. An unstable ruler was threatening their security and prosperity. Indian bankers and merchants conspired with the Company to depose one troublesome nawab and replace him

with another. This can hardly be portrayed as a national betrayal even though the Indian conspirators' names to this day are synonymous with treachery. But Indian national sentiment did not yet exist. Meanwhile the nawabs and their courts, like most within the Mughal hierarchy, were all in some sense foreigners in the eyes of the ordinary people. And court intrigue leading to a change of rulership was the routine mechanism by which powerful interests could secure advantage, letting politics catch up with the realities of wealth and influence. So the Battle of Plassey, often listed as one of the most decisive in world history, was in fact little more than a shoo-in — certainly not military genius against the odds, but simply a well-planned coup d'état against the unsuspecting and unfortunate nawab who had been abandoned by his Indian financiers and allies.

By the time Clive arrived at Fulta, diplomatic efforts to persuade Siraj to return Calcutta had failed. Instead the Nawab wrote exultantly to the Emperor in Delhi that he was author of 'the most glorious achievement in Hindostan since the days of Tamerlane'. By that measure, similar honours in the rematch are due to a British sailor called Strahan. Naval bombardment had quelled the Nawab's artillery in the fort of Baj-baj that dominated the approach to Calcutta. But Clive was still cautious about an immediate assault and ordered an overnight delay. With unexpected time on his hands, 'one Strahan, a common sailor belonging to the *Kent*' took to drinking. Whether through bravado or disorientation, he stumbled forward, waded the moat and 'took it upon his head to scale a breach that had been made by the cannon of the ships'. He emerged on top of one of the bastions and immediately ran into a group of guards. They set upon him but 'he flourished his cutlass, and fired his pistol', gave three loud huzzas and cried out, 'The place is mine!' And near enough it was. The commotion roused his colleagues, who poured into the breach after him and routed the enemy. Strahan fought on with 'incomparable resolution' though his cutlass had been broken off at the hilt.

The triumphant Strahan was immediately charged with a gross breach of military discipline. He pleaded guilty, explaining, 'Why to be sure, Sir, it was I who took the fort, but I hope there was no harm in it.' Apparently there was. As he was led away he complained, 'If I am flogged for this here action, I will never take another fort by myself as long as I live, by God.' His efforts were not needed. Following this action, Calcutta surrendered on New Year's Day 1757 after resisting British naval bombardment for less than an hour.

The British were unanimous that this should not be the end of the affair. Clive had written to London months earlier that, 'I flatter myself that this expedition will not end with the retaking of Calcutta only: and that the Company's estate in these parts will be settled in a better and more lasting condition than ever.' At the same time he had privately written to his father that this was his big chance to 'do great things'. Now it was time for the tricks and chicanery, the plotting of what came to be called a 'revolution' in Bengal.

The first step was to declare war on Siraj-ud-Daula, who was safe at his capital,

Murshidabad. Peace, said the British, could come only if Siraj accepted their terms. These involved not just a full restoration of the 1717 *firman* and lavish compensation for their losses, but a grotesquely wide-ranging extension of the *dastak* (customs exemption) and the right to set up a mint at Calcutta. While diplomatic letters flew back and forth, Siraj decided on a show of strength and marched with his vast army, estimated at 100,000, towards Calcutta. After a bizarre encounter, in which heavy morning fog prevented either side from working out where they were going, let alone who had really won, the Nawab finally agreed to the British terms. Good as they were, some felt cheated of full victory since it was clear that, like the British, the Nawab was playing for time. Writing in Persian and elegantly parodying the tone of Mughal diplomatic correspondence, the British Naval Commander, Admiral Watson, warned Siraj strictly to observe the Treaty or 'I will kindle such a flame in your country as all the water in the Ganges will not be able to extinguish.'

Formal peace, however, had great advantages. It allowed a quick return to business, which cheered the Company's shareholders. It gave Clive time to bribe, plot and intrigue, marshalling allies for an even more profitable outcome. And, with Siraj formally bound by treaty to the Company, he was prevented from forging an alliance with the French, whose stronghold at Chandernagar was both feared and envied by the British Company. When news reached Bengal from Europe that once again Britain and France were at war (the beginning of the Seven Years War), the gloves were off for a trial of strength. The British could not attack Chandernagar without the approval of the Nawab – they were supposedly only merchants, after all. Siraj was dead set against any such action. But after a flurry of meetings, letters, threats and promises, the Company's agent at Murshidabad finally obtained a letter from Siraj which, interpreted extravagantly, seemed to give them the go-ahead. Siraj wrote: 'If your enemy, with an upright heart, claims your protection, you will give him his life; but then you must be well satisfied of the innocence of his intentions; if not, whatever you think right, that do.' John Keay comments: 'only one steeped in Oriental intrigue and conversant with the finer points of diplomatic utterance could possible have seen in this an invitation to make war on the French. Perhaps the whole episode goes to show how adept the Company's servants were becoming in these dark arts.'

Chandernagar succumbed after a fierce battle, by far the costliest of the 200 days. The French never threatened British domination over Bengal again, though the town itself was restored to the French in the eventual international peace treaty, and remained a French colony until 1950, three years after the final curtain fell on the Raj.

Time was fast running out too for the hapless Siraj. At Murshidabad, some of the richest and most powerful interests had come to realize that he was a greater threat to them than the British. Their candidate for the nawabship was Mir Jafar, a Mughal nobleman

related by marriage to Siraj and a commander in his army. Mir Jafar may have been cut from the same cloth as Siraj but he promised them rich rewards in return for their backing. Apparently, there was little subtlety about the plotting. A French observer wrote: 'Never was there a conspiracy conducted so publicly and with equal indiscretion on the part of the English and the Moors. Nothing else was talked about in all their Settlements, and what will surprise you is that, whilst every place echoed with the noise of it, the Nawab, who had a number of spies, was ignorant of everything. Nothing can prove more clearly the general hatred which was felt for him.'

The chief conspirators against Siraj were the Jagat Seth brothers, two Marwari Jains from Rajastan who headed the richest private banking dynasty in India. Their palace at Murshidabad was said to employ 4,000 people. It was lavishly decorated with tiles specially imported from Holland depicting biblical scenes. The Seths feared the money supply would suffer if silver from Europe ceased to flow into Bengal in exchange for traded goods. But for them the grudge against Siraj was personal as well as financial. Siraj had apparently dishonoured one of their female relatives. Rai Durlabh, a Bengali Hindu who was Siraj's *diwan* (chief financial official), was also easing into the conspirators' camp. The third key power-broker brought into the conspiracy was the Sikh merchant Omichand, who had long succeeded in keeping a well-heeled foot in the camps of both Siraj and the Company.

By the end of May a secret treaty had been finalized between the chief British players and Mir Jafar, spelling out not just the alliance but exhaustive terms to reward the Company, the Army and Navy and a large number of individuals. A last-minute hitch threatened the whole deal. Omichand demanded 5 per cent of the treasury at Murshidabad as the price of his co-operation. Mir Jafar would hear none of this. Omichand supposedly then attempted blackmail by threatening to expose the entire plot to Siraj. It was Clive who came up with the notorious solution to the impasse. He persuaded his colleagues to draw up two versions of the treaty, one on red paper, the other on white. Only the red fictitious version included Omichand's pay-off. The real copy in white cut him out entirely. When Admiral Watson refused on principle to be a party to the fraud, it was Clive who persuaded the others to forge his signature. Ever since, moralizers, chief among them Macaulay, have deemed this the most reprehensible of all Clive's actions. In India too Clive has ever more been dubbed 'the forger'. Yet a recent historian of the Raj, Lawrence James, probably gets it right when he cites it as 'a victory for guile over greed'.

Claiming that Siraj was continuing to violate his treaty with the Company, Clive marched north on 13 June 1757 with 3,000 troops. That same day he sent his last letter to Siraj, its tone still belying his real intent: 'The rains being daily increasing, and it taking a great deal of time to receive your answer, I therefore find it necessary to wait on you immediately,

FRANCIS HAYMAN FANCIFULLY DEPICTS THE MOMENT AFTER THE BATTLE WHEN ROBERT CLIVE FIRST GREETS HIS CO-CONSPIRATOR MIR JAFAR, THE NEW NAWAB OF BENGAL.

and if you will place confidence in me no harm shall come of it. I represent this to you as a friend. Act as you please.' In just over a week, they reached striking distance of the Nawab's army of 50,000 troops, who were encamped at Plassey, a few miles south of Murshidabad.

Even at this late stage, Clive was uncertain what to do next. Letters to Mir Jafar were going unanswered and he began to doubt whether the conspiracy would hold. He held a council of war with seventeen senior officers to vote on whether 'on our own bottom it would be prudent to attack the Nabob' or whether they should wait for a clear sign that Mir Jafar would indeed betray Siraj and turn his forces on their own monarch. With the majority, Clive voted for caution. As his army marched under cover of darkness into position at Plassey, they still had little idea whether they were there to make peace, war or something in between. At dawn on 23 June, facing an entire plain of enemy troops, together with the normal array of elephants, cavalry and bullock-drawn artillery, Clive sent a last curt note to Mir Jafar: 'Whatever could be done by me I have done, I can do no more. If you will come to Daudpur I will march from Placis to meet you, but if you won't comply even with this, pardon me, I shall make it up with the Nawab!'

What ensued, though decisive, was a minor skirmish, not a great battle. The Nawab's artillery fired first and Clive's forces thought it prudent to withdraw behind an embankment to relative safety. Four hours of fairly sporadic artillery exchange followed without any closer fighting. The British were still unclear which of the troops facing them belonged to Mir Jafar, how many he commanded or what he intended to do. Meanwhile, a heavy monsoon downpour was drenching the Nawab's powder and inclining him to withdraw until nightfall. Clive too was contemplating something similar and, fed up with wet clothes, he had quit the battlefield in order to change into a dry uniform. At that moment, a British officer, one Major Killpatrick, noticed the withdrawal of one of the enemy's artillery pieces. In defiance of orders he advanced with two guns to take up the abandoned position. Clive returned to the scene, furious at this reckless action. But it was quickly clear that the enemy troops were not counter-attacking. Thousands on the British flanks had turned spectator and were evidently loyal to Mir Jafar. The carefully planned conspiracy would indeed skew the entire contest. Clive immediately ordered a full attack, which succeeded in routing the Nawab's forces almost before they had started. Of Siraj's 50,000 troops, it's thought less than a quarter offered any resistance. The entire affair was over with minimal casualties. The British lost four Europeans and fourteen sepoys. There were fewer than 500 losses on the Nawab's side.

The chief casualty was of course Siraj, who fled but was tracked down and assassinated by Mir Jafar's son not long afterwards. By then Clive had graciously helped Mir Jafar on to the throne and equally graciously helped himself and his co-conspirators to a king's ransom.

———————————

In less than fifteen years, the East India Company had become utterly severed from its old strategy of 'quiet trade'. Thanks to Clive and his colleagues, it had seen off the challenge from the French company for trading supremacy. It had become permanently enmeshed in Indian politics. To further secure or enhance its revenues, it would soon find itself abandoning the pretence of puppet nawabs to become the direct ruler of Bengal. Within fifty years it was in effect governing most of India.

This turn of events leading to an accidental empire has bemused observers ever since. One of Clive's sidekicks, Luke Scrafton, put it down to the nature of Indian society: 'An Englishman cannot but wonder to see how little the subjects in general are affected by any revolution in the government. It is not felt beyond the small circle of the court. To the rest it is a matter of the utmost indifference, whether the tyrant is a Persian or a Tartar.' Even so, the great nineteenth-century French historian Alexis de Tocqueville marvelled that an empire two-thirds the size of Alexander the Great's had been founded against the formal orders of the authorities at home, and that it was to grow despite the deliberate attempts of the East India Company, the British Government and public opinion to halt that advance.

But empire was still the last thing on most Company men's minds. Taking a lead from Clive, they were still focused, entirely legitimately, on loot. In accordance with the terms of the secret treaty, Mir Jafar was forced to dip into his newly won coffers and immediately dole out about £1.5 million as presents to the Company, the military, Clive and his cronies. Omichand of course got nothing. With available sums exhausted, Mir Jafar found he still owed a further one million pounds.

Robert Clive the victor of Plassey had himself walked into Siraj-ud-Daula's treasury shortly after Plassey. Asked later to explain his actions by Parliament, he famously protested: 'An opulent city lay at my mercy; its richest bankers bid against each other for my smiles; I walked through vaults which were thrown open to me alone, piled on either hand with gold and jewels! Mr Chairman, at this moment I stand astonished at my own moderation.'

Clive, who not long before had enjoyed the standard clerk's salary of £10 a year, received £234,000. Under pressure, Mir Jafar later awarded him a promised *jaghir* with a lifetime salary of £27,000. But the protection racket had only just begun.

CHAPTER THREE

NABOBS

'One of the most wicked places in the Universe,' said Clive about Calcutta, perhaps with a smirk of approval. This was a honky-tonk Klondike kind of town, where men drank, strutted and brawled, lived for the moment, worshipped nothing but the green-back, and spent it as quickly as they came by it. This was when Calcutta so dazzled with garish high-living that it became known as 'the City of Palaces'. Though truth to tell, there was enough poverty and overcrowding, open sewers and dismal stews for it already to deserve Rudyard Kipling's later moniker 'The City of Dreadful Night':

Today Kipling's city is instantly recognizable, though this thrilling place is far less of a Black Hole than concerned Indians will have you believe when you tell them where you're heading. But 'the City of Palaces' takes some imagining, even when a remnant of its splendour is staring you in the face.

Demolition and development have of course done their work – this is, after all, one of the most densely

FADED GRANDEUR IN CALCUTTA — AN OCCASIONAL DILAPIDATED BUILDING IS ALL THAT REMAINS OF THE ORIGINAL 'CITY OF PALACES'.

populated cities on Earth. The lawns and gardens mostly went a century or more ago. The wrecking-ball later got most of the houses, turning bungalows for four into life insurance offices for a couple of thousand. But occasionally you'll still find the tattered classical façade of an eighteenth-century bungalow (literally 'of Bengal'), its veneer of yellowing plaster – for so much of Calcutta's original luxury was cosmetic – flaking off like dead skin. You'll be able to make out the *porte cochère*, where visitors could be hauled out of their palanquins without being exposed to the sun. And there might be a perfect Corinthian capital part-obscured by a sign announcing the Purbanchal Ex-Servicemen's Welfare Association or the Office of the Deputy Superintending Epigraphist. In the gloom inside, interior partitions have long since cluttered up the original, extravagant sweep of dining-room–drawing-room–veranda.

These few remaining city 'palaces' are now mostly workplaces. But out near the airport at Dum Dum (birthplace of the infamous exploding bullet), Clive's half-ruined country house plays dangerous host to sixty-odd squatters. In the decade after Plassey, Clive was to become the undisputed overlord of the Company in Bengal. Taking their example from him, the Company's top merchants and soldiers set about reaping the fruits of victory with a speed and determination that was quite breathtaking. However unsavoury this might seem, it was, according to both Company regulations and the norms of post-Mughal power-politics, utterly legitimate. The former acknowledged the need for big personal rewards and incentives. The latter had always been based on a version of winner-takes-all. Indeed, the participants in this bonanza modelled themselves as much on Oriental despots as on English aristocrats. So they were dubbed 'nabobs' as an anglicism of the 'nawabs' whose powers they were beginning to supplant and whose hedonistic lifestyles they now crudely parodied. These nabobs set Calcutta on the road to becoming the Empire's second city. Then they went home determined not just to flash their wads, but to use the loot to buy themselves real power in Britain.

Job Charnock's Calcutta had been all but destroyed during Siraj-ud-Daula's siege and brief occupation. Now a new city began to emerge. What had been three nondescript fishing villages a few generations back would, by 1775, become a city of 250,000 people, including perhaps 2,500 Europeans. The tiger-infested jungle south of the old Fort William was cleared, and a new fort constructed. To prevent history repeating itself, the new Fort William was surrounded by a vast open space, the Maidan, which provided clear line-of-fire and a recreational heart to the city for riding, racing and the regulation evening carriage drive. This was a chance to see and be seen or, as it was known, to *'hawa khana'* (eat the air). By 1804 the Maidan had hosted India's first cricket match: Old Etonians versus Calcutta.

Though the European men outnumbered European women eight-to-one, enough British girls now began to arrive hunting husbands, armed with trunks full of the latest London fashions, to encourage sumptuous balls and an endless round of more tediously genteel visits. There were also romantic boat-trips on the Hooghly – just the amorous couple, forty boatmen and an African slaveboy from Mauritius who had been taught to play the French horn. Soon Calcutta boasted two French hairdressers, several theatres and newspapers, a celebrated performance of Handel's *Messiah* and a Masonic temple. But though all this aped London society, the British inhabitants were too much of a fast-set, too macho, raucous, even vulgar, for this to set the real tone in Calcutta. You're closer to the spirit of the place and times when you imagine the legendary bread-pellet flicking contests that enlivened so many dinners. Those who could snuff a candle out from several yards became the talk of the town. Indeed, the real pulse of the city could be found in its drinking clubs, gambling dens and high-stake card tables. Calcutta's young Sheriff, Alexander Mackrabie, recorded the ex-pat antics in his diary:

September 1775 – In the evening played cards at Lady Anne Monson's: three whist tables and two chess. Quadrille is little in vogue here, Lady Anne is a very superior whist-player. Mr Francis generally fortunate.

November 3 1775 (A party at the Claverings')…*Entre Nous*, the evening was stupid enough, and the supper detestable; great joints of roasted goat, with endless dishes of cold fish. With respect to conversation, we have had three or four songs screeched to unknown tunes; the ladies regaled with cherry-brandy, and we pelted one another with bread-pills *à la mode* de Bengal.

March 8 1776 – We supped at Mr Barwell's and lost our monies. I have lost seven rubbers running. Oh, sad, sad, sad!

Saturday March 9 1776 – There was a ball at Colonel Gallier's, and the French women dancing cotillions as if they had not another hour to live… Miss Howe, who lives with Lady Impey, is going to marry Dr Campbell, who has fewer hairs and more years than I have. There was he capering about and gallanting the lady and exercising her fan; she is not above sixteen… We who did not dance needs must drink. I have got the biles and the indigestion cruelly this morning, and there is General Clavering gone out at six and carried those dear girls with him on horseback, though they were not in bed before two.

THE LUXURIOUS CALCUTTA

LIFESTYLE OF THE NABOBS

IS EXQUISITELY RENDERED

IN JOHN ZOFFANY'S

PAINTING OF SIR ELIJAH

AND LADY IMPEY, THEIR

THREE CHILDREN AND

SERVANTS.

Another significant indicator of the zeitgeist was that, despite all the construction works, for three decades Calcutta lacked a purpose-built church to replace the one Siraj had destroyed. Instead, churchgoers made do with a temporary chapel that served as a customs depot from Monday to Saturday. Mackrabie explained in a letter to his father that Calcutta's few British clergymen were hardly overwhelmed by the spiritual and pastoral burdens of their calling. One thought about little except hunting, riding out most days with Calcutta's large pack of hunting dogs. The second seems to have become obsessed with 'Chinese gardening'. The third concentrated on business by becoming a major supplier of bullocks to the army. In short, 'I endeavour to find some light from them all; but the fear of God is not the kind of wisdom most in request in Bengal.' Indeed, it was said that the main incentive to go to this apology for a church was that it served as a pick-up joint. 'By sanction of ancient custom', any new woman in town, fresh off the 'fishing fleet', would turn up in church while the eager men jostled to be the one to help her down from her palanquin towards a vacant pew.

Maintaining this kind of lifestyle did not of course come cheap. Calcutta rents in the last third of the eighteenth century were higher than they would be again until about 1900. They were certainly on a par with London's top addresses. Since the landlords were Indian, they also hint at the incomes being accumulated by non-Europeans. We know Ruttoo Sircar, for example, owned nineteen houses in Calcutta and lived magnificently off these rents and the interest from loans to Europeans.

Mackrabie shared a house with his brother-in-law Philip Francis, obstreperous scion of the four-man ruling Council of Calcutta. £500 bought them only 'a large, but rather mean house like a barn, with bare walls and not a single glass window'. It was 'surrounded with mosques and pagodas, where they make, night and day, such a cursed clatter with drums, cymbals, horns and pans you would think a legion of devils were keeping jubilee'. There was nothing for it but to move. Finally, in February 1776, Mackrabie tells us: 'We have at last engaged a capital house, the best in town; but such a rent! £100 a month is enormous.'

Once you'd found the right bachelor pad, you had to muster the household to go with it. Mackrabie was so amazed by the extravagance, he described in detail the domestic arrangements for this house he shared with three other young men:

My own establishment consists of a *Sircar* [a broker and interpreter], a *Jemmadar* who stands at my Door, receives messages, announces visitors, and also runs by the side of my palanquin to clear the way. I am preceded in all my peregrinations by two *peons* or running footmen and any number of *Hircarrahs* or messengers… Eight Bearers for my Palanquin complete my Train… Mr F [i.e. Mr Francis] keeps five [horses] and according to the cursed custom of this idle country, has ten fellows to look after them, besides a Coachman to keep the whole in order. He has moreover 12 Palanquin bearers, for no reason that I can learn except his being a Councillor – four *Peons*, four *Hircarrahs*, two *Chubdars* who carry silver staves, two *Jemmadars*. These are without doors. Within: a Head *Sircar*, or *Banian*… Housekeeping Comprador and his mate go to market, two coolies bring home what he buys – *Consomar* takes charge of it. Cook and two mates dress it. Baker in the house. Butler and assistant take charge of Liquor. *Abdar* and his mate cool them. Two Side-Board men wait at Table. House – two *Metranees* [sweeper-women] to clean it, two watchmen to guard it, a *Durwan* to keep the Door. Tailor, Washermen and Ironing Men for each person. *Mashalgees* or Torch-Bearers F [Francis] 4, M [Mackrabie] 2, L [Livins] 1, C [Collings] 1. We make a flaming funeral appearance. Two *Mallies* or Gardeners, Cow and Poultry Feeder and Pork Man…

Let me see:

Mr F	62
Macr	20
L & Coll	28

= 110	

One Hundred and Ten servants to wait upon a family of four People!

Even if labour was very cheap, phenomenal incomes were needed to sustain such lavish lifestyles. Yet neither the duties of the Company servant, nor his private trading activities where the real money was made, were exactly onerous. Sometimes, as the eighteenth-century travel-writer James Mackintosh reported, you needed to do little more than conserve your energy while the money came rolling in:

About the hour of 7 in the morning, his *durwan* opens the gate and the *veranda* is free to his *circars, peons, harcarrahs, chubdars, houccaburdars* [hookah-bearers] and *consumahs* [butlers], writers and solicitors. The head-bearer and *jemmadar* enter the hall, and his bedroom at 8-o'clock… The moment the master throws his legs out of bed, the whole posse in-waiting rush into his room each making three salaams, by bending the body and head very low, and touching the forehead with the inside of the fingers, and the floor with the back part. He condescends, perhaps, to nod or cast an eye towards the solicitor of his favour and protection. In about half an hour, after undoing and taking off his long drawers, a clean shirt, breeches, stockings and slippers are put upon his body, thigh, legs and feet without any greater exertion on his own part than if he was a statue. The barber enters, shaves him, cuts his nails, and cleans his ears. The *chillumjee* [basin] and ewer are brought by a servant whose duty it is, who pours water upon his head and face, and presents a towel. The superior then walks in state to his breakfasting parlour in his waistcoat; is seated; the *consumah* makes and pours out his tea, and presents him with a plate of bread or toast. The hairdresser comes behind, and begins his operation while the *houccaburdar* swiftly slips the upper-end of the snake or tube of the *houcca* into his hand; while the hairdresser is doing his duty, the gentleman is eating, sipping and smoking by turns.

By and by his *banian* presents himself with his humble salaams… If any of the solicitors are of eminence, they are honoured with chairs. These ceremonies are continued until perhaps ten o'clock, when, attended by his cavalcade, he is conducted to his palanquin, and preceded by 8 to 12 *chubdars, harcarrahs* and *peons*… If he has visits to make, his *peons* lead and direct the bearers, and if his business renders his presence only necessary, he shows himself and pursues his other engagements until 2 o'clock, when he and his company sit down, perfectly at ease in point of dress and address to a good dinner, each attended by his own servant. As it is expected that they shall return to supper, at 4 o'clock they begin to withdraw without ceremony, and step into their palanquins so that in a few minutes, the master is left to go into his bedroom, when he is instantly undressed to his shirt, and his long drawers put on, and he lies down on his bed, where he sleeps until about seven or eight o'clock. Then the former ceremony is repeated, and clean linen of every kind, as in the morning, administered… After tea, he puts on a handsome coat, and pays visits of ceremony to the ladies; returns a little before ten o'clock; supper being served at ten. The company keeps together till between 12 and one in the morning preserving great sobriety and decency, and when they depart our hero is conducted to his bedroom… With no greater exertions than these, do the Company's servants amass the most splendid fortunes.

Such extravagant lifestyles were by no means confined to the British. Nor, despite many of the trappings of English society, was Calcutta any kind of British provincial town. Rather it was a sort of Hong Kong of its day, one of the first modern, international cities, populated by a cosmopolitan crowd all hoping to take a cut of the good times. This did not of course make it a melting-pot. But it did foster a certain cheek-by-jowl, live-and-let-live multiculturalism. The city attracted merchants and adventurers from the other European nations who had created trading settlements in India. As Calcutta's pre-eminence grew, they increasingly moved there as the fortunes of their own enclaves diminished. That brought small numbers of French, Portuguese, Dutchmen and Danes. Soon, a handful of Italians and Russians arrived, among them musicians and theatrical impresarios.

There was also a sizeable and wealthy Armenian Christian community, many of them involved in the diamond trade. Armenians had been merchants and settlers in India's main cities since the Emperor Akbar's time, long before the British or even the Portuguese had put down any firm roots. They had certainly been in Calcutta since Job Charnock's day at the end of the seventeenth century. Indeed, if you believe one much-debated gravestone in Calcutta's Armenian cemetery bearing an epitaph from 1630, they may actually lay claim to be the city's true founders.

Before 1800 there were also small but influential Jewish and Chinese communities. A certain Shalom David Cohen, presumed an Arabic- or Persian-speaking Jew, was reputedly such a great friend of the Raja of Lucknow that he was invited to ride on his elephant.

A Tonjon, or Ladies' Carriage.

TRAVELLING IN STYLE —
NO ENGLISHWOMAN
MOVED AROUND
CALCUTTA WITHOUT AT
LEAST FIVE BEARERS.

Later the great Iraqi Jewish trading empire of the Sassoon dynasty expanded from Bombay to Shanghai and Calcutta, the key axis in the lucrative (and entirely legal) opium trade to China, which the Sassoons dominated.

But as we have seen, some of Calcutta's greatest and most flamboyant fortunes were Indian. Today these great merchants, landlords and *banians* are remembered in India only so they can be despised. They are collectively known as *babus*, a vaguely insulting term in Indian English which implies that they are half-anglicized and effeminate, that they are Bengali Hindus masquerading as Muslim nawabs, and that their excessive wealth was somehow ill-gotten. The infamous crew includes Gobindram Mitter, 'the black *zamindar* [landlord]', renowned for his extravagant nautches and his religious patronage. He would honour the goddess Durga by draping her from head to toe in gold and silver during her annual festival, the Durga puja. This left him enough cash to stump up 50,000 rupees to feed a thousand brahmin priests. Later, there was Bhubanmohan Niyogi, who always lit his pipe with a ten-rupee note, and Ramtanu Datta of Hat-Khola, who wore the finest Dhaka muslin *dhoties* (loin-cloths) only once before throwing them away. Ironically, today's Indian millionaires meet less resentment. They are frequently regarded as role models and aspirational heroes, fully deserving all the glamour and glitz, admired rather than reviled for their spectacularly expensive weddings and parties.

THE MAP ON THE WALL
SUGGESTS JOHN
MOWBRAY AND HIS
BANIAN WERE MAKING
THEIR FORTUNES IN
BIHAR AND TIBET,
PROBABLY IN CLOTH,
SALTPETRE AND WOOL.

Even before Plassey, some banians had amassed great wealth. In the boom years after the battle, Indian fat-cats probably got just as much cream as their British clients. As their

historian Peter Marshall puts it, 'The master–*banian* relationship was in many respects a partnership of equals offering substantial benefits to both sides.'

The most powerful *banian* was Nabakrishna Deb, a man so rich he managed to spend half a million rupees on his mother's funeral. Finding his name a bit of a mouthful but well-nigh essential in business-talk, the English rechristened him Nobkissen. (They were always renaming Indians: Siraj-ud-Daula even more absurdly became to some writers 'Sir Roger Dowlett'). Nobkissen had travelled the road to fame and riches side-by-side with Clive. As *munshi* (Persian secretary) to the Company, he had accompanied Clive in the final campaign to overthrow Siraj-ud-Daula. In all likelihood, it was Nobkissen who acted as adviser and translator in all the key diplomatic exchanges between Clive and the Nawab – nuancing the Company's brusque sentiments into the florid and emotive circumlocutions that were the hallmark of Mughal court correspondence.

Nobkissen had allegedly joined Clive in filling his pockets at the Murshidabad Treasury after the Battle of Plassey. Later, he became Clive's own household manager, 'political *banian*' to the Company in Calcutta and a Mughal title-holder to boot. Soon after Clive returned to Britain for the last time, Nobkissen resigned all formal office. The two had obviously been close – when Clive died, his widow sent his former *banian* a picture of her husband and protestations of continuing friendship. For the next twenty-five years, Nobkissen obviously remained one of Bengal's biggest magnates, owning the city's most valuable real estate, revenue-farming vast territories, holding lucrative salt concessions and acting as banker to numerous Europeans from the Governor downwards. He apparently promised one young writer he would make him 'a great man, as he said he had made others'. When he died in 1797 he was worth 10 million rupees (£1 million).

Like other *banians* of this era, Nobkissen worked closely with the English but in no way seems to have envied or adopted their lifestyle. It would certainly never have even crossed his mind to dress in the absurd manner of the European. We know he was a great religious and artistic patron, a benefactor of many learned *pundits* (Hindu scholars) and a scholar in his own right with a celebrated Oriental library. His Hindu faith seems to have been entirely traditional and conservative, although it is unusual that his six wives could all read and write Bengali.

While the British and their Indian partners led separate lives in their separate communities, this did not prevent them socializing together, still less indicate racism on either side. Nobkissen regularly hosted nautches, which must have been glittering occasions attended by the leading lights of Calcutta's diverse high society. The most famous chronicler of every tedious detail of this indulgent and dissolute, celebrity-obsessed and shallow world was the diarist William Hickey, whose name, thanks to the famous *Daily Express* diary column, is even today synonymous with gossip. Hickey described attending one of Nobkissen's nautches:

On Monday night, Rajah Nobkissen gave a nautch and magnificent entertainment to several persons of distinction in commemoration of Miss Wrangham's birthday. As the ladies arrived, they were conducted by the Rajah through a grand suite of apartments into the zenana, where they were amused until the singing began, which was so mellifluous as to give every face a smile of approbation. The surprising agility of one of the male dancers occasioned loud acclamations of applause. The principal female singers called the nymphs and swains to celebrate the festivity of the day and spoke a few complimentary lines suitable to the occasion. After supper there was a ball, which was opened by Mr Livius and Miss Wrangham, who were dressed in the characters of Apollo and Daphne. When the minuets were ended, country dances struck up and continued till past three in the morning, when the company departed highly pleased with the elegant festival. And when the Rajah was attending Miss Wrangham to her carriage, he thanked her in very polite terms for having illuminated his house with her bright appearance.

Though they were called 'masters', it is obvious that the British traders often possessed only a fraction of the power and wealth of the *banians*, their supposed 'servants'. How could it be otherwise? As Warren Hastings put it, 'Young and inexperienced men… some totally ignorant of the language of the country… give their authority and influence to the people who had either acquired their confidence by long personal service or the right of creditors to exact it.' Often the 'master' was a mere minority stakeholder in a joint enterprise between the two, earning a healthy commission by lending his name and duty-free status to his *banian*, but otherwise having little or nothing to do with what was effectively an independent business. Peter Marshall's study of the master–*banian* relationship in Bengal concludes: 'a great deal of what passed as European trade can only have been European in the most nominal sense'.

So though the years after Plassey confirmed there had indeed been a revolution, the claims ever since that British gold-diggers put Bengal out of business need to be treated with great caution. It is true that some Indians and the French lost out. It is also true that the revolution's beneficiaries were other Indians as well as the British. This is hardly surprising since, as we have seen, they were co-authors of the whole affair.

Clive and his fellow conspirators had cleaned out the treasury at Murshidabad immediately after Plassey, leaving the newly installed Nawab, Mir Jafar, with a continuing debt of one million pounds and no evident means to pay it off. Not for the last time, Bengal's wealth had been fantastically overestimated. Mir Jafar was repeatedly forced to reschedule his debts with the Jagat Seth bankers. Every time he did so, he was also compelled to sign over territorial tax-raising rights to the Company, which of course in the

long term further limited his ability to raise revenues to meet his obligations. Mir Jafar also found his customs-income diminishing fast. The Company's *dastaks* (duty-free passes) were now extended to Company servants' private trade. In practice, almost anyone, Indian or European, who wanted to trade within Bengal found it more profitable to buy customs exemption from the nabobs than pay the taxes properly due to the Nawab. Up country, British traders and their hired goons intimidated, sometimes violently, those locals who did not immediately choose to do business according to the terms set by the mobsters.

Mir Jafar understandably became increasingly resentful of the Company. Meanwhile, his troops and officials became equally disillusioned with him, since he frequently failed to find the cash to pay their wages. He might have expected to look to Clive, grateful beneficiary of the huge *jaghir*, to help him reassert his authority. But poor health had forced the victor of Plassey back home to England to soak up the glory and revel in his new peerage, even if it was of the second division Irish variety. Clive was succeeded as Governor of Bengal by first John 'Black Hole' Holwell, then Henry Vansittart. Neither man thought much of Mir Jafar. Now, having been irrevocably sucked into Bengali politics, the Company's chieftains found it easy to turn king-maker again. In October 1760, scarcely three years after his installation, Mir Jafar was eased into retirement in favour of his son-in-law Mir Kasim. Vansittart and

Holwell accepted with gratitude the lavish presents that the new Nawab put their way. Meanwhile the Company was ceded the revenues of yet more tax districts.

But there was a problem. Mir Kasim was able, energetic and wanted to be his own man. Grappling with the notorious abuses of the dastak, he astonished everyone in 1763 by abolishing all internal customs dues. His case was simple: 'The trade which has been carried out by the English merchants… makes the name of the English stink in the nostrils of a Hindu or a Muslim.' Overnight, all *dastaks* were worthless. Of course free trade in Bengal wouldn't do at all. The last thing the nabobs really wanted was a level playing field. It was time for yet another revolution. Conspirators were gathered, an army sent north, and Mir Jafar was restored to the nawabship in place of Mir Kasim. Of course, Mir Jafar's first move was to renew the *dastak* and scatter 'presents' all round yet again. Vansittart was utterly unapologetic about his big bonuses: 'We are men of power, you say, and take advantage of it. Why, man, what is the use of station if we are not to benefit from it?'

The Company's Directors in London were, as ever, aghast at this turn of events but powerless to rein in the excesses. Most galling of all, while private individuals raked in the cash, the Company found it was not enjoying similar profits and was instead becoming burdened with ever increasing military costs. Gradually, in the years after Plassey, a national debate began which came to absorb the British Parliament and public opinion as well as the Company for much of the next century. The debate boiled down to one simple question. The East India Company, one of a number of competing European trading companies, had suddenly found itself in an unrivalled position to fulfil all its ambitions in India. The question was: what should those ambitions be? And since it was patently obvious to everyone that this now involved issues far wider than commerce, the question was inescapably bigger: what were Britain's ambitions and interests in India?

Broadly speaking, the Directors in London reiterated, increasingly ineffectually, their one perennial policy: the Company should stick to business and avoid extra expense, distraction and scandal. 'You seem so thoroughly possessed of military ideas,' they wrote to the Council in Calcutta, 'as to forget your employers are merchants.' In Bengal, however, the Company's nabobs were becoming ever more exasperated with what they now saw as the absurd and impractical pieties of a group of penny-pinching Londoners at Head Office. In practice, they anyway had a virtual carte blanche. Distance forced London to set policies so broad that they amounted to little more than platitudes. It took not less than a year to receive an instruction from London relating to breaking news in Bengal. So most specific directions from London were way out of date. If they weren't, but were unpalatable, they were easily evaded.

The more far-sighted observers were already entertaining more expansive visions. As early as 1759, Robert Clive secretly wrote to William Pitt, the most powerful minister at

Westminster, to suggest that the sovereignty of Bengal itself was up for grabs. Nawabs could be easily dispensed with altogether, 'but so large a sovereignty may possibly be an objective too extensive for a mercantile company'. Wouldn't it be better, asked Clive, for the Government and nation to get involved directly?

Pitt did not reply. But successive administrations were forced to grapple with the same dilemma. On the one hand there was alarm and embarrassment that the Company's nabobs in India were such free agents, had become so deeply involved in India, and were so beset by war and scandal. Surely something must be done? On the other hand the Government was mightily relieved that they were not directly implicated in ruling such distant, trouble-some territories. Look at all the trouble they were having with the colonies in America! Moreover, even if they wished to get more involved, was this constitutionally acceptable? By its Charter, the East India Company held effective licence to operate as a private company without interference. Nothing upset an eighteenth-century Englishman more than the thought that overbearing authority might encroach on his ancient rights and liberties.

These questions became inescapable after 1765 when any pretence to independent Indian rule in Bengal evaporated. The ousted nawab Mir Kasim had fought to recover his throne with vigour, proving far less of a pushover than his predecessors. The Company had effectively supplied and trained both armies, so for the first time in decades the two sides were evenly matched. Unlike Plassey, this was a vicious war of several fiercely contested battles, with high casualties on both sides. When the Company failed to halt its advance, Mir Kasim carried out a threat to massacre all the English prisoners he held. At least forty-nine were murdered at Patna on 4 October 1763 in a long-forgotten incident that lays far better claim than the legendary 'Black Hole' to live in infamy. Mir Kasim also took this opportunity to murder the Jagat Seth brothers. Meanwhile, the Company found their troops restive and close to general mutiny for the first time. They only succeeded in restoring discipline through brutal exemplary justice: twenty-five of the sepoy mutineers were blown from the muzzle of their own guns.

Mir Kasim had also succeeded in winning allies who perhaps recognized this was their last opportunity to resist the dramatic recent shift in power towards the British. The Nawab of Oudh, the vast province north-west of Bengal, realized that the Bengal story would be repeated before too long in Oudh unless the Company was checked. Meanwhile, the Mughal Emperor himself, Shah Allam II, decided that the British were an even greater threat than the Afghans or the Marathas to the wreckage of his empire. Although the Emperor lacked any of the authority or power of his illustrious predecessors, he retained residual influence by virtue of his office, from which most other titles and offices in India still formally derived.

The decisive battle came at Buxar, close to Varanasi, on 23 October 1764. Though the British lost close to a thousand troops, their victory over the allies cemented the Company's mastery of northern India. As the historian Percival Spear put it: 'Hitherto they [the British] had been rivals and manipulators of existing authority; their power was fortuitous and hedged with doubt; the issue was still open. It was now unchallenged.' Mir Kasim lost everything but his freedom and died years later in abject poverty, his last known address being a tent outside Delhi. The restored Nawab, Mir Jafar, conveniently died a few months after Buxar so the Company took the opportunity to reduce the office to nothing more than a figurehead, though one that was still expected to distribute 'presents'. The Mughal Emperor also had little choice but to switch over to the British side, driving the best deal he could muster. Meanwhile, Oudh found itself on the road to becoming a client state with very little real independence. The defeated Nawab lost territories and revenues and was encouraged into a defensive alliance with the Company that at great cost guaranteed him safety from the Marathas or Afghans. Of course the enemy within turned out to be a greater threat than the enemy without and the Company got much the better of this bargain. From now on there could be no external threat to Bengal, while the cost of defending it was effectively borne by the buffer state of Oudh.

In April 1765 a new Governor arrived in Bengal and took immediate stock of the situation. 'It is scarcely a hyperbole to say that the whole of the Mogul Empire is in our hands,' he wrote to the Directors in London. 'We must indeed become the Nabobs [Nawabs] ourselves in fact, if not in name, perhaps totally so without disguise… Since commerce alone is not now the whole of the Company's support, we must go forward, to retract is impossible.' And yet Bengal's new master was determined to pursue 'a plan of moderation', asserting in the same letter that 'I mean absolutely to bound our possessions, assistance and conquests to Bengal, never shall the going to Delhi be a plan adopted… by me'. Instead, the new Governor believed his mission was to put his own corrupt house in order. 'See what an Augean stable is there to be cleansed,' he wrote. He would wage a war on 'rapacity and luxury' however many enemies that made him. Finally he signed off: 'I am determined to return to England, without having acquired one farthing addition to my fortune.' Bengal's new Governor, back in India for the third time, was, of course, Robert Clive.

Four months later, the Mughal Emperor Shah Alam II sat on a makeshift throne perched on top of the dining table in Clive's tent at Allahabad. The impromptu ceremonial was there to mark what was in effect the first formal, constitutional and legal recognition of British rule in India, what came to be known as the Raj. The Emperor declared, 'at this happy time our royal *Firman*, indispensably requiring obedience, is issued'. This granted the Company the *diwani* of Bengal, Bihar and Orissa 'from generation to generation, forever and ever… as a free gift'. The office of *diwan* gave the Company rather than the nawab responsibility for collecting taxes and administering civil justice. The revolution was complete.

THE MUGHAL EMPEROR GRANTS CLIVE THE *DIWANI* OF BENGAL. THE GRAND SETTING IS PURE FICTION — IT ACTUALLY TOOK PLACE IN A TENT.

The news sent the Company's stock price in London through the roof, with investors salivating at the prospect of tapping supposedly inexhaustible Bengali riches. Even William Pitt, now heading the administration at Westminster as Lord Chatham, looked on the *diwani* as 'a kind of gift from heaven' which might deliver 'the redemption of the nation'. Yet exemplifying a mounting national hypocrisy, Pitt simultaneously expressed the most fastidious distaste for these same nabobs who had secured heaven's bounty:'The riches of Asia have been poured in upon us, and have brought with them not only Asiatic luxury, but, I fear, Asiatic principles of government. Without connections, without any natural interest in the soil, the importers of foreign gold have forced their way into Parliament by such a torrent of private corruption as no private hereditary fortune could resist.' Quietly, however, the toffs began to condescend to hold their noses and try trade in India themselves. They might have been blue-blooded but they still got excited about the promise of big money prizes.

The nouveaux riches are rarely restrained. What use is cash if you don't flash it? So the nabobs snapped up estates, married well and decked their wives out with jewels, glitzy outfits and a world of interiors to die for. Thomas Rumbold, for example, allegedly started his working life as a waiter at White's Club in London. By the time he retired from the Governorship of Madras not that many years later he was worth a cool million pounds. It was enough to tempt a bishop's daughter up the aisle. To keep her happy, he bought her a cradle for their baby 'covered with cloth of gold, ornamented with pearls and diamonds… [with] rockers of solid gold'. What really rankled was that this pushed prices up for ordinary hard-working aristocrats. With so much nabob money sloshing around, the cost of a country estate was soaring. And as for the wages that half-decent servants were now demanding…

But though their lifestyles tended to excess and their tastes seemed irredeemably vulgar, there is little evidence that the few dozen nabobs who came back to Britain with big fortunes were planning anything more radical than to ease themselves into the establishment. At each general election more followed Clive's lead and bought their way into Westminster. In 1770, for example, the borough of New Shoreham held a nabobs' auction, with opening bids for its parliamentary seat invited above £3,000. Meanwhile, cheese-monger's son Richard Smith ploughed part of his fortune into contesting the seat at Hindon. He set up a stall in the town square, where he offered five guineas to everyone who voted for him. This kind of bribery and corruption was hardly new. Indeed, it was long sanctioned by tradition. But apparently there was a difference between an old pot and a new kettle. And certainly the nabobs set about abuse so brazenly that even the most diehard defenders of the existing electoral system found it hard to marshal a defence. Once their wallets got them to Westminster, however, there is no evidence that the nabob MPs – twelve in 1761, twenty-seven by 1780 – acted as any kind of cohesive bloc. However much the ruling elite sneered, nabobs were not about to undermine the moral and political fibre of

Britain, whatever that might have meant in the louche and sleazy world of mid-eighteenth-century aristocratic politics. What really motivated the critics of course was envy and snobbery. Egad, these nabobs included the sons of a cheesemonger and a carpenter. Some of them were even Scottish!

In the summer of 1772 a new comedy opened at the Haymarket Theatre which was billed as 'a pointed and judicious satire on the… conduct of a certain great trading Company'. The 'hero' of Samuel Foote's *The Nabob* is Sir Mathew Mite, an inn-keeper's son who is sent to India after being caught stealing pies. Every theatregoer would have understood the unforgivably gauche Mite as a thinly veiled side-swipe at Robert Clive, who had returned from India for good in 1767. Having made his ill-gotten fortune, Mite attempts to turn himself into a gentleman and tries to enter Parliament by buying the constituency of 'Bribe'em'. He splashes out on antiques in the hope he'll be mistaken for a connoisseur but is so ignorant that the dealers sell him fakes instead. In another scene, he gets elocution lessons so he can josh and curse at London's top clubs without being found out. But Asiatic vice has been imported along with the plunder. Mite wears a silk nightgown and admits he is contemplating starting a seraglio in London stocked with luscious 'blacks from Bengal'. At least Mite's proclivities were heterosexual. The entirely unsubstantiated press gossip at the time about Robert Clive had him attending homosexual orgies dressed up as the prophet Mohamed (with the other participants including the Pope and the Holy Roman Emperor)!

The Nabob ends with virtue triumphant and Mite receiving his comeuppance. The aristocratic heroine prissily explains, 'The possessions arising from plunder very rarely are permanent; we every day see what has been treacherously and rapaciously gained, as profusely and rapidly squandered.' Mite retreats wounded and confused. Like Clive, he cannot come to terms with the lack of 'gratitude of the country to those who have given it dominion and wealth'.

By the time the play opened, however, drastic events were throwing into doubt whether conquest had indeed brought wealth. In April 1769 the Company's stock crashed. Ever since the *diwani*, it had been absurdly over-valued. The bubble suddenly burst when news reached London that there was once again regional conflict in the south and that the French might mount a renewed challenge from Mauritius to British naval supremacy. Panic plunged the share price far lower than either threat warranted. But any chance of recovery evaporated with the first reports in 1770 of a famine of biblical proportions affecting most of Bengal.

When the monsoon of 1769 failed, nature effectively condemned millions of Bengali peasants to death. But the charge at the time and ever since has been that Bengal's new rulers must take responsibility for the scale of the suffering. Various estimates suggest between one sixth and half of the population died. It took a century before an official report properly investigated the calamity. Sir William Hunter combed the records to compile his grim account:

> All through the stifling summer of 1770 the people went on dying. The husbandmen sold their cattle; they sold their implements of agriculture; they devoured their seed-grain; they sold their sons and daughters, till at length no buyer of children could be found; they ate the leaves of the trees and the grass of the field; and in June 1770 the Resident at the Durbar [of Murshidabad] affirmed that the living were feeding on the dead. Day and night a torrent of famished and disease-ridden wretches poured into the great cities… The streets were blocked up with promiscuous heaps of the dying and dead… Even the dogs and jackals, the public scavengers of the East, became unable to do their revolting work, and the multitude of mangled and festering corpses at length threatened the existence of the citizens.

Of course, while the peasants starved, Calcutta's nabobs continued to party with abandon. There seem to have been no organized efforts at famine relief. Worse, British traders and their associates were almost certainly among the most enthusiastic hoarders and profiteers. It is of course impossible to calculate how many would still have died regardless of who ruled Bengal. Widescale famine was hardly new to India. But the victims in 1770 could expect neither the traditional support mechanisms of the old social structure nor the energy and zeal which characterized later British administration and which acknowledged the welfare of the people as a responsibility of power. Far from relieving the distress, the Company enforced revenue collection assiduously and increased it by 10 per cent in 1771. The *zamindars*, the landholders who under the continuing Mughal tax regime were responsible for collecting the assessed taxes from the peasants, were forced to squeeze their tenants mercilessly to attempt to extract the full amount. Even so, in most cases the sums required were simply not available. Up to two-thirds of the *zamindars*, the traditional ruling class, were ruined. Their successors were new men, often *banians*, who had no links to the land or the locality. They tended to treat the office of *zamindar* as a business and sometimes lacked any sense of obligation to the community.

The longer-term consequences were as devastating as the impact of the famine itself. At least one-third of the cultivated land fell into disuse. Clive had called Bengal 'the paradise of the earth' whose agriculture and manufactures were 'sufficient not only for its own use, but for the use of the whole globe'. This indeed had been the underlying principle motivating every decision and action the Company had made in India. In fact Bengal's economy took forty years to recover.

By 1772 the Company found itself deeply in the red. Bengal, far from being Pitt's 'redemption of the nation' and delivering the anticipated £2 million revenue surplus back to Britain each year, had driven the Company heavily into debt, its main creditors being Indian bankers and its own employees. There was no alternative than to suspend dividend payments and go cap-in-hand to the Government for a £1 million bail-out.

Far too much was at stake for Parliament to let the Company go bankrupt. But the price of intervention in the Company's finances was a measure of parliamentary scrutiny and control of its activities. The general perception was that something would have to be done about India before Britain too was permanently corrupted. The 1773 Regulating Act became the first of many subsequent pieces of legislation to involve the state more directly in the affairs of the Company and the administration of British India. Once the Company was forced, through its own failings, to concede this principle, its independence was bound to diminish even if officially British India remained the Company Raj until 1857.

Somebody obviously needed to carry the can for such a debacle. There was near unanimity as to who that should be. Parliament and press turned on the victor of Plassey. It was all Clive's fault. In particular, it seemed to beggar belief that Clive was still enjoying his annual £27,000 *jaghir*, regardless of the perilous state of the Company's finances. Mir Jafar had cunningly awarded the *jaghir* to Clive on land whose revenues were ceded to the Company. So Clive's employers, the Company, were in effect also his tenants. By continuing to collect his *jaghir* he seemed the worst kind of voracious landlord, abusing not just distant Bengalis but the British share-owning public as well.

To Horace Walpole, he and his cronies were worse than the Spanish conquistadores notorious for their brutal colonization of South America:

> The groans of India have mounted to heaven, where the heaven-born General Lord Clive will certainly be disavowed. Oh my dear Sir, we have outdone the Spaniards in Peru! They were at least butchers on a religious principle, however diabolical their zeal. We have murdered, deposed, plundered, usurped – nay, what think you of the famine in Bengal, in which three millions perished, being caused by a monopoly of provisions, by the servants of the East India? All this is come out, is coming out – unless the gold that inspired these horrors can quash them.

For the record, Clive had left India three years before the onset of famine. The Company did indeed have monopolies of provisions – but salt, betel and opium weren't exactly part of a peasant's staple diet.

Sympathy for the Bengali peasantry may have been as much rhetorical as genuine. Like today, the late-eighteenth-century press was only really interested in foreign news if it involved domestic scandal. But the newspapers then were far more merciless and scurrilous than our own timid tabloids. They lied and libelled grotesquely in their vendetta against the man some of them now dubbed 'the King of Sodom'. An anonymous contributor to the *Gentleman's Magazine* explained that when Clive had said, '"Let there be a monopoly of the necessaries of life, for the benefit of my family and friends," he signed the death warrant for two millions of his fellow-creatures.' Bengal, he wrote, was once a paradise on earth but was now a forest where tigers roared and the jackal howled.

Though not yet fifty, Clive was now ill and depressed and could only cope with his constant stomach cramps by resorting to increasing quantities of opium. But neither doubt nor remorse was among his afflictions. Indeed he seems to have relished responding to the venom of his critics and waged one last great campaign to rescue his reputation in Parliament: 'I have been examined by the Select Committee more like a sheep-stealer than a member of this House. I am sure, Sir, if I have any sore places about me, they would have been found; they have been probed to the bottom; no lenient plasters have been applied to heal: no, Sir, they were all of the blister kind, prepared with Spanish flies, and other provocatives.'

Westminster has always had a soft spot for humour. The House burst into gales of laughter and applause when he turned on his chief rival Lawrence Sullivan who was 'so assiduous in my affairs, that really, Sir, he has entirely neglected his own'.

Finally on 21 May 1773, the House of Commons moved to a free vote on a motion of censure against Clive, which was designed to ruin him. Clive had concluded his defence with impressive simplicity: 'Before I sit down, I have one request to make to the House. That when they come to decide upon my honour, they will not forget their own.' The motion was rejected. Instead of being condemned for abusing his power, Parliament passed an amendment acknowledging that 'Robert Lord Clive did… render great and meritorious services to this country.'

Clive had held on to his fortune. But his reputation, though formally salvaged, would clearly always remain clouded by scandal. Less than eighteen months later he was dead. Illness and depression seem to have overwhelmed him. He slit his throat at his house in Berkeley Square on 22 November 1774.

––––––––––

The aftermath of Plassey had been astonishingly greedy and through its excesses it had damaged not just Bengal's economy but the Company's long-term commercial interests. But a lot of the later distaste for the revolution can now be seen to be just that, a deep-seated revulsion at any overthrow of any old order, however corrupt and despotic. Edmund Burke, the godfather of Conservatism, damned the nabobs more eloquently than most: 'Animated with all the avarice of age and all the impetuosity of youth, they roll in [to Bengal] one after another; wave upon wave; and there is nothing before the eyes of the natives but an endless, hopeless, prospect of new flights of birds of prey and passage, with appetites continually renewing for a food that is continually wasting.'

Though Burke's critique was rational, most of the accusations against the nabobs reeked far more of snobbery, jealousy and hypocrisy than real concern for India. What had really rankled with the British aristocracy was that the nabobs were arrivistes and impertinent upstarts. What also offended them was that the relatively few and spectacularly immodest individuals who had taken the risks and done the work reaped the rewards. Cue a high-minded crusade against corruption and the gradual articulation of a moral purpose to British rule. Yet imperialism didn't vanquish greed. It merely nationalized it.

The nabobs' avarice and vulgarity have also fatally tarnished their subsequent historical reputation. Imperial chroniclers, who might have been inclined to celebrate the Raj's true founding fathers, instead shied away from them with fastidious distaste. The later ideology of Empire castigated individual acquisition, even though its raison d'être was international larceny. But in today's world of fat-cat bonuses and global patent enforcement, the nabobs' excesses, though scarcely excusable, seem more familiar. Many people would now wearily accept them as inevitable – the flip-side, they might argue, of individualism and entrepreneurial energy.

By 1773, however, it was clear that the Wild East needed taming. Sleaze and scandal had characterized the first phase of what had become – largely accidentally – Britain's rule in India. The private emperor Clive and his rogue traders might have won Bengal and minted it personally. But the Company was broke and the British public was disdainful, if jealous, of anyone who made it back from India. What was needed was someone who could turn British India into something more than a treasure-chest. That man was Warren Hastings – and during his period as Governor-General, Briton and Indian would meet, mingle and exchange ideas on a more friendly and equal footing than they were to do again for over 200 years.

CHAPTER FOUR

AN INDIAN LOVE AFFAIR

A s a full-on assault on the senses, the definitive
Indian experience remains today, as it was in the
eighteenth century, to visit the *ghats* (waterside
steps) along the Ganges at Varanasi. In fact this scene, in what
is often claimed to be the world's oldest living city, has
probably changed little for over 2,000 years. Every day at
dawn, the first of thousands of pilgrims arrive to begin their
ritual bath in the waters of the holy river, here at the heart of
the Hindu universe. On the steps leading down to the water,
ash-coated, naked *sadhus* (holy men) contemplate the Divine.
Nearby, fat brahmins sit cross-legged, surrounded by pupils
eager to absorb the mysteries of the Vedas, India's ancient
Sanskrit scriptures. Elderly widows, clad in distinctive all-
white robes, launch small *puja* offerings of flowers, sweets and
spices into the water. Soon, they too will make the same
journey, cremated at the riverside so that their soul can be
released from the perpetual cycle of birth and rebirth.

Robert Clive had seen little and cared less for Indian
culture. His successor Warren Hastings soaked it up with
enthusiasm. Striking far inland, he made the long and

BENARES, AS DEPICTED BY WILLIAM HODGES, THE FIRST PROFESSIONAL EUROPEAN LANDSCAPE
ARTIST IN INDIA AND TRAVELLING COMPANION OF WARREN HASTINGS.

arduous trip to Benares (as Varanasi was then known) in the company of the painter William Hodges, the first professional western artist to tour India and commit to canvas what it was really like. Far from being alienated by the visceral squalor, chaos and idolatry by the holy river, Hastings was becoming convinced that Europe and Christendom held no monopoly on civilization and that prejudice was the fruit of ignorance. Hastings acted in the belief that the British were privileged to have discovered a vast store of knowledge and culture of far greater long-term value than India's raw wealth. He became chief patron to a wide range of British efforts to get to grips with India on her own terms, all shot through with extraordinary excitement at the discovery of this new civilization.

Yet Warren Hastings was not in Varanasi on vacation, soaking up the timeless essence of India as the Ganges flowed by. And he had other travelling companions besides the artist Hodges. A small army stood by to assist him in browbeating the ruler of Benares into coughing up large amounts of cash to help the Company meet escalating military costs.

As we'll see in Chapter 7, Hastings was a complex man whose career expresses many paradoxes. His famous impeachment by Parliament, a seven-year marathon to dwarf the Clinton saga, will forever associate him with sleaze – even though he had in fact done much to end the corrupt excesses of the post-Plassey years and was ultimately acquitted. His frequent military engagements with Indian rulers inexorably extended British power in India, even though his honestly held policy was to try and avoid conflict, claiming that British dominion over India was 'an event… I never wish to see'.

History tends to remember Hastings as a sleaze-ridden military adventurer, the 'King of the Nabobs'. Hastings's visit to Benares was used by the prosecutors at his impeachment as evidence of precisely these flaws. Yet the visit also demonstrates a remarkable other side to Warren Hastings, common among his contemporaries, which has been largely and unfairly eclipsed. For a single generation in the late eighteenth century, Britain and India seemed on the brink of an entirely different relationship to the one that did later emerge with the Raj.

Warren Hastings was appointed Governor of Bengal in 1772 and soon afterwards took up in addition the new post of Governor-General, shouldering overall responsibility for all the East India Company's affairs in the subcontinent. By then he had already clocked up over twenty years of Indian experience. One of the main reasons he had landed the job was that over the course of his career he had been too careless and too generous, and had possessed too many scruples to become obscenely rich. But he was unusual in other ways too. Unlike the old guard, he didn't drink much, and didn't get involved in racketeering by bullying or beating the locals. Most importantly, Hastings was interested in Indians, not just profiting from them or sleeping with them. By the end of his career he would conclude, 'I love India a little more than my own country.'

As dysfunctional childhoods go, Warren Hastings's takes some beating. He was born in 1732 into a once great family, whose connection to the manor of Daylesford in the Cotswolds stretched uninterrupted from the Domesday Book until poverty forced its sale a few years before Warren's arrival. His mother, Hester Warren, of humble yeoman farming stock, died giving birth to her only son (hence his unusual name bestowed at the double ceremony burying the one and christening the other). Within months, his blue-blooded father, a thoroughly ungodly vicar, had abandoned him for good to run off with a shopkeeper's daughter, and then hopped it again to the West Indies, where he married a third time and was nonetheless seen fit to serve as Rector of Christ Church, Barbados. In later life Warren Hastings would only once mention his father. He simply wrote, 'There was not much in my father's history worth repeating.'

Warren now became the charge of his impoverished paternal grandfather, who in turn put him into care with an illiterate foster-mother from the village. Hastings recalled a home worn by 'the pressure of absolute want'. Yet the family's shame and reduced circumstances seem to have steeled the young boy. He later wrote that his favourite pastime as a child had been to lie dreamily on the banks of a stream overlooking the family's former estate: 'Then, one bright summer's day, when I was scarcely seven years old, I well remember that I formed the determination to purchase back Daylesford.' It would remain his life's mission.

At eight years old, Warren Hastings was sent to London to stay with a still well-connected uncle. He received no affection but an excellent education as a boarder at Westminster School. But within a few years his uncle died, it turned out with debts rather than assets, and Hastings was taken out of school effectively destitute. A distant relative living in Streatham became the new guardian. Hastings completed his formal education in a style as far removed from Westminster as one could imagine. Nevertheless, a routine course in merchant's book-keeping helped him gain a writership in the East India Company. He sailed to Bengal aged seventeen in January 1750.

For the next fourteen years, Hastings was knee-deep in silks, calicos and muslins. Unlike Clive and most of his predecessors, however, he took immediate pains to study the local languages, quickly mastering Hindustani, Bengali and the court tongue, Persian. After the inevitable two years' tedium of ledger work, he went up-country as one of the Company's agents in Kasimbazar, at the heart of Bengal's textile production. Though he dabbled in coffee and salt, he quite remarkably failed to turn the post to his personal advantage. Instead, he was coming to the notice of his superiors, admired for his competence and intelligence, even if his views were already considered a bit suspect. Clive for one felt Hastings paid too much attention to the opinions of 'the natives' who, whether

Moslem or Hindu, were he felt equally 'indolent, luxurious, ignorant and cowardly' and had to be ruled by 'such a force as leaves nothing to the power of treachery and ingratitude'. Hastings begged to differ, insisting, 'if our people, instead of erecting themselves into lords and oppressors' stuck to trade on fair and equitable grounds, 'the English name, instead of becoming a reproach, will be universally revered'.

To Hastings, the abuses of the *dastak* were especially reprehensible. In 1763 he used his new post as a junior Council member at Calcutta to oppose the majority and side with Mir Kasim, who was trying to reform or abolish the grotesquely unequal levies. Unfortunately for Hastings, Mir Kasim responded to the Company's intimidation by murdering his British prisoners. Though Hastings reluctantly stayed loyal to the Company in the war that followed, he refused on principle to vote for the restoration of Mir Jafar or the reintroduction of the *dastak*. As soon as the victory at Buxar ended the

'I LOVE INDIA A
LITTLE MORE THAN
MY OWN COUNTRY' —
THIS MUGHAL
MINIATURE CAPTURES
WARREN HASTINGS
IN AROUND 1782.

آنقدر فرق زقدر تو بود تاکیفو ل   أہ بودتاہمواالبذرعقل اول

أہ بودتاہمواالبذرعقل اول   انقدر فرق زقدر تو بود تاکیفو ل

conflict, Hastings resigned his post and returned to England. Few returning nabobs came back with smaller fortunes or hazier prospects.

Luckily for Hastings and British India, his career-break was brief because it corresponded with the turmoil at home about how to manage the Company's affairs in India and rectify its notorious abuses. Within a few years, he was back in India, first in Madras as Deputy Governor, then back to Bengal in 1772 in his new post as Governor. From the start, he did not hide his conviction that changes were urgently needed. Too many of his colleagues erred through basic ignorance: what did 'gentlemen of Cumberland and Argyllshire' really know of India? As for the House of Commons, which was becoming increasingly involved in questions of governance, they too were ill-informed 'of the laws of being, of the manners and customs of the inhabitants, or of the forms of government'.

Hastings knew his main task was to corral the Wild East into some kind of order. Only by curtailing the disreputable excesses of his colleagues could Bengal become governable and the Company return to profit. Unlike many other senior Company officials, his horizons were far broader than Calcutta. Throughout his career, he toured extensively and witnessed with dismay the after-effects of the famine. 'It is an exhausted country and has been much oppressed,' he wrote, acknowledging that Company heavies had reduced village weavers to 'absolute and irredeemable vassalage'.

Ironically, his first move in his war against corruption was to give himself and many British colleagues a massive pay-rise – while simultaneously banning many of the kickbacks and commissions that they had come to regard as their right. Hastings was a pragmatist, and he and others did not change their old ways overnight. But by abolishing the hated *dastak* and replacing it with a low, uniform customs duty of 2.5 per cent, he did more than anyone to end the mobsters' protection racket. One young nabob, John Shore, wrote home complaining that a lucrative career was now well-nigh impossible.

The most senior Company servants were banned from all private trade, while most others were prevented from trading in grain and other staples. Another prohibition precluded private opium trade, which Hastings had personally found very profitable. Instead, to make up the Company's losses resulting from the end of the *dastak*, opium became a government monopoly. This was critical, as the tea trade with China was now the Company's most significant activity. British cuppas depended on Chinese opium trips.

Hastings put most of his immediate energy into an overhaul of the justice system. But in fostering the rule of law over Indians, Hastings was convinced 'the people of this country do not require our aid to furnish them with a rule of conduct or a standard of property'. He would do it their way. So the untold story of the founding administrative principles of what became the British Empire was that, far from being infused with arrogance and prejudice at its outset, it was based upon respect. Thanks to Hastings, British judges resisted pressure from London to substitute English common law or Roman law for existing ancient Hindu and Muslim codes. To do so would have been 'wanton tyranny'. Bengal was 'a great nation' and certainly had no need for any supposedly 'superior wisdom' to impose alien laws from afar. Instead, Hastings aimed 'to found the authority of the British Government in Bengal on its ancient laws, to point the way to rule this people with ease and moderation according to their own ideas, manners and prejudices'.

Though Hastings had great respect for Indian civilization, this was also first-class politics. His obvious role model was Akbar who had, in many ways, faced similar challenges. The Mughals had come as a small band of Muslim outsiders but had built their empire on religious tolerance and assimilating the best aspects of Hindu society into a new syncretic culture. Hastings also appreciated that the best basis for effective rule was continuity and respect. New laws and administrative systems would take root with Indians only if they accorded with what 'time and religion had rendered familiar to their understandings and sacred to their affections'.

The first practical problem was to establish what those ancient, and mostly unwritten, laws were. To do so, Hastings took the remarkable step of gathering eleven leading brahmin pundits in Calcutta with a brief to codify in Sanskrit, India's ancient, sacred language, the basic tenets of Hindu civil law (criminal law was mostly Muslim and more accessible). Because no English speaker had yet fully mastered Sanskrit, these were then translated into Persian. Finally, under Hastings's direction, a young scholar, Nathaniel Halhed, translated the new code into English. In 1776 this was published as the *Code of Gentoo* [Hindu] *Laws*. Two years later an equally extraordinary work followed. Halhed's *Grammar of the Bengal Language* required the preparation of the first typographic fonts in Bengali, a feat completed, again with Hastings as sponsor, by Charles Wilkins and an Indian craftsman. With reason, Wilkins became known as the Caxton of India. Later it was Wilkins who succeeded in becoming the first European to become fully proficient in Sanskrit (with the exception of a handful of earlier Jesuit missionaries who raided Sanskrit literature for very specific and limited purposes). Wilkins's accomplishments justifiably demanded more than prosaic tribute:

> *See patient Wilkins to the world unfold*
> *Whate'er discover'd Sanskrit relics hold*
> *But he perform'd a yet more noble part*
> *He gave to Asia typographic Art.*

It is difficult at this distance, and with the awesome resources of accumulated scholarship at our instant disposal, to appreciate the magnitude of the achievement of these early oriental scholars. Holding down day jobs with the Company as mundane writers or slightly loftier justices, they devoted their spare time to rigorous study. With amazing rapidity, and without the benefit of any existing manuals, they mastered these wholly alien scripts and languages. Then they applied their new-found skills with equal zeal to both the practicalities of reformed administration and the wider pastures of pure scholarship. Over the next few decades, these Orientalists would explore every aspect of Indian culture and civilization, voraciously digesting every ancient text that could transmit knowledge about the subcontinent's history, philosophy, science, linguistics, religion, art, flora, fauna and topography.

The new system kicked in remarkably quickly. It routinely involved Englishmen administering justice, often in the vernacular, with Hindu pundits or Muslim *maulvis* (judges or legal scholars) sitting at their side. Although the comparisons are inappropriate, one might still be forgiven for comparing that to the white-dominated police and justice systems in multicultural Britain today. In civil law, most sentences and penalties remained as they had been before the British arrived. Hastings retained similar respect for the Muslim criminal codes that remained under the jurisdiction of Indian judges. He explained to a jurist in London that, 'This is as comprehensive, and as well defined, as that of most states in Europe, having been formed at a time in which the Arabians were in possession of all the real learning which existed in the western parts of this continent.' The fact that he found some of it 'barbarous' was immaterial. It was their law, and not to be needlessly or illegitimately altered.

In the longer term, Hastings's plan was to withdraw Europeans from the revenue and court systems of all Bengal's districts, returning local power to Indians. In the meantime he attempted to protect the peasantry as much as possible from any continuing abuses of power by the Europeans. To do that he specifically invited allegations against Company officials. A complaints box was set up outside every district tax-office (though sadly, we do not know how much they were used). You still find them in almost every public institution in India – a symbol of equality before the law, though rendered almost impotent by bureaucracy and inertia.

What most impresses about Warren Hastings is his breadth and energy. In one document you find him monitoring the activities of the new postal system he had introduced throughout Bengal. In another you find him pondering the possibilities of building a canal across Suez to cut drastically the journey time to and from Europe. He sets out the ideas that led to the establishment of the first public granaries as a defence against future famine, and introduces a national mint at Calcutta to protect the currency from abuse and adulteration. Ironically for a Governor-General who would later become overwhelmed with regional conflict, his instincts were for journeys of discovery rather than military expeditions. He commissioned James Rennell's map series surveying Bengal all the way north from Calcutta to Assam and Bhutan. Looking today at this folio of exquisitely rendered maps completed in 1779, one cannot fail to marvel at their accuracy and detail.

One of the Governor-General's pet projects, financed from his own pocket, was the extraordinary trip to Bhutan and Tibet of his friend George Bogle in 1774. No Briton had

THIS MINIATURE, DATING FROM C.1650, DEPICTING MYSTICS FALLING INTO A HOLY TRANCE, WAS PART OF WARREN HASTINGS' INDIAN ART COLLECTION.

ever been to Tibet (though some Jesuits had briefly visited some decades earlier). So Hastings himself compiled a memo summarizing all the available information about the legendary mountain kingdom ruled by the Dalai Lama. Such a trip would fascinate 'thousands of men in England... in search of knowledge'. This would excite 'ten times' the interest of the habitual military accounts of 'victories that slaughtered thousands of the national enemies'. Hastings also drafted a set of objectives for Bogle's mission, some practical, others delightfully quixotic. Among other tasks, Bogle was asked to bring back two yaks; to find out whether in Tibet it really was 'very common for one lady to have several husbands' (and if so work out how anyone knew who a child's father was); to plant potatoes along the entire route; to consider the possibilities of trading in rhubarb; to discover whether one could go on from Tibet to Siberia; and to keep a detailed diary of everything he discovered without neglecting everyday details like Tibetan cookery.

Although Bogle did not make it to Lhasa, he and his Bengali assistants did spend five months with the Panchen Lama at Tibet's second city, Shigatse. Bogle was able to learn Tibetan, but unable in return to explain to the Panchen Lama the Holy Trinity. He got the answers Hastings needed about polyandry. It was indeed common, and paternity was determined either by looks or left to the mother to nominate.

Bogle returned safely to Calcutta in July 1775, bearing a request from the Lama to rebuild a Buddhist sanctuary in Calcutta that had been destroyed by Siraj-ud-Daula. Hastings happily obliged. He also acted as 'Founder and Protector' of Calcutta's first Greek Orthodox Church and Patron of the Mahommedan College, donating the land himself and establishing a centre for Islamic scholarship under the direction of Maulana Majuddin, which translated into English and analysed countless Arabic and Persian texts. In supporting the construction of St John's Church, Hastings even saw to it that members of his own nominal faith, the Church of England, at last had a proper place of worship.

In matters of religion, Hastings seems to have inclined to universalism. A classic product of the liberal enlightenment, his wide-ranging intellectual curiosity was tempered by personal reticence in matters of faith. His biographer Keith Feiling describes it as 'a mystic confidence, more Oriental than Christian, that his life was borne along as part of a long beneficial process'. There was a world of difference between the late-eighteenth-century deist, finding meaning and value in many spiritual quests, and the tub-thumping evangelicals who soon held sway in British and British Indian society, convinced that Truth was a Christian monopoly. Like his predecessors, Hastings did his best to keep the missionaries at bay. They were banned from all Company territory on the grounds that their proselytizing might prove an affront to Indian society and so cause political difficulties for the British. Later history demonstrated how justifiable these fears were – but by then salvation was prized more than sensitivity or security.

Although Hastings was evidently a polymath of wide and divergent enthusiasms, it is clear that he was most profoundly and personally affected by his encounter with Hinduism. There is no doubt that acquiring all this knowledge was useful. Indeed, to cajole sceptical Directors in London perennially obsessed with the bottom line into paying for some of this scholarship, Hastings had repeatedly to emphasize its utility. Yet in his private letters to Marian, his wife and soul-mate, it is clear that the Hindu way of life and mind-set had truly got under his skin. There is nothing calculated or political about his quoting to her from the *Bhagavad-Gita* (Divine Song), one of the greatest Hindu sacred texts. The *Gita*, he told Marian, contained precepts that had become 'the invariable rule of my latter life'. This could be distilled into one essential rule: 'Let the Motive be in the Deed and not in the Event. Be not one whose motive for Action is the Hope of Reward. Perform thy Duty. Abandon all thought of the consequence.'

Thanks to Hastings, the poetry and metaphysical wisdom of the *Gita* reached a far wider audience than Marian. In the teeth of opposition from his continually obstructionist Council, Hastings had managed to obtain for Charles Wilkins the official post of Printer to the Company. He had also ensured the Company placed substantial orders with Wilkins for copies of Halhed's *Grammar*. Further successful lobbying by Hastings, together with these profits from sales, allowed Wilkins to go on a six-month sabbatical to Benares (Varanasi). Brahmins – members of the highest Hindu caste, the priesthood – were very reluctant to teach 'the language of the gods' to non-Hindus, but Wilkins did find in Benares a distinguished Kashmiri pundit, Kasinatha, who would take him on as a student. So, having become the first British Sanskritist, Wilkins worked with the pundit to translate the *Gita* for the first time into English. In 1784 the work was complete and Hastings himself penned an extraordinary Introduction to the English text, in the form of a public letter to the Chairman of the East India Company in London.

Hastings first chooses to highlight the work's literary merits. It displays 'a wonderful fertility of genius and pomp of language into a thousand sublime descriptions'. Judging translations is always difficult, but Hastings believes the English text is on a par with the best French versions of Homer or Milton. Notwithstanding this, Hastings deliberately warns the reader against adopting too Eurocentric a perspective in approaching the work. European standards are 'by no means applicable to the language, sentiments, manners, or morality appertaining to a system of society with which we have been for ages unconnected, and *of an antiquity preceding even the first efforts of civilization in our own quarter of the globe*' (author's italics).

Hastings warns the reader that this is not an easy read: 'Many passages will be found obscure… others will be found cloathed with ornaments of fancy unsuited to our tastes'. Reassuringly, however, 'few [passages] will shock either our religious faith or moral sentiments'. And if the reader struggles with certain sections, this could be a limitation of the western mind not the eastern mystic, because they are 'elevated to a track of sublimity into which our habits of judgement will find it difficult to pursue them'.

Hastings then bravely attempts to explain to a British readership, perhaps for the first time, the underlying spiritual purpose of Indian meditation. Devotees aim to 'divest their minds of all sensual desire, but that their attention be abstracted from every external object, and absorbed, with every sense, in the prescribed subject of their meditation'. Hastings is obviously deeply impressed with this way of pursuing 'the contemplation of the Deity, his attributes, and the moral duties of this life'. He demonstrates this through a personal story:

> I myself was once a witness of a man employed in this species of devotion, at the principal temple of Benares. His right hand and arm were enclosed in a loose sleeve or bag of red cloth, within which he passed the beads of his rosary, one after another, through his fingers, repeating with the touch of each (as I was informed) one of the names of God, while his mind laboured to catch and dwell on the idea of the quality which appertained to it, and shewed the violence of its exertion to attain this purpose by the convulsive movements of all his features, his eyes being at the same time closed, doubtless to assist the abstraction. The importance of this duty cannot be better illustrated... than by the last sentence with which Krishna closes his instruction to Arjuna, and which is properly the conclusion of the Geeta: 'Hath what I have been speaking, O Arjuna, been heard *with thy mind fixed to one point*? Is the *distraction* of thought, which arose from thy ignorance, removed?' [Hastings's italics]

Hastings is thus able to recommend the *Gita* without hesitation, boldly attesting to its spiritual as well as literary merits, and ranking it in power and purpose alongside the Gospels. It is 'a performance of great originality; of a sublimity of conception, reasoning and diction, almost unequalled; and a single exception, among all the known religions of mankind, of a theology accurately corresponding with that of the Christian dispensation, and most powerfully illustrating its fundamental doctrines'.

Hastings then effectively defends Hinduism against the common blanket criticism of idolatry, the most visible manifestation of the religion, and one that tended instantly to repel Christians rather than encourage deeper investigation. He wonders whether 'a doctrine so elevated above common perception did not require [it] to be introduced by such ideas as were familiar to the mind, to lead it by a gradual advance to the pure and abstract comprehension of the subject'.

So much for the merits of the *Gita*. Hastings knew the trickier task was to convince the Company's top brass that exploring these abstruse realms was not entirely pointless. He owns up frankly that 'the study of Sanskrit cannot, like the Persian language, be applied to official profit'. Nevertheless, he does suggest it is fundamentally 'useful to the State'. This is because Hastings refuses to couch utility narrowly, demeaning culture by reducing it to a political or economic equation. Instead the benefits of greater mutual understanding are intangible, and of far greater value.

> Such studies, independently of their utility, tend, especially when the pursuit of them is general, to diffuse a *generosity of sentiment*, and a disdain of the meaner occupations of such minds as are left nearer to the state of uncultivated nature; and you, Sir, will believe me, when I assure you, that it is on the virtue, not the ability of their servants, that the Company must rely for the permanency of their dominion. [author's italics]

Oriental studies, however, do more than improve the 'moral character and habits of the service':

> Every accumulation of knowledge, and especially such as is obtained by social communication with people over whom we exercise a dominion founded on the right of conquest, is useful to the state: it is the *gain of humanity*: in the specific instance which I have stated, it attracts and conciliates distant affections; *it lessens the weight of the chain by which the natives are held in subjection; and it imprints on the hearts of our own countrymen the sense and obligation of benevolence*. [author's italics]

Hastings above all hopes such study will curtail the scourge of prejudice:

> It is not very long since the inhabitants of India were considered by many, as creatures scarce elevated above the degree of savage life; nor, I fear, is that prejudice yet wholly eradicated, though surely abated. Every instance which brings their real character home to observation will impress us with a more generous feeling for their natural rights, and teach us to estimate them by the measure of our own.

In a remarkable conclusion, which can hardly have endeared him to his masters, Governor-General Hastings then goes straight on to predict the end of British rule in India. 'These [writings] *will survive when the British dominion in India shall have long ceased to exist, and when the sources which it once yielded of wealth and power are lost to remembrance.*' Hastings's statement is unforgettable, both for its candour and its foresight.

Before Hastings, Robert Clive frequently referred to Indians as 'blacks' and had a low opinion of many of their supposed characteristics, though he was certainly not a scientific racist in the Darwinian sense. After Hastings, no Governor-Generals ever explored India with such an open or unprejudiced mind. Familiarity bred contempt and British global hegemony increasingly seemed proof of her moral, intellectual and even biological superiority. Yet Hastings was not a one-off, skewing a sorry story for one moment into life-affirming, but ultimately inconsequential, redemption.

For a start, not all Hastings's predecessors were thugs or wide boys. The smarmy John Zephaniah Holwell, who briefly succeeded Clive as Governor, tends to be remembered only for his racy account of the Black Hole. But he also cast himself as a very different kind of hero in his 'Interesting Historical Events, Relative to the Provinces of Bengal and the Empire of Indostan' (1766). In it, Holwell reveals that the loss of Calcutta to Siraj deprived him not just of his liberty, but of a manuscript he was translating of 'the Shaftah': 'As that work opened upon me, I distinctly saw, that the *Mythology*, as well as the *Cosmology* of the *Egyptians*, *Greeks* and *Romans* were borrowed from the doctrines of the Bramins contained in this book' (Holwell's italics).

Holwell's readable book shows off his journalistic skills far more than his scholarship. He complains that Hindus have been badly misrepresented: 'All the modern writers represent the *Hindoos* as a race of stupid and gross *Idolaters*.' Holwell is hardly surprised by this treatment, since, he jokes, most of the authors have been Catholic. But it is nonetheless 'injurious'. It is also absurd since Catholics are greater idolaters than Hindus, who 'from the earliest time have been an adornment to the Creation'. In their own way, Holwell has no doubt Hindus are 'approaching the Deity'. This approach was sufficiently attractive for Holwell, who chose to describe himself as a 'Christian Deist', to emulate pious Hindus by becoming a vegetarian.

In one of the earliest attempts to analyse what we would now call racism, Holwell tries to account for this prevailing prejudice: 'Ignorance, superstition, and partiality to ourselves, are too commonly the cause of presumption and contempt of others.' Ultimately, we think we are best through ignorance, 'a conclusion natural, though absurd!' Holwell does not have a problem with loving one's own religion providing that this does not 'from an intemperate zeal of religious vanity (now so much in fashion) presume to condemn, depreciate or invade the religious principles of others'.

The problem, according to Holwell, is that superficial encounters with other cultures can narrow minds rather than broaden them. Simply to say natives worship 'this stone, or monstrous idol… only serves to reduce in our esteem our fellow creatures to the most abject and despicable point of light'. If, however, one studies this culture in greater depth, one discovers that 'such seemingly preposterous worship had the most sublime, rational source and foundation'.

Holwell's encounters with Hinduism were clearly first-hand, not just theoretical. He describes in detail the great annual *Durga Poojah* festival 'usually visited by all Europeans (by invitation)' and includes in his book a beautiful pull-out plate section of drawings he did himself capturing different aspects of Hindu iconography. Like Hastings, he concludes with a startling comparison: he is 'amazed that we should so readily believe the people of *Indostan* a race of stupid *Idolaters*; when, to our cost, in a political and commercial view, we have found them superior to us'.

So, in men like Holwell, Hastings had forebears of a similar mind-set. His Orientalist followers would be of far greater significance. Though he claimed to be 'an unlettered man', Hastings lit the touch paper for one of the most explosive and significant intellectual renaissances in history. As we will see (Chapter 9), the Orientalists did ultimately lose their fierce cultural war with the Anglicists, who grew utterly convinced of the superiority of the West and the worthlessness of native cultures. But their defeat could not erase their achievements. The work of the Orientalists ensured the world had one history, one that could no longer be told from an exclusively Judaeo-Christian and western perspective. Its languages were seen to share common roots. Its cultures and people were also inextricably linked, of common parentage and self-evidently therefore meriting equal rights. These were the preconditions for multiculturalism, even if they were eclipsed for 150 years. Of course, in situations like these there is also always the temptation of the 'what might have been'. If the Orientalists had not lost out to the Anglicists – and it was touch-and-go who would prevail – India and the world might well have taken a different route, and, just maybe, been spared some of its nineteenth- and twentieth-century horrors.

The greatest Orientalist was indubitably Sir William Jones. Indeed, though biographers are prone to overrate their subjects, Garland Cannon surely does not over-egg it in describing Jones as 'one of the most remarkable men of all time'. He was certainly amongst the most prolific, packing into his short life of forty-seven years more careers than seems possible. Arabist, classicist, philologist, historian, judge, philosopher, grammarian, Sanskritist, poet, legal scholar, musicologist and astronomer – it is no exaggeration to say that Jones the polymath mastered, rather than dabbled in, every one of these disciplines. Above all, Jones was renowned for his skills as a linguist. He knew so many languages that George III once joked that he knew every language except his own (he was Welsh). This was unfair as Jones did know Welsh – just not as well as he knew English, Latin, French, Italian, Greek, Arabic, Persian, Sanskrit, Spanish, Portuguese, German, Runic (ancient Scandinavian), Hebrew, Bengali, Hindi, Turkish, Tibetan, Pali, Pehlavi, Deri, Russian, Syriac, Ethiopic, Coptic, Swedish, Dutch and Chinese. His mother deserves the credit. Whenever he asked a question as a small child she replied, 'Read and you will know.'

Jones spent only the last decade of his life in India. When he arrived there in 1783 to take up a post as judge in the Supreme Court in Calcutta, he was already one of the most famous scholars of his age, though as yet mostly ignorant of Indian history or literature. However, his

Arab and Persian studies had by then made him perhaps the first European to shed his Eurocentric perspective. As the Preface to his *Grammar of the Persian Language* put it:

> Some men never heard of the Asiatic writings, and others will not be convinced that there is any thing valuable in them; some pretend to be busy, and others are really idle... we all love to excuse, or to conceal our ignorance, and are seldom willing to allow any excellence beyond the limits of our own attainments: [we are] like the *savages*, who thought that the sun rose and set for them alone, and could not imagine that the waves, which surround their island, left coral and pearls upon any other shore.

Here was a European who was comparing his compatriots to savages, not the natives! En route to India for five long months aboard the *Crocodile*, Jones had found plenty of time to reflect on what lay ahead:

> When I was at sea last August... I found one evening, on inspecting the observations of the day, that India lay before us, and Persia on our left, while a breeze from

THE ORIENTALISTS REALIZED INDIA'S ANCIENT CIVILISATION MATCHED THAT OF ANCIENT GREECE AND ROME. THOMAS DANNIELL'S PAINTING SHOWS THE MEENAKSHI TEMPLE AT MADURAI.

HASTINGS WAS ONE OF THE FIRST EUROPEANS TO UNDERSTAND THE SPIRITUAL DEPTHS OF HINDUISM. THIS MINIATURE SHOWS KRISHNA'S CELESTIAL FIGHT WITH INDRA.

Arabia blew nearly on our stern… It gave me inexpressible pleasure to find myself in the midst of so noble an amphitheatre, almost encircled by the vast regions of Asia, which has ever been esteemed the nurse of sciences, the inventress of delightful and useful arts, the scene of glorious actions, fertile in the productions of human genius, abounding in natural wonders, and infinitely diversified in the forms of religion and government, in the laws, manners, customs, and languages, as well as in the features and complections [sic] of men. I could not help remarking how important and extensive a field was yet unexplored, and how many solid advantages unimproved.

Jones's use of the term 'unexplored' was entirely justifiable, even though normally one needs to substitute the more accurate phrase 'as yet undiscovered by white men'. Eighteenth-century Indians knew almost nothing about their history or ancient literature, so that India's pre-Moghul identity and in particular the golden ages of the Mauryas and Guptas had literally been forgotten. The great twentieth-century Indian linguist Suniti Kumar Chatterji has acknowledged the vital role played by European Orientalist scholars in overcoming this amnesia:

As an old people, worried and wearied by our domestic trials and tribulations, we had for some centuries gone to sleep… and in that sleep we had lost the real knowledge of ourselves, our doings, our relations with our neighbours, and our duties to ourselves. We had nothing but some shreds of our past memories, some dim recollections of what we were and what we did. We had not yet learned to draw out anything from the vestiges of our civilization which fortunately were still with us, as an inheritance of value of which we had no idea.

Jones was a big disappointment to the social scene in Calcutta because he declined almost every supper invitation. Nevertheless, within months of his arrival, he sent out a circular letter proposing the establishment of a learned society to foster Oriental study. It met for the first time on 15 January 1784. Today, nearly 220 years later, you can go to the Asiatic Society's premises in Park Street at the heart of Calcutta and ask to see the minutes of this inaugural meeting. A massive, dusty volume will arrive, its pages disturbingly brittle as you turn them. The ink is faded on each ochre sheet, but the calligraphy is exact and Jones's original vision for the society is still clear and penetrating:

Investigation of whatever is rare in the stupendous fabric of nature; correcting the geography of Asia by new observations and discoveries; tracing the annals and even traditions of these nations… and bringing to light their various forms of government, with their institutions, civil and religious; examining their improvements and methods of arithmetic and geometry – its trigonometry, mensuration, mechanics, optics, astronomy and general physics; their systems of modality, grammar and rhetoric and dialectic; their skill in chirurgery and medicine, and their advancement whatever it may be, in anatomy and chemistry. To this you will add researches into their agriculture, manufacture and trade, and whilst you enquire into their music, architecture, painting and poetry, will not neglect those inferior arts, by which comforts, and even elegances of social life, are supplied or improved. If now it be asked, what are the intended objects of our enquiries within these specious limits, we answer MAN and NATURE; whatever is performed by the one, or produced by the other.

Astonishingly, the Asiatic Society lived up to these expectations, serving as the launch-pad for energetic activity in almost all of the listed fields. In a few glorious decades these would indeed give India back its lost heritage, reveal to the rest of the world the full scale of the subcontinent's achievements, and uncover remarkable connections between East and West, cultures far less separate than either had yet imagined.

After this initial meeting, the minutes show the society met almost weekly and got straight down to business. First, they heard a paper on 'two pillars situated in the north of Patna'. Next, they discussed the links between Arabic, Persian and other Indian tongues. A discourse by Jones himself on orthography followed. By February, the society was taking the first steps towards dramatic discoveries. The note that they have found 'agreement between Greek and Hindu chronology' might at first seem strictly for the anoraks. In fact, achieving this (and it actually took another decade) for the first time locked Indian history into a known timeline, allowing the two separate narratives to be lined up side by side and synchronized. This was the key to dating India's great dynasties and her ruined cities. For the first time it became possible to establish, for example, when Askoka lived or which Indian monarch was the contemporary of Alexander the Great.

Despite being the world's most celebrated linguist, Jones had told Charles Wilkins that 'life is too short and my necessary business too long' for him to emulate Wilkins and learn Sanskrit. Ironically, it was the 'necessary business' of being a judge rather than the calling of pure scholarship that drove Jones, after a year in India, to change his mind. Rather than rely solely in court on the pundits, Jones wanted to scrutinize Hindu legal texts himself in order to ensure the justice he dished out was as accurate as possible. However pragmatic the motivation, he fell almost instantly in love with what he called the 'celestial tongue' expressed so perfectly by its poets and dramatists. Jones translated a near-forgotten, 2,000-year-old play *Sakuntula* into English and outraged certain English critics by dubbing its author, Kalidasa, 'the Shakespeare of India'. The play was an instant sensation in Europe and

America and was translated into eighty languages. By the end of the nineteenth century it had entered the canon, nominated as one of the hundred best books in the world. But Jones did not just introduce Indian literature to the West. No less an Indian nationalist than Jawarhalal Nehru, India's first Prime Minister, said of Jones and other Orientalist colonials that 'India owes [them] a deep debt of gratitude for the rediscovery of her past literature'.

Jones's studies in Sanskrit literature, philosophy, astronomy and law utterly convinced him that classical India was as great as ancient Greece or Rome. Today, in the twenty-first century, that may not seem so shocking a notion. To many people, the shape of the world 2,000 years ago may not even seem that relevant or important. But in the eighteenth century, which deeply revered classical antiquity and looked for classical sources to legitimate almost every aspect of modern society, this was an intellectual bombshell. Suddenly, an entirely unknown ancient civilization had been uncovered, populated by giants to match Plato, Virgil, Homer and Cicero. No wonder people breathlessly talked of the dawn of a new renaissance.

In February 1786, about six months after taking up Sanskrit, Jones gave his 'Third Anniversary Discourse' to the Asiatic Society. From his studies he concluded that Sanskrit in many ways surpassed Greek or Latin. He was also able to announce what many regard as his greatest discovery – that the three great ancient tongues were linked.

> The Sanskrit language, whatever be its antiquity, is of a wonderful structure; more perfect than the Greek, more copious than the Latin and more exquisitely refined than either; yet bearing to both of them a stronger affinity, both in the roots of verbs, and in the forms of grammar, than could possibly have been produced by accident; so strong, indeed, that no philologer could examine them all three, without believing them to have sprung from some common source, which, perhaps, no longer exists.

This discovery gave birth to the science of linguistics and the world of comparative philology. For the first time it was clear that languages belonged to families that had sprung from common ancestors. There was effectively one Indo-European culture. As Jones said with relish, 'East and West are now inseparable.'

By this time Jones too can be described as an Indo-European. Two centuries before Hare Krishna, hippies' ashram trips, and the search for karma cola, William Jones was composing poetry in Sanskrit and spending hours a day in the company of pundits. When the court was not in session he retired to what he called his *ashram* (hermitage) at Krishnagar, where he wore white brahmin's robes and tended a large pet turtle called Othello. He was especially proud when the Maharaja, with the approval of the brahmins, declared him a Hindu, just one caste down from the priests themselves. In fact, Jones was a more devoted Christian than Warren Hastings. But his own faith enhanced rather than undermined his

THE GREAT ORIENTALIST
SIR WILLIAM JONES AT
HIS DESK. BESIDE HIM IS
A STATUE OF THE ELE-
PHANT GOD GANESHA,
PATRON OF LEARNING.

respect for Hinduism: 'I am no Hindu, but I hold the doctrine of the Hindus concerning a future state to be incomparably more rational, more pious and more likely to deter men from vice, than the horrid opinions inculcated by Christians on punishments without end.'

Sadly, Jones soon had the chance to discover whether Hindus or Christians were right about the afterlife. In early 1794 he was working furiously to complete his magnum opus, a complete digest of Hindu law in eleven volumes. On its completion he planned to return to England and rejoin his wife, who had just set off home because of ill-health. Ignoring a painful swelling in his side, he stepped up his work-rate still further so that he wouldn't miss the boat. He collapsed on 20 April and died a few days later. Calcutta's pundits apparently wept without restraint as he was borne to South Park Street Cemetery. The East India Company erected a huge monument to his memory in London in St Paul's Cathedral. It is an apt tribute to Europe's love affair with India, all the more remarkable given its location within an Anglican church. Jones is dressed as a brahmin and his hand rests on a volume of Hindu scriptures. On the pediment there is even a four-armed figure of Vishnu.

In the decades after Jones's death, the West remained enthralled by something that historians have dubbed Indomania. The Asiatic Society flourished as one of the world's most influential centres of scholarship. Its journal, *Asiatick Researches*, sold by the thousand in Europe, and was in such demand that it even fell victim to a pirate edition. His successors at the society, such men as Henry Colebrooke and James Prinsep, were scholars as eminent as their mentor and made discoveries of equal significance about Hindu culture and Indian history. By raiding the past, they were dramatically affecting their own times, and thereby influencing the shape of the future. Without the work of the Orientalists, a proud and self-confident all-India identity, the prerequisite for nationalism, might never have emerged in the same way. In fact, from early in the nineteenth century, Bengali intellectuals seized on the new discoveries to help them articulate a radical, progressive vision for Indian society which was all the stronger for being rooted in some of its finest and oldest traditions. By any definition, that is a Renaissance.

Yet history has been incredibly unkind to Jones and the Orientalists. First, in the nineteenth century their achievements were increasingly belittled or rubbished. Victorian imperialists, Christian evangelists, liberal modernizers and jingoistic bigots all decided that India had little or nothing to teach Great Britons and that the English language and British values were the subcontinent's only hope. They thought the Orientalists were guilty of over-romanticizing traditional India's superstitions and customs, which they considered inhumane and irrational. The Orientalists' enemies preferred to stay ignorant in order to preserve their prejudices. In that way they could justify the Raj as the salvation of a land which would otherwise remain irredeemably primitive and evil.

Later, in the post-colonial world of the late twentieth century, the Orientalists were found guilty of a far more heinous crime than being hopeless romantics. As we have seen, Warren Hastings pointed out in his introduction to the *Gita* that Oriental studies were 'useful to the state'. Even the great scholar Jones only took up Sanskrit to help strengthen the grip of British judges in laying down the law for their Indian subjects.

Notwithstanding the praise from Nehru himself, Indians have therefore found it hard to lionize these Britishers. To the Palestinian–American critic Edward Said, whose influential broadside *Orientalism* was first published in 1978, the Orientalists were agents of imperialism rather than detached scholars. Said and his followers argued that all their knowledge was assembled, structured and deployed to perpetuate colonialism's 'hegemonic power' in the East. Orientalism according to this interpretation was an especially pernicious form of cultural imperialism, distorting its history, colonizing its learning and subjugating the Orient's past to an oppressive western mind-set.

It's a compelling theory. But Indian and western academics have more recently been fighting back. David Kopf, an American professor, recently suggested:

Said's Orientalism… has virtually nothing to do with the actual development of Orientalism in India, or with the human beings who promoted it in the nineteenth century, or with Orientalism as cultural policy, social activism and scholarly achievements. Greatly influenced by French deconstructionists such as Jacques Derrida, Said transformed Orientalism into a dragon that might be destroyed with his book.

The Indian historian O. P. Kejariwal has also courageously leapt to the Orientalists' defence. He calls Jones 'the Copernicus of history' precisely because he was able to free himself from the fixed perspective of his own outlook. Jones realized that only once the history of the East was properly known could one begin to tackle the history of mankind. To Kejariwal, far from being a hegemonic agent, Jones was 'the first scholar to have looked at the East without a western bias'.

Two hundred years on, it is clear the Orientalists merit less controversy and more credit on two counts. They were indeed Company officials, at least in part motivated by the thought that Oriental studies would be useful to the Company in India. Notwithstanding this, they clearly served humanity by bringing the peoples of the world closer together. They did so in ways that fundamentally disprove Kipling's conviction a century later that East and West could never find common ground. Today, we are finally returning to this view of the world first fashioned by the Orientalists. We call it multiculturalism. Secondly, the Orientalists gave India back her history and culture, which became vital aspects of her emerging national identity. Arguably, in that way the Orientalists contributed far more to Indian nationalism than they did to British colonialism.

CHAPTER FIVE

GOING NATIVE

At first sight you might think you'd have trouble finding the tomb of Major-General Charles Stuart in Calcutta's South Park Street Cemetery. There's no Register of Graves at the gate, and the burial ground is a densely packed 'Who Was Who' of British India, chock-a-block with monument after monument recalling great deeds, gentle dispositions and sudden, pitiful ends. Broken columns, Grecian urns, Egyptian obelisks and pyramids, Roman colonnaded temples and Palladian cubes are scattered by the dozen. Every classical rule of architecture is displayed cheek-by-jowl as if the place were a capricious source book of western civilization.

Luckily, amid the classicism, one tomb stands out. There is nothing unusual about its size, materials or condition. You are drawn towards it purely because of its exuberant, incongruous style. The tomb is topped by a Mughal-shaped dome, with small *shikharas* (curved temple-style towers) at each corner. The canopy protects a simple, four-sided shrine, entered via an arched gateway whose angular columns look like they are carved from sandalwood. Every available surface is a riot of decoration, in contrast to the restraint and severity

'HINDOO STUART'S INDIAN-STYLE TOMB WITH ITS DOMED ROOF,

STANDS OUT FROM THE REST.

of the tomb's stiff-upper-lip neighbours. The frieze, though much eroded, contains relief sculptures of what look suspiciously like Hindu deities, some in apparent cross-legged benediction. Meanwhile, the jambs leave no room for doubt. Curvaceous representations of the Goddess Ganga and Prithvi Devi, Goddess of the Earth, protect the soul of the departed English officer. For Major-General Charles Stuart was more commonly known as 'Hindoo' Stuart, and apparently took several of his favourite idols into his coffin for company.

Stuart was just one of a significant cast of Europeans who were motivated by neither loot nor detached scholarship. Instead, these men, whom the writer William Dalrymple has aptly dubbed 'the White Moghuls', began to love the culture of their adopted home so much that some of them effectively 'went native'. They readily shed many of the habits of their homeland to take up Indian clothing, lifestyle, food, women, values and even religion. A full 200 years before the first hippies hit the subcontinent, to chill out to its spiritual vibes in their cannabis-enhanced haze of supposed self-discovery, these eighteenth-century adventurers had 'found themselves' in India.

If the Orientalists' greatest assets were their open minds, the White Moghuls are best characterized as full-hearted. The Russians would use an even better term for them. They would describe them as 'big souls'.

The Orientalists deeply admired Indian history, culture and religion. But their interest was essentially scholarly and often purely antiquarian. Without belittling their achievements, it would be fair to say that many had far better relationships with dead Indians than live ones. They tended to glorify the past golden age and compare it with what they regretted was the reduced, enervated culture of contemporary India. The White Moghuls were men of an entirely different stamp, living life to the limits as well as in the library.

Rather than being the offspring of the European enlightenment, the White Moghuls were successors to the European adventurers who had been coming to India for 200 years and had, in many cases, become fully integrated within multicultural Mughal society. Ever since the early seventeenth century, Europeans had arrived in India at a very tender age. So it was natural that some had 'crossed over' and built their lives as mercenary soldiers, merchants, officials and even musicians in the service of the Great Mughal Empire and its subsidiary courts. In these early days, opportunities within the East India Company had been largely confined to its small coastal factories and were entirely dwarfed by the wealth, culture and majesty of the Mughals. It is not surprising, therefore, that some Britons 'went native', absorbed into a culture that had flourished precisely because it was open to talent, regardless of its origins. In many cases these men had all but shed the culture of their birth. They took Mughal rank, served in its armies, changed their names, married Indian women, and embraced Islam, a process that necessarily involved circumcision. These were not men planning to make a quick fortune and head home. Instead, within a generation, the historian loses track of them as their families merge entirely into Indian society.

By the late eighteenth century, the power balance was well on the way to being reversed. Few Europeans were likely to look to the residual Mughal presence in Delhi as the honey-pot it had once been. Power, influence and opportunity were instead increasingly transferring to the Presidency cities of Calcutta, Madras and Bombay, where the predominant culture was European. Nevertheless, Britons continued to fan out across the subcontinent in increasing numbers. They went as ambassadors to native courts, as soldiers and officers attached to their armies, as traders sourcing business deep inland, and as explorers, artists and scholars seeking subjects and inspiration far removed from the claustrophobia of the big cities. Just like their predecessors, many of these men found the predominant Indian culture both attractive and welcoming. A few did indeed choose to remain isolated, aloof and celibate, their only option if they wished to mix solely with their own kind. But it is hardly strange that many, perhaps the majority, changed their lifestyles and outlooks to suit their surroundings.

Indeed, the only reason it does seem strange is that later the Victorians, fired with evangelical zeal and fully fledged racism, increasingly frowned on open Indianization, pushing it underground though never entirely eradicating it. What they also tried their best to do was to erase this chapter from history. As we saw earlier, for example, the second edition of Captain Williamson's *Vade Mecum* entirely omitted the lengthy section found in the original that gave newcomers useful advice about native women. It would all have been too shocking for Victorian society. Thus too Victorian biographers deliberately suppressed evidence about their subjects' Indian *bibis* or wives and their 'country-born' children. They tended even to downplay evidence that their characters mixed openly and equally with Indians or admired Indian religion or culture. William Dalrymple explains:

> In the 1780s to 1800s, there's no embarrassment at all about talking about their posh Mughal wives, their Anglo-Indian children, the fact that they've converted to Islam. The same biographies reprinted in the 1830s and 1840s have those passages omitted. I mean deliberately erased. It's not an accidental thing, it's a deliberate cover-up. It's a kind of Stalinist air brushing. It's like the removal of those figures who had fallen out of favour with the Communist Party, from photographs that happened in 1930s Russia. It's a deliberate rewriting of history by the Victorians to disguise this multiculturalism.

This happened because, by the mid-nineteenth century, the moral fibre of the Raj was thought in some way to depend on something akin to apartheid. Even by dressing for

COLONEL JAMES TODD
WAS ONE OF MANY
COMPANY MEN TO 'GO
NATIVE' AND LEAVE THE
RESIDENCY CITIES FOR
STATES WHERE THERE
WERE FEW EUROPEANS.

dinner every night in full evening dress, the British were demonstrating that they were a race apart. By maintaining their 'standards', they were constantly reaffirming to themselves their superior civilization. Sweating profusely and wearing clothes wholly inappropriate to a jungle in the middle of the monsoon were small prices to pay. No one would have dreamt of turning up, like their predecessors a generation or two earlier, in loose-fitting pyjamas, a flowing gown from Lucknow and a turban.

This Victorian veil is only now being lifted. What William Dalrymple and others have rediscovered is a far more tolerant, open encounter between Britons and Indians than the shamefully starched rigidity and mutual incomprehension that followed. Dalrymple goes so far as to call it 'the vibrant multiculturalism of the East India Company'.

Several remarkable late-eighteenth- and early-nineteenth-century careers have recently been re-examined to throw this multiculturalism into focus. The lives of Claude Martin and Samuel Palmer in Lucknow, James Achilles Kirkpatrick at Hyderabad, and David Ochterlony and William Fraser in Delhi reveal fascinating degrees of cultural hybridity. At least in their personal and social lives, these men 'went native' to a far greater extent than their contemporaries in the coastal Presidencies (who, as we saw in Chapter 1, were likely to have had Indian mistresses and Anglo-Indian children but otherwise remained culturally British).

In the late eighteenth century, Lucknow, the capital of Oudh, was one of the world's great playgrounds. Under the patronage of its fabulously wealthy nawabs, the culture at court and in the city deliberately replicated and in many ways outdid the former glories of Agra and Delhi at the height of the Mughal Empire. The nawabs were renowned for both their culture and their decadence, their libertine ways epitomized by a portrait in the city's art gallery of the last nawab, Wajid Ali Shah, proudly exposing one nipple. So Lucknow was definitely the place to be if you were an Urdu poet, a ghazal singer or musician, a nautch dancer or an exquisitely mannered courtesan, offering not just virtuoso sexual services but poetry, philosophy and refined conversation to educate your clients. Not surprisingly, Lucknow was also a magnet for Europeans. William Russell, the great Victorian correspondent for *The Times*, later wrote, 'Not Rome, not Athens, not Constantinople, not any city I have ever seen appears to me so striking and beautiful as this.'

John Zoffany's famous painting *Colonel Mordaunt's Cock Match* captures the atmosphere of the Lucknow court perfectly. A mixed group of Indians and Europeans gossip and lounge around while attending a cock fight. There is little formality and many are in casual dress. They are surrounded by a wider circle of spectators, including Lucknow's famous musicians and dancing girls. In the centre, the Nawab, Asaf-ud-Daula, rises to greet a jacketless Mordaunt, who, as well as organizing cock fights, was the handsomely rewarded commander

A COCK-FIGHT AT THE COURT IN OUDH — WARREN HASTINGS ONCE OWNED THIS PAINTING WHICH FEATURES MANY OF HIS EUROPEAN AND INDIAN FRIENDS.

of the Nawab's bodyguard. Among the many European spectators, some cradle fighting cocks, while others smoke pipes or are deep in conversation with Indian colleagues. The artist Zoffany himself holds a pencil at the back of the picture, and stares straight out of the canvas. The elegant officer at the front of the cushioned dais is Colonel Claude Martin.

The son of a cooper from Lyon, Martin came with little or no education to India in 1751, aged just sixteen, to serve with the French Compagnie's forces. When their fortunes declined, he transferred his allegiance to the East India Company. He was linked to the British Company for the rest of his career, much admired by both Warren Hastings and his successor Lord Cornwallis, though even when he was promoted to the rank of Major-General he refused to adopt British citizenship. From 1776 onwards, Martin made his home in Lucknow and became one of the Nawab's closest confidants. His eclectic preoccupations included supervising the Nawab's arsenal, farming indigo, dealing in horses, supplying trinkets and mechanical curiosities to the court and experimenting as a metal caster, producing several serviceable cannon. Spectacular self-made wealth allowed him to build for himself no fewer than seven flamboyant palaces, one of which boasted its own prototype air-conditioning system. His greatest palace, Constantia, was built to house his own mausoleum. It's a sort of Indo-European Xanadu straight out of *Citizen Kane*. Martin even deserves the credit for becoming the Indian subcontinent's first aviator. Just a few years after Montgolfier's first European flights, Martin built a hot-air balloon and made several pioneering trips, though he wisely refused to take the Nawab along for the ride.

Martin's household was every bit as decadent as the Nawab's. It included two eunuchs, a transvestite, an in-house firework maker, and Martin's seven mistresses. Martin's unembarrassed candour about these women means we know more about them than about most other similar *bibis*.

In India, as in Europe, Africa and America, the late eighteenth century was a period in which it was both legal and common to own slaves. It was likewise permissible in all these continents to have sex with girls whom we would regard as still children. In India, Hindu and Moslem girls tended to marry or start having sex at around twelve. But it is worth remembering that in Britain child prostitution was rampant and that the age of consent for girls remained twelve until 1885. In the majority of cases, Martin appears to have bought his mistresses when they were very young. Some were the daughters of prostitutes, others were illegitimate Eurasians. For example, the youngest mistress, Sally, just fourteen when Martin died at sixty-five, was the cast-off daughter of an English officer who abandoned both her and her mother when he returned to Britain. Three of Martin's mistresses, including his favourite Boulone, were sisters.

Though we may find this grotesque, it is clear that Martin was devoted to his *bibis,* however unequal the relationship. In his rambling will, which is part confessional autobiography, Martin explains (without punctuation): 'God may give them their reward they are innocent of any Guilt I am culpable on the Sin if they have Committed any by having partook of my bed they owed Compliance to my Command as theirs Duties Having every reason to be well satisfied of their Services'. At this, Martin's biographer, Rosie Llewelyn-Jones, sensibly comments: 'It is fruitless to speculate on the degree of coercion or the amount of pleasure that the seven young women may have experienced when ordered to his bedroom. Life for abandoned or abducted girls, especially those of mixed blood, was precarious enough, even if they did not starve to death or end up in brothels.'

Boulone, whose portrait still hangs at Constantia, is buried in its grounds in a small and elegant Muslim mausoleum. She and her sisters were noble-born, which had not prevented their father, a minor nawab, from selling them into slavery when he lost his fortune. By the time Martin died, he and Boulone had been together for twenty-five years. In his will, he left her and the other *bibis* and their families substantial legacies. He also set out in detail her story:

> My faithful girl called Boulone, or Lise, who has been most faithfully attached to me, and (about whom I) never had the smallest room to complain since I acquired her, which was when she was about nine years old... That said girl I acquired for the consideration of a sum I paid to one Carriere, a Frenchman, who had acquired her by purchase from a cruel and inhuman father and mother of her... I brought her up as a child I loved, and I educated her with all the tenderness of a father, took proper care to learn her principle of religion, and learned her great modesty and decency, and to read and write, for when at age of reason she should choose any one of her pleasure for either husband or companion. As I proposed to marry her to any one of her caste if she chose it, she choosed never to quit me... she persisted that she would live with me; according, I keep her, and as she has always been extremely attached to me, I have endeavoured to make her as happy as I had it in my power, and I have every reason to praise her conduct, character of chastity and modesty; and I may say to her credit that since we lived together since the year 1775, we never had a word or bad humour one against another.

Having looked after his women and children, the bulk of Martin's vast remaining fortune was left to charity. Bequests went to the poor in Lucknow, Calcutta, the French station at Chandernagar and his birthplace Lyon, with specific instructions that children of all religions should benefit. Though a Catholic by birth, Martin's religious beliefs were clearly as unconventional as his lifestyle:

I worshipped Him as I had been taught in my infancy, though avoiding all the priestly ceremony; but as still many doubts crowded on my mind, I could never cease enquiring the true path of religion, and worshipping the Omnipotent Creator or God, and I endeavoured to learn the religion of other nations and sects; and though I found mostly every other nations and sects as ridiculous in their ceremony as I thought the religion I was educated in, still I found a similarity in the substances of every religion of nations and sects [with which] I have been acquainted, all professing sound morals, and the recommendation to do all the good possible to other creatures, to worship only one God the creator of all, and to be charitable to all other creatures, to do penances for sins – in short, every principle of religion as good as any of the several sects of the Christian religion.

But Martin's greatest posthumous project was to found schools in Lyon, Calcutta and Lucknow, the latter in Constantia itself. His will explains his motivation: 'I want to thank all those who have been around me by making their life easier after my death. I also want to give the children of both Lyon and India, the instruction I received with so much difficulty. I want to make it easy for young people to get access to knowledge, especially the sciences.'

The La Martiniere Schools survive to this day. Those in Lucknow and Calcutta are among the subcontinent's finest, oldest and most famous schools. Every day at assembly, the boys continue to sing a hymn in honour of their founder, Claude Martin. Yet as we shall see in Chapter 9, by a strange irony, the rigid Anglo-Saxon ethos of the schools has always been almost entirely at odds with Martin himself and with what we can deduce from his will were his multicultural intentions. There is therefore no better symbol of the end of the complex, morally ambiguous era of the White Moghuls than La Martiniere, the perfect English public school.

The career of General William Palmer, sometime British Resident (Company Ambassador) at Lucknow, Gwalior and Pune, demonstrates that men far more conventional than Claude Martin adopted similar lifestyles naturally, and without embarrassment or damage to their careers. If anything, until about the 1820s it was a definite advantage for a British Resident to live with a begum (aristocratic Muslim woman) or two. They enhanced his status at court while the *zenana* provided him with useful local knowledge and a wide circle of contacts. So the *bibi* was not just a 'sleeping dictionary'. She was also something of a passport.

In an unfinished but intimate family portrait, variously attributed to both Francesco Renaldi and John Zoffany, (see pages 118–19) Palmer is shown in his military-style red-

coat surrounded by his Indian womenfolk, their children, and servants. Palmer is looking adoringly at his chief woman, who is wearing the finest jewellery. This is Begum Faiz Baksh, the daughter of a Delhi nobleman, whom Palmer first met at Lucknow and with whom he would live for thirty-five years. She is shown sitting on the ground and cradling their baby, named Hastings after his godfather Warren. Controversy has raged over the identity of the other woman, seated to Palmer's left. Some art historians suggest that she is Faiz Baksh's sister Halima, while others insist that her pose demonstrates she is Palmer's second *bibi*. It seems entirely possible that she was both.

It is unlikely that Faiz Baksh and Palmer ever married, no doubt principally because of their different faiths. It does not in any case seem as if formal wedlock was much of an issue at the time. Hastings, and his elder siblings William and Mary, were all baptized and sent to school in England, as had been Palmer's three other mixed-race children, the offspring of an earlier partnership in the West Indies with a Creole woman called Sarah. All six children did well when they returned to India, and there is no evidence that their mixed-race origins were later much of a disadvantage. Begum Faiz Baksh, however, remained a Muslim, and was eventually buried near the main mosque in Hyderabad.

SIR DAVID OCHTERLONY, DRESSED IN INDIAN COSTUME, ENJOYS A NAUTCH AT THE BRITISH RESIDENCY IN DELHI, C. 1820.

In fact, Hyderabad played host to a British Resident (ambassador) at the very end of the eighteenth century who did undergo a formal marriage ceremony to his Indian lover, one of the few senior Company officials to do so. In 1800 news of the secret wedding between James Achilles Kirkpatrick and Khair un-Nissa (meaning 'Excellent among Women') reached Calcutta and London and caused a considerable stir. It was rightly appreciated that in order to marry the Muslim noblewoman, Kirkpatrick must have converted to Islam.

The marriage had come about because of extraordinary boldness on the part of Kirkpatrick's would-be bride, what would today be called Girl Power. Khair un-Nissa saw Kirkpatrick for the first time when he was out riding and fell for him instantly. She sent messengers to him with billets-doux, but he rejected her advances. So she persuaded her mother and grandmother to accompany her on an uninvited visit to Kirkpatrick's *zenana*, ostensibly to visit his concubines. Kirkpatrick later confessed in a letter to his brother that a 'long nocturnal interview' followed, during which he had 'a full and close survey of her lovely person'. She repeatedly declared her love for him, claiming 'that her fate was linked to mine'. To begin with, Kirkpatrick 'attempted to argue the romantic young creature out of her passions'. But eventually 'the ultimate connection took place'. Kirkpatrick commented, 'I must have been more or less than man to have held out any longer.'

By all accounts, the romance endured for the rest of their lives, though there is no reason to believe Kirkpatrick gave up his concubines. Khair un-Nissa, like any married Muslim noblewoman, was expected to spend the rest of her life secluded in purdah. So Kirkpatrick built for her a *zenana*, the Rang Mehal, fit for a Mughal princess. Behind its high walls, there were shady pavilions, soothing fountains and richly decorated chambers decorated with delicate fretwork. Because she could not leave this cloistered Oriental paradise, Kirkpatrick thoughtfully erected a large, plaster scale-model of a Palladian villa in the Begum's garden. This was a model of the new Residency Kirkpatrick had built at the other end of the complex. So though she could never visit, Khair un-Nissa was nonetheless able to see exactly how and where her husband lived.

What William Dalrymple has suggested is a political dimension to this relationship which, without diminishing the romance, makes it more than just a love story. Like Lucknow, Hyderabad was a cosmopolitan and sophisticated independent Muslim kingdom whose court, thanks to the fabled diamond mines of Golconda, was blessed with almost unimaginable wealth. Kirkpatrick's match may well have helped the British Resident to know the mind and maintain the allegiance of Hyderabad's monarch, the Nizam of Hyderabad. Certainly, in 1798 he had pulled off a diplomatic master-stroke in persuading the Nizam to switch allegiance from his historic allies, the French, to the British. As a result, a 14,000-strong French sepoy army surrendered to Kirkpatrick's tiny corps of guards.

Henceforth, Kirkpatrick was known at court as Hushmat Jung ('Magnificent in Battle'). Yet there is every chance that Kirkpatrick's marriage, far from aiding the British cause, was made at the cost of him turning into something akin to a double agent. Dalrymple has discovered documentary evidence in Persian of a secret deal between Kirkpatrick and the Nizam's Prime Minister, which seems to have been the price he had to pay for obtaining the Nizam's permission for him to marry Khair un-Nissa. In this compact, which was unknown to Calcutta, Kirkpatrick swears to 'give an unequivocal support to his Highness's Government so long as he remained Resident, and also to remain grateful for ever'. This new evidence of course encourages all sorts of intriguing speculation. Is this really more of a spy thriller than a love match? Could Khair un-Nissa have sneaked into Kirkpatrick's *zenana* not because she thought he looked sexy on horseback but because she was some kind of Mata Hari, working for the Nizam or one of the court factions, on a secret mission to win over the British supremo?

Even without knowing about Kirkpatrick's secret agreement with the Nizam, the Company's top brass in Calcutta were unsettled by the news of his marriage. The Governor-General, Richard Wellesley, immediately ordered an investigation, which privately concluded that Kirkpatrick's actions had 'tarnished the National reputation'. As the eighteenth century gave way to the nineteenth, Wellesley's disapproval was a sign that attitudes to inter-racial relationships were quickly changing. Nevertheless, Wellesley's concerns were primarily political rather than religious or racial. The main anxiety was that Kirkpatrick's match, by favouring Khair un-Nissa's family, might alienate another important faction at court. In any event, Kirkpatrick's actions were not thought sufficiently serious to cost him his job, nor his children their place in either Muslim or English society. Saheb Allum and Saheb Begum also answered to the names of William George and Katherine Aurora, sometime residents of Hyderabad and Brighton.

The last stronghold of the true White Moghul was probably the British Residency in Delhi early in the nineteenth century. By then the Mughal court was decayed and powerless, but the Emperor remained official overlord of most of the subcontinent and therefore still possessed considerable powers of patronage. Britain's official representatives to the court therefore played a crucial diplomatic and military role. The men posted there were the antithesis of the later archetypal, pith-helmeted British diplomats. Delhi was the new Company frontier, a dangerous six-month journey from Calcutta through Maratha territory. Life in the city bore little or no resemblance to the British seat of power in Bengal. Sir David Ochterlony, Britain's first Resident to Delhi, was known to the locals as 'loony Akthar' (Crazy Star). Every evening he would process through Old Delhi with all thirteen

OVERLEAF:
THIS INTIMATE GROUP
PORTRAIT SHOWS WILLIAM
PALMER WITH HIS LONG-
STANDING INDIAN
PARTNER, FAIZ BAKSH,
THEIR CHILDREN, AND
ANOTHER WOMAN WHO
MAY WELL HAVE BEEN
HIS OTHER MISTRESS.

of his wives, each astride her own elephant. He dressed as a local and threw wild nautch parties. An Indian miniature survives portraying exactly this scene (see page 115). Ochterlony lolls on cushions in Oriental splendour, nonchalantly surveying his dancing girls while puffing on an enormous, elegantly coiled hookah. The Indian artist captures the sumptuous Oriental decoration of the Residency's tiled floor, its Persian carpets and the array of lavish costumes. But he also depicts pure European elements. A copybook Regency fanlight pierces the façade above the main entrance. Meanwhile, conventional portraits of stern-faced forebears stare down on Ochterlony's debauchery. All in all, it's the most complete visual expression of this fusion between East and West.

Ochterlony's assistant, William Fraser (Fraser Sahib), went even further. During his thirty years in Delhi he acquired a Rajput beard, six or seven legitimate wives, fifty children, and a private army of a thousand sepoys. He refused to eat beef or pork, wore Indian robes (but a Scottish tam-o'shanter on his head) and infinitely preferred the company of Indians. He had certainly left his home near Inverness far behind.

William was one of five Fraser brothers to make their careers in India. Only one of them made it back to Scotland. Certainly, in many ways, despite his Indian ways, William was a pioneering British empire-builder. Among his many claims to fame, he was responsible for recruiting the first Gurkhas into British military service (where they serve to this day). A friend commented on his daredevil nature that 'whenever there is a war anywhere, he throws up his judicial functions and goes off to it'. He seems to have been an instinctive autocrat, who used his personal charisma and authority to command the loyalty of his sepoys and to annex, pacify and administer vast tracts of northern India. Unlike later imperialists, however, Fraser's skills were not honed on the playing fields of Eton or Haileybury, the school set up in Hertfordshire by the Company in 1805 to mould its Indian personnel. Instead, William Fraser explained in a letter to a younger brother that the best preparation for India was 'personal intercourse with natives of all denominations and castes, to acquire idiom, dialect, manner, local knowledge, knowledge of custom, character, prejudice, religion, internal arrangement, ancient hereditary habits and distinguishing characteristics'.

To his friend, the French botanist Jacquemont, William Fraser was 'half Asiatick in his habits, but in other respects a Scottish Highlander, and an excellent man with great originality of thought, a metaphysician to boot, and enjoying the best possible reputation of being a country-bear'. Ochterlony's successor as Resident, Sir Charles Metcalfe, seems to have been wary that the 'self-willed' Fraser was a bit of a loose cannon and 'might drag the Government into mischief'. Nevertheless, Metcalfe acknowledged that Fraser's intimacy with the natives was his greatest strength and extremely useful. Mere usefulness does not account for his patronage of Ghalib, Delhi's finest Urdu poet. It is an equally inadequate explanation for his evident passion for Mughal painting, which saw him both build a great collection of historic miniatures (now in the Metropolitan Museum in New York) and commission from local artists some of the first modern Indian paintings of everyday Indian subjects.

Fraser's brothers and friends were fully aware that, as Jacquemont put it, he had 'as many children as the King of Persia, but they are all Hindus or Muslims according to the religion of their mamas'. Yet it is interesting that, like many sons before and since, he did his best to keep the truth about his sex-life from his parents back in Scotland. Instead he disingenuously wrote to his father that, 'It is enough for me to reflect how many valuable women are to be had in Britain, to hinder me from risking the charms of a hundred or more in India. So I must wait until I go home, and then it will be too late.' In fact, perhaps because of all his wives and children, Fraser never made any attempts to go home. Or rather, for him and many others, India had become far more home than Britain. As William Dalrymple puts it, 'that was where they belonged'.

As was normal throughout Indian history, a new hybrid people had emerged. This wasn't just a product of what has been dubbed 'sexual imperialism'. Nor was it, as Innes Munro put it in 1780, simply because it was cheaper to maintain 'a whole *zenana* of Indians than the extravagance of one English lady'. Though some White Moghuls simply relished the obvious attractions of a harem, for others it had clearly been a genuine marriage of minds as well as bodies. As their letters and wills indicate, devotion and love could be colour-blind. Certainly India's open-minded sensual code, embodied in the *Kama Sutra*, encouraged the understanding of pleasure and its place in the cycle of life. But this unique moment in the British–Indian encounter probably owes just as much to more universal instincts of sex, love and companionship. These were damaged, but never wholly eradicated, by Victorian prudery and prejudice, racism and hypocrisy, the noxious cocktail by which the empire was later supposedly 'made respectable'.

It was far easier to break into Muslim society than the exclusive and mysterious world of brahminical Hinduism, which makes 'Hindoo' Stuart a rarity even among White Moghuls. Judging by what little we know about him, he also outdid a notoriously wild and weird bunch in sheer eccentricity. Born in Ireland around 1757, Stuart arrived in India while still a teenager to take up a military career. Over the next forty years, he rose straight up through the ranks, from cadet to major-general, serving first in a European regiment, then with the Native Infantry, latterly commanding his own regiment, the Saugor Field Force (and taking the opportunity to build a Hindu temple at Saugor). Quite what first drew Stuart to Hinduism is not clear. This was not some gradual, intellectual awakening. Instead he must have been instantly and totally smitten. From almost as soon as he arrived in India, he developed the habit of walking every morning from his house to the Hooghly, the branch of the Holy Ganges that passes through Calcutta on its way to the Bay of Bengal. There, he would bathe and pray in the manner of a devout Hindu, a ritual he was to perform daily for the rest of his life. His Hinduism was therefore on open display to the whole of Calcutta. As far as one can tell, this does not seem to have set back his career.

Over fifty years, Stuart also accumulated a large collection of Hindu devotional sculptures. Unlike other collectors of the time, who were academics, connoisseurs or simple souvenir-hunters, Stuart seems to have used his collection for its original purpose. To him, they were far more than works of art. When he went on leave to Britain in 1804, he took a number of these household gods with him, no doubt so he could keep up his devotions. Much of his collection ended up in the British Museum and so you can still admire idols there that were once worshipped by an Irishman, rather than simply pilfered or purchased as exotic objects of display.

Even by today's standards of non-conformity, some of Stuart's attitudes seem far-out. In 1800, he became a frequent and vigorous correspondent to the *Calcutta Telegraph,* urging European women to wear saris instead of impractical and unattractive western fashion. Years later he published these letters, and those from various outraged women in reply, in a deliciously silly volume entitled 'The Ladies Monitor, Being A Series of Letters First published in Bengal On the Subject of Female Apparel Tending to Favour a regulated adoption of Indian Costume And a rejection of Superfluous Vesture By the Ladies of this country With Incidental remarks on Hindoo Beauty, Whale-Bone Stays, Iron Busks, Indian Corsets, Man-Milliners, Idle Bachelors, Hair-Powder, Waiting Maids, And Footmen'.

Stuart's thesis begins in a way that brooks no argument: 'The dress of the Brahmin ladies stands, confessed, as yet unrivalled in the world, for its elegance and simplicity.' It is, maintains Stuart, without doubt more suitable than the absurd corsetry then in fashion in Europe and therefore Calcutta. Rejecting the suggestion that British women would look indecent in saris, he sensibly points out that 'indecency is a term whose bounds are merely relative'. After all, the delicate sensibilities of British women are not offended by their palanquin-bearers, who wear nothing but a loin-cloth. Stuart's mission, he declares unambiguously, is first and foremost to get English women to wear less: 'I am a professed enemy to superfluous vesture; and... my aim is to reduce their dress, as far as is consistent with our manners, to an imitation of the Indian costume.' Stuart reserves especial loathing for European stays and busks, the prodigious structural engineering women strapped themselves into in order to hold their bellies in, project their breasts out and allow their dresses to balloon grandly up and over towards the floor. These, Stuart feels,

are not just cumbersome but positively dangerous. Using iron busks in a country with so much lightning exposes a woman to the risk she might 'instantly be reduced to ashes'. 'This is no laughing matter, ladies,' Stuart warns, 'for I am absolutely serious.' How much more sensible to cast them off, glut Bengal with a new supply of scrap metal and lower the price of iron for farmers who need new wagon-wheels: 'In God's name dismiss these treacherous bosom-friends, and consign them to the FORGE to be converted into swords for the protection of our coast.' Instead women should 'let nothing ruder than their lovers' arms be henceforth admitted to the pressure of their lovely forms'.

It gradually becomes apparent to the reader that Stuart's enthusiasm for the sari is not motivated solely by its practicality. He explains that the Hindu woman tends to bathe fully dressed in public, changes her sari 'while yet in the river, and necessarily rises with wet drapery from the stream… Had I despotic power, our fair ones should soon follow the example; being fully persuaded it would eminently contribute to keep the bridal torch for ever in a blaze.' At this point, in a sort of eighteenth-century Ode to the Wet Tee-Shirt, Stuart launches into verse:

> *How oft, where Ganges rolls the rapid stream,*
> *Have I beheld the lovely Brahmin dame,*
> *Just rising from the flood, in all her pride;*
> *Her thin, wet clothes, in vain her beauties hide;*
> *In folds adhesive, fondly they embrace*
> *Her lovely limbs, displaying every grace;*
> *While the charmed eye surveys without controul,*
> *And bears delicious poison to the soul.*
>
> …
>
> *Soft thrillings seize on every vital part,*
> *And nought but heaven can save the prostrate heart.*

Stuart mounts a persuasive case for western women to ignore what he calls the 'fashion dictators of Europe'. They should, he insists, forget 'the Mother Country', free their minds and strip off. He was at a dinner party, he explains, where the women were all complaining that they did not know how to wean British men off Indian girls. One of the men argued the women were so poorly dressed they had only themselves to blame: 'believe me, the Ganges… establishes very different standards of beauty and it is unreasonable to expect that we should fall in love with such a mountain of clothes, however fine or brilliant they may appear'. At this point, no doubt moved by his own 'Bridal Torch', Stuart feels more verse rising up:

But first, retrench such num'rous folds of clothes;
And Nature's bounties, modestly disclose.
Let robes adhesive, your fair limbs invest:
And, to imagination, leave the rest.'

It is hardly surprising that European women took umbrage at Stuart's master-plan. As one properly, but primly, observed, they wanted to be admired for 'the internal decoration of our minds', not the outward charms of their curves as seen through wet fabric. What is especially revealing, however, is the degree to which the women couch their ripostes using derogatory racist assumptions that Stuart would never have used. Thus 'Maria' writes to the paper complaining Stuart has 'transferred every becoming grace of dress and person to *our sooty sisterhood*' (author's italics). He is probably not good enough for white women, argues Maria. Instead, 'let him rage among the race of TAWNY SYBILS, whose allurement are best suited to the libertine mind'. Stuart admits he finds such generalizations revolting. He rails in reply against those small-minded English who call Indians 'Blackee' or refuse to eat pilau in case it turns them into a Hindostanee. He argues that 'the chief purpose of travelling into foreign countries' is to 'free the mind from prejudice'. If we retrench, 'in vain then do we travel'.

In a small way, this exchange, dated 1800, perfectly captures the moment of transition in British India, as the old, easy-going norms of fraternization and mutual discovery are eclipsed by censoriousness and racism. The early, overwhelmingly male era of the rogue traders and adventurers was on the wane. Missionaries and a far greater number of European women were arriving in Calcutta. Neither were likely to find the old ways admirable or even acceptable. To them, as one correspondent put it, Stuart was a victim of 'enervated Oriental ideas, imbibed on the banks of the Ganges'. The outraged writer continued, 'I would seriously advise this Hindoo gentleman... to desist railing against the British fair'. 'His vitiated taste' was only too obviously derived 'from the precincts of a Harem'.

Stuart seems to have delighted in pleading guilty. Indeed, the rest of the volume seems designed to shock. The harem, Stuart argues, is not such a bad institution, citing with admiration the case of Muhamad Ali Khan, Nawab of Karnataka, who had 'no less than 758 children, in the space of thirty-six years'. Monogamy is impractical in India because too much available pleasure diminishes 'the sweet attractive grace of Virgin-Modesty'. One attractive option is to sleep with prostitutes, members of a regulated institution under the protection of magistrates. Although prostitution is far better organized than in Europe, Stuart nonetheless favours the harem, explaining that he is a realist and that 'when so large a field presents itself to the gratification of the passions, the purer joys of the matrimonial state lose their attraction on the youthful mind'. At least, Stuart argues, the harem preserves the institution of marriage, albeit as polygamy rather than monogamy.

Finally, with one last smirk, Stuart turns his attention to the side-saddle, which decorum dictates British women use while riding. This is absurd, argues Stuart, since that way they fall off much more frequently: 'If ladies must ride a horse, Nature directly points out the safest and most simple mode.' This is, of course, to do as most nations in the world do, and 'bestride the naughty saddle like a man'. In the past, perhaps, British women were 'sans culottes... and doubtless, under such circumstances, it would have been unreasonable to expect that their delicacy should be exposed to the rude friction of the saddle'. But now 'soft, linen pantaloons' were available which 'will tend to secure them against injury'. What is more, Stuart reassures his readers, these pantaloons were even cleverly designed to avoid the disaster of inadvertently revealing an ankle.

For all this lubriciousness, Stuart should not be regarded as some dirty old man or prototype sex tourist. In 1808, he brought out an altogether more serious book, his *Vindication of the Hindoos*, which mounts a valiant and passionate defence of Hinduism from recent assaults by missionaries. Like Jones fifteen years earlier, Stuart has no doubts about 'the excellence of the moral system of the Hindoos'. But unlike the great Orientalist, Stuart rests his case not on books but on twenty-seven years' direct experience of 'the mass of the people', much of it on military service in rural Bengal. Different backgrounds nonetheless deliver very similar conclusions. Stuart explains:

'HINDOO' STUART WAS CRITICISED BY HIS SUPERIORS FOR OVER-INDULGING THE RELIGIOUS SENSIBILITIES OF HIS TROOPS.

Wherever I look around me, in the vast region of Hindu mythology, I discover Piety in the garb of allegory; and I see Morality, at every turn, blended with every tale: and as far as I can rely on my own judgement, it appears the most complete and ample

system of Moral Allegory, that the world has ever produced... I must do them the justice to declare that I never met with a people, exhibiting more suavity of manners, or more mildness of character; or a happier race of beings, when left to the undisturbed performance of the rites of religion.

Stuart of course goes one big step further than Jones, and announces that he is a Hindu. In the course of his book, he refers to 'my beloved Durga' (the goddess-consort of Shiva, focus of Calcutta's greatest annual festival of Durga-puja). Later he swears 'by the beard of Brahma' that there is nothing indecent about the Shiva lingam – the devotional, symbolic phallus which is the focus of Shiva worship. 'I have half a dozen myself in London,' he adds, attempting to convey the sublime tantric mysticism of the Hindu world-view:

communicating male and female light,
which two great sexes animate the world.

Finally, in one revealing passage in his book, Stuart leaves no room for doubt about his new faith: 'But *in thus admitting my conversion to Hinduism*, it does not absolutely follow that I reject the doctrines of Christianity; for if I believe Krishna to be Narayan, the Spirit of God floating on the face of the waters, who descended to the earth for the benefit of mankind, I entertain, I conceive, of a notion not very inconsistent with Christianity'. Perhaps that explains why Stuart was ultimately content to be buried in an Anglican cemetery, albeit along with his favourite idols, rather than being cremated and consigned to the Ganges. Unfortunately, the more intriguing question of why the Church was happy to bury him in such circumstances remains a mystery.

The bulk of Stuart's book is a prescient warning about the dangers of denigrating or interfering in Indian customs or beliefs. Stuart is appalled at the 'pious zealots who inconsiderately annex the idea of barbarism to every religious system not blessed with the sacred light of Gospel dispensation'. Not only are missionaries 'obnoxious', they are also dangerous, in that public confidence is 'the chief security of our precarious tenure in Hindostan'. In those circumstances, attempting to convert the native is 'impolitic, inexpedient, dangerous and unwise'. Not to put too fine a point on it, it is simple 'insanity'. If, Stuart asks, their religion is insulted, 'what confidence can we repose in the fidelity of our Hindu soldiers?' As the nineteenth century progressed, Stuart's warnings were fated to be forgotten – yet he was all but predicting the Indian Mutiny of 1857.

In the eighteenth and early nineteenth centuries, Company and British regiments had modelled themselves on Mughal units and fully catered for the diverse religious persuasions of their troops. Indeed, a regiment might well have benefited from the blessings of a Brahmin priest, a Muslim imam and a Protestant chaplain. Stuart certainly encouraged his own sepoys to come on parade sporting impressive Rajput moustaches or brightly coloured caste marks on their foreheads. But the tide was beginning to turn against facial hair, Indian feelings and commonsense. Stuart's commander-in-chief ticked him off on the appearance of his men. Their 'preposterous overgrowth of… Cheek Moustaches and immoderately large whiskers' was somehow bad for discipline and might exacerbate religious distinctions between the troops which were already 'sufficiently embarrassing to the public service'.

Later they would legislate against such cultural self-expression. But in the 1820s, this was still a subject for debate, not diktat. When Stuart died in April 1828, his obituary in the *Indian Gazette* strikes an apt note for its times. The tone is one of mild surprise, not moral disapproval: 'General Stuart had studied the language, manners, and customs of the natives of the country with so much enthusiasm, that his intimacy with them, and his toleration of, or rather apparent conformity to, their ideas and prejudices, obtained for him the name of "Hindoo" Stuart, by which, we believe, he is well known to many of our readers.' Within a few years, those same readers would probably not have dared mention his name unless it was to ridicule his views or denigrate his memory.

The era of the White Moghuls was drawing to a close. Yet their passion for India did not disappear without trace. On the contrary, returning nabobs with Orientalized tastes had started a fashion back home for all things Indian. One old India hand was said to have rented a house in Soho Square in London for his wife and six Indian concubines. Rumour had it they all shared a bedroom, with the women's beds all arranged in a circle around his.

In translating his Indian lifestyle to Blighty lock, stock and barrel, this White Moghul was highly unusual. But Indian art, architecture, food, music, literature and even health fads were coming into vogue in Britain on a far wider scale, disseminated both by returning Britons and by the country's first Asian visitors and settlers. Sometimes these were genuine imports from the subcontinent. More often they were fanciful impersonations of what Britain imagined to be the fruits of the mysterious and magnificent Indian Orient. Either way, 200 years before bhangra and chicken tikka masala, a fusion culture of a kind was emerging in fashionable British society.

CHAPTER SIX

FIRST FUSION

D eep in the picture postcard Cotswolds, a quiet valley plays host to one of Britain's oddest country houses. This is quintessential England where the towns and villages answer to names like Moreton-in-Marsh, Bourton-on-the-Water, Upper Slaughter and Stow-on-the-Wold. By that measure, Sezincote ought to be rechristened Taj-in-the-Vale.

The Emperor Akbar himself would have felt instantly at home had he set eyes on Sezincote. It is in the vibrant hybrid style he pioneered, combining traditional Hindu and Persian Muslim details. A bulbous Mughal dome crowns the building. At each of its four corners, a *chatri* (minaret-style open pavilion) rises up above the roof, which itself overhangs the façade, thanks to an elegant *chaja* (projecting cornice with deep brackets). The central arch of the main entrance shares the 'true' proportions of the grand entrances to the forts and mosques of Delhi and Agra. The decorative stonework includes carved lotuses, delicate Rajastani peacock-tail arches and chunky Hindu pillars. Imagine then how disappointed Akbar might have been to go inside this promising palace in search of audience halls and *zenanas*,

AMIDST FLAGSTONES DAMPENED BY SUMMER DRIZZLE.

SEZINCOTE'S MUGHAL DOME IS REFLECTED IN THE POND.

fountained courtyards and domed pavilions. Instead, he would have discovered a perfectly run-of-the-mill late-eighteenth-century English country house.

Sezincote was built for Charles Cockerell, a nabob who left India quite obviously determined that India shouldn't leave him. There's even a small temple in the grounds dedicated to the sun god Surya. Moreover, the gardens and terraces are scattered with sculptures of Nandi, the joyful bull whose sacred task is to serve as vehicle for Shiva. The overall effect is of an exuberant, unabashed Oriental theme park, an excellent symbol of how far India had captured the British imagination by the early nineteenth century.

The earlier generation of returning nabobs had lacked the self-confidence to do anything so outré. Their highest aspiration had been to acquire landed estates and ease their way into the establishment. To do this, they had naturally tended to play safe, which meant neo-classical. Of course, this could not spare them the satirists' bile. Instead, they shared the perennial fate of social climbers, which was to be sneered at for their vulgarity even as they desperately clung to the coat-tails of convention.

The great Clive, for example, exulted in his title, Baron Clive of Plassey. But the grand house he had built for him by Henry Holland and 'Capability' Brown at Claremont in Surrey was a copy-book example of Georgian restraint and reserve without, of course, the slightest Indian flight of architectural fancy. Instead, Clive took the best advice in art his money could buy and hot-footed it to Paris and Italy on an extensive shopping expedition. No doubt he was thrilled with his Gobelins tapestries, his substandard Tintoretto and his dubious Guido Reni. But of course the cognoscenti tittered that he had paid well over the odds for them.

The change came, as we saw in Chapter 4, when Warren Hastings opened his own eyes and mind to India, and became chief patron to the Orientalists, who spread knowledge and respect for the subcontinent around the world. Nevertheless, for all his Indian experiences, Warren Hastings remained an eighteenth-century English gentleman. To him, his greatest achievement was probably marshalling the means to buy back the Hastings family's ancestral seat at Daylesford in what was then Worcestershire (now Gloucestershire). The house he began building there at vast expense in 1788 was naturally neo-classical. But Hastings's architect was allowed a slight indulgence at the back of the building where a single, vaguely Mughal, dome surmounts the rotunda. Only a few years later, the same architect, Samuel Pepys Cockerell, was allowed by his brother Charles to let rip down the road at Sezincote.

Warren Hastings's interiors at Daylesford were the first in England to conjure up a version of India. The sculptor Thomas Banks designed great chimney pieces to fire the imagination every bit as effectively as their hearths warmed the toes. Here were maidens in saris carrying water jugs on their heads as they sashayed through the palm trees bearing platters groaning with Bengali fruit. In one, cavorting elephants herald Lakshmi, the goddess of wealth. In another, dancers, musicians and a fat-bellied entertainer attend an effete prince, who sits under a canopy nonchalantly smoking a hookah. Hastings furnished his rooms with Indian ivory, stacked his library with Oriental manuscripts and planted Bengali mangoes and peaches in his beloved gardens. While Old Master paintings remained de rigueur, the Rembrandt and the Correggio were confined to the 'picture room'. Hastings instead gave pride of place in the principal entertaining rooms to modern western paintings of India and his collection of Indian miniatures. Here hung several paintings by William Hodges, who had been with Hastings on their trip to Benares in 1780 (see pages 82–3). Here too hung Zoffany's riotous Lucknow scene, *Colonel Mordaunt's Cock Fight*, featuring his old friends the Nawab of Oudh and General Martin (see page 111).

One might expect the estate of a former Governor-General to be full of eastern promise. But within a few years, the taste for India had even spread to those who had never been further east than Margate. Like all trends, this one spread because of the glamour, allure and exclusivity of the style's original exponents, and the accessibility and affordability of something similar, albeit suitably adapted to the mass market. Few people could afford a house like Sezincote, even if they had wanted to make such a strong statement. But there were thousands of people who could demonstrate their refinement, modernity and cosmopolitanism by purchasing one of Thomas and William Danniell's aquatints of 'Oriental Scenery'. Meanwhile, those of yet more modest means could probably stretch to some Staffordshire pottery inspired by a Danniell scene, or perhaps do up a boudoir with some wallpaper featuring a Mughal ruin or Hindu folly picturesquely set in an eastern Arcady.

Thomas Danniell was an innkeeper's son who had started his career painting decorative scenes on carriages. After minor success as a landscape artist, he set out in 1785 for India, taking along as assistant his nephew William. In Calcutta, the pair started off by working as picture restorers and framers. With the exception of Hodges's brief trip, no European artist in India had yet made any kind of living through landscape. John Zoffany, Tilly Kettle and Francesco Renaldi, for example, worked almost exclusively to commission as portrait-painters. The Danniells took a different tack, quickly embarking on a series of views of Calcutta, which they were enterprising enough to engrave and publish as twelve aquatints. The profits were sufficient for them to amass the funds for a far more ambitious venture. In 1788 they headed north-west on what became a three-year odyssey across North India. They took with them a handful of servants, a huge stock of artists' materials, an odd assortment of camping gear and a pram as makeshift milometer, to help them map their route. They went up the Ganges to Benares and Allahabad, reached the Mughal marvels of Delhi and Agra, where they painted the Qutb Minar, the Taj Mahal and the Red

OVERLEAF:
THE ROPE BRIDGE WAS
240 FEET LONG AND
COULD BE SOON
ERECTED AND REMOVED'
WROTE THOMAS
DANNIELL OF HIS
PAINTING OF SRINAGAR
IN THE FOOTHILLS OF
THE HIMALAYAS.

Fort, and headed north into the hills, even reaching Srinagar in the mountain kingdom of Garhwal near the remote Himalayan source of the Ganges. Later, they made a similarly ambitious journey through equally uncharted territory west and south of Madras, though by now their fortunes allowed them a far bigger retinue and the occasional comfort of a palanquin. On this trip, they were able to commit to their sketch books the radically different architecture and history of the south's Dravidian Hindu civilization. Finally, they headed west to Bombay. By the time they set off home in 1793 they had produced over 1,400 drawings as well as a considerable number of landscapes in oil.

The Danniells' nine-and-a-half-year stint in the East resulted in no fewer than six volumes of 'Oriental Scenery' aquatints published between 1795 and 1808. Of course these proved far more collectable than their earlier scenes of Somerset. But it is interesting that the picturesque aesthetic prized by the Danniells was little different whether applied to Wookey Hole or the foothills of the Himalayas. Like all the most marketable modern art, the overall effect was not too radical. The India that proved a sure-fire success in English drawing-rooms was as much a product of western expectations as eastern reality. The English already knew how they liked their nature. So the Danniells obliged in India. Their best-selling scenes tended to feature an exotic jumble of ruins casually strewn about a romantic landscape, preferably peppered with craggy boulders, dramatic gushing torrents and perhaps, a distant shepherd boy watering his flock.

The Danniells' conformity to, or rather mastery of, an existing aesthetic should not, however, disguise their extraordinary achievement. Though they chose to portray India in a certain way, they had made remarkable, pioneering journeys to do so, visiting and documenting places that no European had ever reached before. The scenes they selected are indeed imbued with an inescapably romantic aura. But the architectural proportions and sculptural detail are invariably accurate, with William often using a form of camera obscura to ensure the underlying content was as scientific as its mood was exotic. Recently, an Italian photographer, Antonio Martinelli, returned to the scenes of many Danniell aquatints and, in similar light, set his tripod up in what he calculated was the same spot as the artist's easel. Published side by side, the modern photograph and eighteenth-century aquatint are often near identical. In their way, therefore, the Danniells were the artistic equivalents of the Orientalist scholars, collecting archaeological and historical data and spreading a compelling message about the wealth of Indian civilization.

There were those who bravely tried to do something similar with Indian music. In 1792 the great Oriental scholar Sir William Jones had himself studiously tried to penetrate its mysteries in a learned treatise 'On the Musical Modes of the Hindus'. As so often with Jones, ancient supersedes modern and abstract theory receives more attention than musical performance and practice. This was all part of Jones's quest for pure Sanskrit culture unsullied by the supposedly debased influence of contemporary music with its Muslim Mughal overtones. But it did not exactly assist Europeans to understand, let alone enjoy, the Indian music they were likely to encounter. So even those Europeans who snapped up Danniells' aquatints, adored *Sakuntala* and other Sanskrit poetry and considered Halhed's *Code of Gentoo Law* their idea of a good read, tended to reach for Haydn and the harpsichord as an antidote to Indian music. As one pained listener put it: 'Their screeching notes break in upon all conversation, and come upon the sense with so little harmony, that it is difficult to avoid rushing into the street with both hands to your ears – an action which I detected myself performing much more frequently than my politeness justified.'

Familiarity, however, did breed a certain fondness as well as contempt. As William Hamilton Bird, a Calcutta-based musician, put it, the music was 'wild but pleasing when understood'. Soon, he and other musically literate members of Calcutta society such as the Fowke family and Sophia Plowden decided to rise to the challenge of collecting some of the songs they frequently heard at nautches. This was no easy feat since Indian music was rarely written down and defied easy translation to the western stave, with its demand for a time signature, a key and a regular scale. Once they had committed a draft on to sheet music, the natural tendency was to arrange it and add harmonies to make the sound more 'pleasing'. By the time the music was then read back off the page by, say, flute and harpsichord, it bore little resemblance to the original song. But what this lacked in authenticity it made up in popularity. Such was the taste for the East that what were called 'Hindoostanee Airs' became, albeit briefly, an unlikely English musical sensation. Musical scholars remark that they most closely resemble Scottish folk songs. To an eighteenth-century English ear, Scottish music, with its weird bagpipe drone, was probably quite exotic and alien enough.

Further English editions of these airs successfully ironed out any residual Indian, or even Scottish, sound. A few, such as 'An Indostan Girl's Song', retained at least by name the romance of India. Others, though they were still called 'Hindoo Airs', were given improved titles. Thus 'Sakia, fusul bararust' ('Cupbearer, it is the season of Spring') mutated into the rather more mundane 'Crazy Sally'. Yet although scarcely an echo of the authentic India now remained, its distorted imprint on the English imagination survived. Popular operas in the early nineteenth century included *A Trip to Bengal*, *Englishmen in India*, *Indian Nuptials* and *The Choice of Harlequin* or *The Indian Chief*. Needless to say, the subcontinent had become little more than a convenient and exotic backdrop for opera's stock characters to spend a couple of hours doing dastardly deeds, triumphing heroically, falling in love and dying tragically.

After a show, there's nothing the English like more than going for a curry. In late-eighteenth-century London, that wasn't a problem. Britain's first Indian restaurant, the

Norris Street Coffee House, opened in 1773. Since it was situated on Haymarket it was even handy for the theatre. A decade later, a fashionable store on Piccadilly chose to highlight its curry. An ad in the *Morning Herald* for Sorlie's Perfumery Warehouse boasted that not only did curry taste good, it 'renders the Stomach active in Digestion – the Blood naturally free in Circulation – the Mind vigorous and contributes most of any Food to an increase of the Human Race'. Whatever its aphrodisiac properties, the new-fangled craze for chicken curry clearly upset some plain English folk, the type the French call *rosbifs*. In an anti-nabob tract by Henry Mackenzie called 'Influence of the Neighbourhood of a rich Asiatic', published in 1785, one 'John Homespun' complains: 'Our barn-door fowls, we used to say, were so fat and well tasted, we now make awkward attempts, by garlic and pepper, to turn into the form of curries and peelaws.' One 'rich Asiatic' with a definite taste for curry was Warren Hastings. Not content with the pre-packaged curry powder from Piccadilly, he decided to grow his own. A section of the hothouse in his beloved kitchen garden at Daylesford was devoted to chillies. He was so proud of them that he used to mail them to his old colleagues from India.

Within less than a generation, curry was clearly commonplace in London, which even had its first Indian-run Indian restaurant. As advertised in *The Times*, the Hindostanee Coffee House on George Street near Portman Square offered 'the Nobility and Gentry... the Hookah, with real Chillum tobacco, and Indian dishes, in the highest perfection, and allowed by the greatest epicures to be unequalled to any curries ever made in England'. The story of its remarkable proprietor Sake Dean Mahomed appears below.

Soon afterwards, housewives were obviously themselves experimenting extensively with Indian cuisine. If you sent off by mail order to a Mrs Turnbull of 57 Queen's Garden, Hyde Park, she would send back by return one of no fewer than a hundred different curry recipes. One, for example, mixed turmeric, cardamom, coriander, ginger, black pepper, red pepper, caraway seeds and cloves. Mrs Turnbull had thoughtfully reached an arrangement with Beeces Medical Hall in Piccadilly who would save the housewife the inconvenience of sourcing and grinding all the different ingredients herself. All you had to do was add water and pour it over meat. The result was possibly the first cook-in sauce, reliably delivering an exotic taste of the Orient with none of the hassle or anxiety. What was more 'The whole recipe will not cost more than seven shillings and is enough to last a family 5–6 months allowing a curry for every day.'

Arguably the greatest cultural import from India to Britain has been neglected because it was taboo: personal hygiene. As noted above, light, soft, affordable cotton had given the nation the option of clean modern underwear for the first time. Until around the end of the seventeenth century, Britons were either strangers to undies or wore uncomfortable woollen ones that they changed infrequently, stifling the stench under several outer-layers.

But if Indian wonder-textiles had long since given the British the chance to stay clean, they had still not developed the habit of washing themselves as well as their clothes. An etiquette manual from 1782 advises wiping the face daily with a clean cloth. But it warns against using water because this could overexpose the individual to cold or sunburn. Certainly, even in high society, bath-time was an extremely irregular occurrence. A doctor in 1801 noted that 'most men resident in London and many ladies though accustomed to wash their hands and faces daily, neglect washing their bodies from year to year'. At the London Hospital in 1789, 126 patients shared one bath located in the basement. The more fashionable St George's Hospital on Hyde Park also owned a bath, but claimed never to use it. Certainly, since the end of the Roman Empire, few houses or even palaces in Britain had possessed a bathroom. As late as 1812, even the Lord Mayor of London couldn't persuade his Aldermen to put a simple shower into the Mansion House. The request was turned down 'inasmuch as the want thereof has never been complained of'.

But gradually India helped teach Britain how to wash. No Briton visiting the East Indies could fail to be impressed by the compelling evidence of India's dedication to cleanliness. From the daily ablutions in holy rivers, temple tanks and mosque fountains, to the water-features within the harems and pavilions of Mughal palaces, running water was central to both Hindu and Muslim ritual and architecture. To them both, cleanliness really did equate to godliness. Some daring Britons, chief among them returning nabobs, began to try it and agreed. It was well known, for example, that the Duke of Wellington had developed in India his novel habit of taking a daily bath. This was the hero of Waterloo, no less — a sweet-smelling example not be sniffed at. By 1829, with the shocking candour one might expect from a notorious radical, William Cobbett could write in his Advice to a Lover that 'there never yet was, and never will be, love of any fond duration, sincere and ardent love, in any man towards a "filthy mate"'.

The truth was, baths had become fashionable among the fast set in Regency England. Taking their cue from the flamboyant ne'er-do-well the Prince of Wales, people flocked to Brighton and immersed themselves in sea-water. Since the sea was horribly cold, few people could swim, and public exposure of flesh was out of the question, the wealthy resorted to elaborate bath houses that had sprung up along the front, offering heated, piped sea water. There was little doubt that by the 1820s, Brighton's undisputed Bath Moghul was the enterprising Sake Dean Mahomed, one-time proprietor of the Hindostanee Coffee House, now the renowned impresario of Mahomed's Baths.

When the Prince of Wales decided to express his fondness for Brighton by building there the most ritzy des-res in England, he chose 'Eastern luxury' as his theme. Originally he had been set on Chinese, but the story goes that after visiting Sezincote, he summoned his architects and told them to switch to Indian. Humphrey Repton and John Nash both headed for Sezincote, pored over Danniells' aquatints and lifted wholesale some of the designs and ornamentation they found there. For example, architectural features from India's most important mosque, Delhi's Jama Masjid, serve as decorative motifs at Brighton for the stable windows. By the time the Brighton Pavilion was finished in 1823 it must have fulfilled the King's every fantasy, which was, as Nash put it, that 'the Pavilion should assume an eastern character, and the Hindoo style of Architecture was adopted in the expectation that the turban domes and pinnacles might from their glittering and picturesque effect, attract and fix the attention of the spectator'. This was the apogee of the Indian style in Britain. And you should have seen the bathroom!

Naturally it was en suite from the King's bedroom, its principal feature being a marble plunge-bath the size of a small swimming-pool, supplied with hot and cold fresh and sea water, and an elaborate set of pulleys to lower the now corpulent monarch gently into the water. In addition there was a smaller bath, a shower bath, a douche bath and a vapour bath. Every last detail had been approved by the King's own personal bathroom adviser, Sake Dean Mahomed, who now proudly bore the splendid title 'Shampooing Surgeon to His Majesty King George IV'. Whenever George or later his successor William IV came to town, Mahomed was on hand to help at bath-time. Sadly, the title and its responsibilities would lapse when Victoria came to the throne. She did not even have a bath at home in Buckingham Palace and saw no need for one during brief stopovers in Brighton. On the Queen's orders, the magnificent bath-room at the Pavilion was demolished and its marble turned into mantelpieces.

'Shampooing' was Mahomed's trade-mark speciality, and it had nothing to do with washing hair. The word was derived from the Hindi *champi*, which means 'to massage'. At Mahomed's Baths, the client sat with his body enclosed by a flannel tent that fully protected his modesty. Perfumed and medicated steam prepared according to Mahomed's secret recipe was then wafted through pipes into the enclosure. The masseur gained access to his client through flaps in the tent and proceeded to give a therapeutic massage using 'herbs and essential oils… brought expressly from India, and… known only to myself'. Any potential customers who doubted the efficacy of the technique were no doubt reassured by the books they could browse or purchase in the bath-house foyer. Testimonials from fashionable and noble clients featured in *Cases cured by Sake Dean Mahomed, Shampooing Surgeon and Inventor of the Indian Medicated Vapour and Sea-Water Baths, Written by the Patients Themselves*. Meanwhile the science was more fully explored in *Shampooing, or Benefits Resulting From the Use of The Indian Medicated Vapour Bath, As Introduced into this Country by S. D. Mahomed (A Native of India)*. This latter book was so successful it ran to three editions over nearly twenty years. Meanwhile, Mahomed's Baths became so popular that copy-cat establishments sprang up in Brighton, forcing him to place advertisements in the papers confirming he was the only true

Shampooer in town. He was certainly the only one to get the seal of approval from one of Brighton's top physicians. Dr Gibney of the Royal Sussex and Sea-Bathing Infirmary referred patients to Mahomed and wrote a book of his own (*A Treatise on the Properties and Medical Application of the Vapour Baths*) which acknowledged the medical profession's debt to Mahomed. Self-publicist extraordinaire he may have been, but knowing what we now do about physiotherapy and complementary medicine, we can safely conclude he was no quack.

The truth was that Mahomed's vapour bath owed more to the *hamam* or Turkish bath than to anything one could find on the subcontinent. But *champi* or massage was indeed an ancient Indian art and Mahomed's genius was to trade on his nationality for all it was worth. As well as impregnating his baths with secret Indian herbs and spices, Mahomed also offered tooth powder 'just introduced from India'. He claimed this was 'the first ever offered to the public in this country'. But in fact 'Asiatic Toothpowder' and 'Toothbrushes, from Indian hair and pattern' had been available for decades to the British, who nevertheless tended to brush their teeth about as often as they took a bath.

It is clear from his marketing literature that Mahomed focused his 'pitch' to potential clients around two different aspects of India. The first was health and hygiene, an obvious core attribute of a bath-house, and one in which Indian superiority was almost self-evident. As Mahomed put it in 'Shampooing': 'To the Hindoos, who are the cleanest and the finest people of the East, we are principally indebted for the Bath... [and] with them the Medicated Bath has been brought to such perfection as to supersede the necessity of internal remedies for disease.' But to attract British clients, Mahomed knew cleanliness would never suffice as his primary strategy. He also had to lay on indulgence and luxury, qualities for which India was, of course, equally renowned. So a visit to Mahomed's Baths was an exotic escape into an Oriental oasis.

The visitor arrived from the King's Road into an entrance hall decorated by a mural of 'Moguls and Janissaries... represented in rich dresses, and the Muses... in plain Grecian attire'. Ladies then proceeded upstairs and into the care of Mrs Mahomed (of whom more below). Gentlemen headed down a corridor whose walls were adorned with 'a profusion of trees laden with fruits and rich foliage... Birds of the gayest colours are represented also winging their rapid flight through sylvan groves, and Hebe is seen reclining on the ambient air, and strewing the earth with flowers, symbolical of the efficacy of the Medicated Baths, which are prepared... from... the growth of India.' The waiting rooms continued the Indian theme. They featured a Rajah's mausoleum, and 'a superb pagoda surrounded by a variety of figures in the costume of the country making their profound salams'. There was a Hindu temple boasting 'an enormous idol' and a temple carriage, 'the celebrated car of Jaggernaut'. On another wall, opposite some Brahmins, were 'a group of native musicians

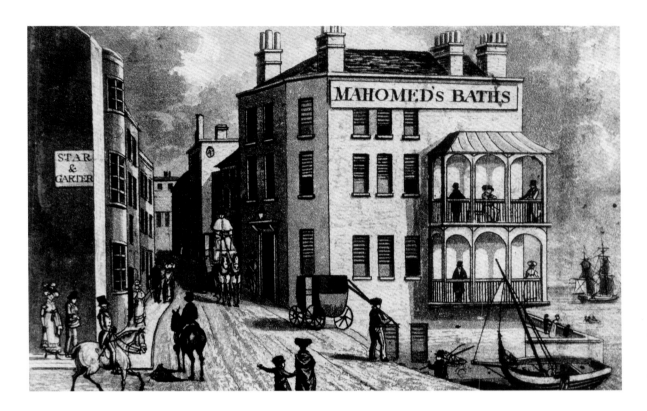

sitting beneath the umbrageous trees of that prolific soil'. By the time the clients took their turn in the eight bath-rooms, where the wood was painted to look like bamboo, they must have congratulated themselves on an Indian experience to rival that of the King's in his Pavilion. They then submitted themselves to the soothing ministrations of Mahomed's team of masseurs with their Indian essential oils. Finally they emerged, pampered and reinvigorated, with stories to tell their friends and glowing tributes to write in the visitors' book (of which two were impressively reserved for 'Ladies and Gentlemen of the Nobility').

Such therefore was the Shampooing Surgeon's success that a lengthy 'Ode to Mahomed' was even published in the *New London Magazine* in July 1822. And despite its hyperbole, this tribute to the 'Dark Sage' was not all poetic licence:

> *While thus beneath thy flannel shades.*
> *Fat dowagers and wrinkled maids*
> *Re-bloom in adolescence.*

> *I marvel not that friends tell friends,*
> *And Brighton every day extends*
> *Its circuses and crescents.*

THE BEST BATH IN BRIGHTON — SAKE DEAN MAHOMED'S BATH-HOUSE OCCUPIED A PRIME SPOT ON THE SEA-FRONT.

BRIGHTON'S BATH MOGHUL, SAKE DEAN MAHOMED WAS HONOURED WITH THE TITLE 'SHAMPOOING SURGEON TO HIS MAJESTY KING GEORGE IV'.

Sake Dean Mahomed remains fascinating because he is himself a fusion figure whose identity owed as much to Britain as to India. In fact, he should perhaps be seen as the reverse of the White Moghuls in India, the first of many Indians to 'go native' among the English with as much enthusiasm as Fraser, Ochterlony, Kirkpatrick, 'Hindoo' Stuart and their ilk did in India. Like them, he took up with a well-born local woman, adopted the native religion, spawned a large Anglo-Indian family, socialized with the higher echelons of his new country's society, and became deeply enamoured of its culture. Among so many claims to fame, he became the first Indian author to write and publish a book in English. This was not 'Shampooing', but a fascinating volume brought out nearly thirty years earlier which adopted the latest, most polished English literary style, the 'epistolary narrative', or series of imaginary letters. This book, entitled *Travels*, relates Dean Mahomed's remarkable life story long before he reinvented himself at the age of fifty as a restaurateur and shampooing surgeon. Indeed, what *Travels* seems to demonstrate is that Dean Mahomed was well on the way to turning himself into an English gentleman even before he left India.

Sake (that is, 'Sheikh' or 'venerable one') Dean Mahomed was born in 1759 in Patna, capital of Bihar. His family were noble-born Muslims distantly related to the Nawabs of Bengal. But ever since Plassey, just before Dean Mahomed's birth, the East India Company had offered far better prospects than the rump court at Murshidabad. Dean Mahomed's father was recruited into the Company's Bengal army as an officer. A military career with the Company also beckoned for the son. When Dean Mahomed was just eleven, he was invited to a British tennis party, where he met an Irish cadet from Cork, Godfrey Evan Baker. He joined Baker's entourage and spent the next twelve years travelling across North India with Baker and gaining seniority alongside his patron. The two seemed to have acted as a tight-knit double-act. Baker's role as quartermaster involved provisioning the regiment, which necessarily required close contact with the local populations from whom the necessary produce had to be extracted. The role of quartermaster was always a lucrative one, and it is highly likely that Dean Mahomed profited alongside Baker. Eventually Captain Baker was given command of his own battalion, and managed to procure for Dean Mahomed a commission as ensign, commanding his own company of Grenadiers. The two officers participated in fierce action against the Marathas and in Warren Hastings's shabby campaign at Benares in 1781 to oust its ruler Chait Singh, who had refused to meet the Company's enhanced demands for cash. In this last campaign, Mahomed was promoted again, to the rank of *subadar* (lieutenant). Even so, he seems to have found the experience of reducing the countryside, imposing the Company's authority and punishing rebels less than glorious.

Dean Mahomed, of course, was far from unique among Indians in seeing senior service with the Company. In 1771, for example, the entire civil government of Bengal's thirty million people was in the hands of just 187 British administrators. Not surprisingly, they were dependent on tens of thousands of Indian colleagues and subordinates. Similarly, Indians outnumbered Europeans in the Company's armies by around eight to one. The Bengal army at the time had 27,277 Indian officers and sepoys but just 522 European officers and 2,722 European soldiers (many of them Continental Europeans rather than Britons, including French, German and Swiss prisoners of war). At least at officer level, close bonds like those between Baker and Mahomed were still, in the eighteenth century, not that unusual.

What was extraordinary was Mahomed's next move, which was to resign his commission and emigrate. Baker's career had come to an abrupt and inglorious end in 1782 when he was accused of extorting money from Indian villagers. Though an investigation did clear his name, Baker decided to return home to Cork. Mahomed's decision to go too is simply explained but begs many questions. He writes that, 'I should suffer much uneasiness of mind, in the absence of my best friend.' Moreover, he had the 'desire of seeing that part of the world'.

Dean Mahomed arrived in Cork aged twenty-five in 1784. There were already at the time several thousand other Indians in Britain and Ireland. But his compatriots were almost all poor *lascars* (sailors), *ayahs* (female servants and nannies), and *bibis* (mistresses). Mahomed by contrast was a gentleman and seems to have been quickly absorbed into the Anglo-Irish Protestant establishment, which included a distinct nabob set. He devoted himself to formal studies in English literature, and quickly fell in love with a fellow student, Jane Daly, who was still a teenager and came from a good Protestant family. Whether because of his race, her age, or their prospects, the two decided to elope rather than seek the approval of her family for their marriage. Their wedding in 1786 nonetheless proves that he was accepted by the clergy as a Christian and that the couple had sufficient means to post the substantial wedding bond needed of an eloping couple. In any event, Dean and Jane Mahomed lived comfortably in or near Cork for the next twenty years, with Dean Mahomed publishing by subscription his autobiographical *Travels* in 1793. The family did not move to England until 1807. Only then did they begin to reinvent themselves as an extraordinary 'shampooing' double-act.

The Mahomeds remained successful and active until around 1845, by which time he was well into his eighties. Dean Mahomed died, just a few weeks after Jane, in February 1851 at the age of ninety-two. A substantial clan of children and grandchildren was already flourishing, with several training in western medicine to become some of the earliest British doctors of Asian origin. One of them, Frederick Akhbar Mahomed (1849–84), did pioneering research which for the first time proved the connection between high blood pressure and kidney damage.

Yet for all his integration into British society, Dean Mahomed's career demonstrates not only the extent but also the limitations of acculturation or fusion in the eighteenth and

nineteenth centuries. Although he spent over sixty-five years in Ireland and Britain, his 'crossing over' to native culture remained, like the White Moghuls in India, only a partial achievement. In his manners, education, outlook and social and family life, he was effectively British. Yet throughout his career, whether by choice or necessity, Dean Mahomed still traded as an Indian every bit as much as the White Moghuls, for all their harems and turbans, were inescapably British. There certainly seems pleasingly little evidence that Mahomed experienced any racism. Yet he remained an outsider of a sort, if only by being regarded as exotic. At least in the first generation, and often thereafter, the differences between cultures seem to remain.

This exoticism, however, wasn't just something Britons were observing about Indians and the mysterious Orient. From the late eighteenth century onwards, a parallel process had also begun. A handful of intrepid Indians were starting to explore the equally intriguing Occident. The first to blaze this trail was a young nobleman from Oudh, Abu Taleb Khan. Unlike Dean Mahomed, he had no plans to settle in Europe. And unlike Britain's marginal and transient population of poor servants and lascars, he was a man of means and leisure, effectively a wealthy tourist. The simple motivation for Abu Taleb's journey seems to have been that he was at a bit of a loose end. An adventure appealed to him and offered the bonus of a darn good story to tell back home. His book of *Travels*, originally written in Persian, recounts the trip he made between 1799 and 1803 from Calcutta via Africa to Britain and Ireland, and thence home via France, Italy, Malta, Constantinople and the Persian Gulf. In essence, the book observes Europeans in their native habitats and reports back to his compatriots the strange ways of these exotic, foreign lands. The book reads like a quixotic early guidebook for real or armchair travellers. Not surprisingly, it is crammed with useful advice and entertaining anecdotes about the English.

The first problem, naturally, was the weather. In fact it was so bad, his ship had to divert to Ireland. Abu Taleb's urgent need, of course, was for a bath. So he was horrified by the facilities in Dublin: 'In this city there are but two hot baths… They are not properly fitted up; and are so small, that with difficulty they hold one person; and even then the water does not rise above his middle. Being a case of necessity, I bathed in one of them… The fact is that in winter the people of Dublin never bathe.'

Despite their filth, Abu Taleb took to the Irish, later concluding they were 'not so intolerant as the English, neither have they the austerity and bigotry of the Scotch'. He took little time to notice that 'their great national defect, however, is excess in drinking', in particular 'immense quantities of a fiery spirit called *whiskey*'. Indeed, after one dinner too many in which 'I was so intoxicated that I could scarcely walk', he grew wary of Irish hospitality.

He seems to have always been cold, and the heating in his lodgings was desperately inadequate: 'Notwithstanding I had all my doors and windows shut, and had three blankets

INDIA'S FIRST TOURIST IN BRITAIN, ABU TALEB KHAN LOVED THE WOMEN BUT HATED THE ENGLISH CLIMATE AND SORELY MISSED INDIAN BATHS.

on my bed, I felt the frost pierce through me like an arrow. The fire had scarcely any effect on me; for while I warmed one side, I was frozen on the other.' He was nonetheless thrilled to see his first snow and hastened to jot down some of the strange local rituals brought on by cold weather: 'What I am now about to relate will, I fear, not be credited (by my countrymen) but is, nevertheless, an absolute fact. In these countries it frequently happens that the ponds and rivers are frozen over; and the ice, being of sufficient strength to bear a great weight, numbers of people assemble thereon and amuse themselves in *skating*.'

Abu Taleb soon became convinced that climate is at the root of most of the fundamental differences in culture between the two countries. And like many single travellers, his keenest cultural interests turn out to be sexual. Because, he speculated, 'the excessive cold prevents their sitting idle', it was natural for the British and Irish to keep their minds occupied, which preserved them 'from wandering to, or dwelling on things that are improper'. Moreover, loose living was scarcely possible without loose clothes. The cold weather made them 'accustomed to wear a number of tight-made clothes, which are troublesome to take off, and are very inconvenient for lying down: thus they are prevented from indulging in indolent habits during the day'.

Arriving in London, Abu Taleb had similar problems with the local standards of hygiene. The lodgings booked for him by friends turned out to be unsuitable. He moved to new ones 'where there were both hot and cold baths, and where I enjoyed the luxury of daily ablution'. But his friends begged him to move, complaining that these new lodgings were on a street where half the houses were 'inhabited by courtesans'. Abu Taleb insisted on staying put, admitting he was 'much gratified by seeing a number of beautiful women, who frequently visited at the house'. Though his friends were concerned no decent people would call on him at such an address, he happily reports that 'even ladies of rank, who had never in their lives before passed through this street, used to call'.

Native etiquette was at first confusing. He received an 'invitation card' from a lady, stating she would be at home on a certain evening. 'At first, I thought it meant an assignation,' he writes, adding in disbelief that when he arrived at her house there were three or four hundred other guests. The hostess had no time other than to ask each guest after their health. A servant then thrust a cup of tea at them after which they were expected 'to depart and make room for others'. Nevertheless by attending a number of these odd occasions, Abu Taleb was soon the talk of the town. He was even presented to the King and Queen at court. 'Ladies of quality' were by now falling over themselves to send him opera tickets, and he 'had an opportunity of obliging many young Englishmen by transferring the tickets to them'. Abu Taleb had discovered he had more of a taste for boxing-matches than for opera, boasting he attended over a hundred bouts.

The newspapers had by now started to dub him 'Prince' Abu Taleb, while charity bashes advertised that 'the Persian Prince' would be in attendance. Abu Taleb admits he found it quite impossible to deny a title he had never claimed. Of course, now that he was a royal, the party invitations really started piling up in earnest: 'In these parties I enjoyed every luxury my heart could desire. Their viands were exquisite, and wines exquisite. The beauty of the women, and their grace in dancing, delighted my imagination; while the variety and melody of their music charmed all my senses... I freely confess, that, during my residence in England, I... gave myself up to love and gaiety.'

Close study of the nightlife did leave some time for sightseeing. But the bad language of the English and their eagerness to rip-off tourists appalled him. It was 'disgusting' that 'when a stranger wishes to visit the House of God or the Tomb of the Kings (I mean the Cathedral of St Paul and Westminster Abbey) [he] is obliged every ten minutes to take out his purse and pay another and another fee. The same vile practice exists at the Tower, and at most of the public buildings, and ought to be abrogated.'

Out of town, the tourist experience was more pleasant. Oxford met with his approval, 'a very ancient city [where] all the public buildings are constructed of hewn stone, and much resemble in form some of the Hindoo temples'. Then it was on to Blenheim, which was 'without comparison, superior to anything I ever beheld'. From there, it was only a short onward hop to stay at Sezincote with his friend Mr Cockerell, who was in the midst of building his new house. It is interesting that, for all the Cockerells' efforts there to create a unique Oriental fantasy, the Indian architecture fails to get a mention. Finally, Abu Taleb went to stay with Warren Hastings at Daylesford, where he was much taken with the great man's devotion to 'his farm-yard and dairy'. Great men in India, Abu Taleb observed, do not normally become closely acquainted with the finer details of cheese-making. After Daylesford, Abu Taleb was set to continue his tour of the Cotswolds. But the chance to inspect prize herds and the countryside's other attractions failed to entice him. You sense his relief as he politely curtails his trip: 'As, previous to my leaving London, Cupid had planted one of his arrows in my bosom, I found it impossible to resist the desire of returning to the presence of my fair one.'

As Abu Taleb seems to have spent much of his British visit horizontal, it was unfortunate that he found sleeping arrangements so deficient:

The beds, and mode of sleeping in England, are by no means to my taste... They spread a sheet, two blankets and a quilt; all of which are closely tucked under the bedding, on three sides, leaving an entrance for the person to creep in next the pillows; which always reminded me of a bear climbing into the hole of a large tree. The bed being broad, and the clothes stretched out, they do not close about the neck, and, for a long time, do not afford any warmth; and if a person turns about incautiously, the four coverings separate, and either fall off the bed, or cause so much trouble that sleep is completely banished. All my other Indian customs I laid aside without difficulty, but sleeping in the English mode cost me much trouble. Our quilts, stuffed with cotton, and lined with muslin, are so light, and adhere so closely to the body, that they are infinitely more comfortable and warmer than blankets; and although it may be objected, that to sleep the whole season with the same quilt next to the body is an uncleanly custom, I reply, that *we* always sleep in a night-dress, which prevents the quilt touching the skin; whereas the English go to bed nearly naked, and use the same sheets for a fortnight together.

Britain, it seems, was not yet ready for the duvet.

Although Abu Taleb enthusiastically devoted himself to gossip, anecdote and trivia, he did not shirk the responsibility of drawing more serious journalistic conclusions from his unprecedented access to the native peoples of Britain. In particular, he recognized that it was an 'unpleasant' part of his duty to his countrymen to enumerate the defects and vices of the English. This turns into thirty-two pages of opprobrium, though by way of balance he does also muster six pages of English virtues.

The most serious deficiency of the English was 'want of faith in religion' which inevitably led to dishonesty, particularly among the lower orders who never resisted the chance of pocketing something if they thought they would get away with it. Abu Taleb also noticed that the English showed 'contempt for the customs of other nations' and unreasonably preferred their own 'although theirs in fact may be much inferior'. For example, he had frequently encountered people who ridiculed Islam. 'From my knowledge of the English character, I was convinced it would be folly to argue the point philosophically with them.' Nevertheless, he could not resist, by way of riposte, questioning the validity of baptism, through which a clergyman somehow procured the salvation of a baby's soul, 'who could not possibly be sensible what he was about'. The English were prone to 'selfishness', the litany continued, and were naturally irritable, unlike the French. Abu Taleb was particularly struck by English 'pride or insolence', which he perceptively concluded was the result of their being 'puffed up with their power and good fortune for the last fifty years'. He found 'this self-confidence... more or less in every Englishman' and was convinced it blinded them to danger and changing circumstances until these hit them in the face. Pride and egotism were connected to 'the eighth defect of the English' which was 'vanity and arrogance'. This manifests itself, for example, in absurdly over-inflated scholarship: 'for as soon as one of them acquires the smallest insight into the principles of any science, or in the rudiments of any foreign language, he immediately sits down and composes a work on the subject and... circulates books which have no more intrinsic worth than the toys bestowed on children'. Abu Taleb even found the 'transcendant' (sic) and 'angelic' Sir William Jones guilty of this offence, since his *Persian Grammar* apparently included some basic errors. Yet Abu Taleb did not seem to have looked carefully in the mirror and noticed the deep irony of his levelling the charge of the under-researched book.

Abu Taleb's cheek in castigating the English 'want of chastity' is also notable, even though this was undoubtedly one of the best researched sections of the book. He professed himself deeply shocked by 'the great degree of licentiousness practised by numbers of both sexes in London'. The sinful city witnessed 'the reprehensible conduct of young women running away with their lovers, and others cohabiting with a man before marriage'. He tells us that the parish of Marylebone alone was home to a reputed 'sixty thousand courtezans, besides which there is scarcely a street in the metropolis where they are not to be found'. He then gave the future traveller a list of some useful addresses!

Women were such a special subject for Abu Taleb that they got an appendix all of their own. In its own bizarre way, the tract 'On the Liberties of the Asiatic Woman' is both a tribute to mutual cultural exploration and emblematic of its tensions and limitations. Abu Taleb had noticed early on that the English worshipped Liberty and were utterly convinced that they were the world's most free people. Women in particular rushed to boast to him how free they were in modern, nineteenth-century England. Then they enjoyed berating Abu Taleb for the sorry state of 'the women of Asia [who] have no liberty at all, but live like slaves, without honour and authority, in the houses of their husbands'. Abu Taleb, however, drawing upon his experience of both societies, remained utterly convinced that Asian women were far more liberated than their English sisters.

He pointed out, for example, that 'by the laws of England, a man may beat his wife with a stick' so long as he doesn't break any bones. This restraint Abu Taleb himself considered 'salutary', but not exactly a sign of freedom. He went on to observe that if an English wife 'should be so far lost as to commit a disgraceful action', the cuckolded husband was 'authorized by law to take away all her property and ornaments, to debar her from the sight of her children, and even to turn her out of the house'. He was also astonished to learn that if the husband obtained proof of 'her misconduct' he could divorce her and leave her utterly penniless and without property. How could it be, wondered Abu Taleb, that 'if a divorce takes place, the mother, who for twenty years may have toiled and consumed herself in bringing up her children, has to abandon all to the father, and full of grief and affliction, leave his house'? This utterly convinced Abu Taleb that 'English women, notwithstanding their apparent liberty... are by the wisdom of their lawgivers, confined in strict bondage'.

On the other hand, Muslim women in India would share rights to the children after a divorce. Moreover, although they were confined to purdah, they were 'much more mistresses of their own conduct' although their greater freedom did mean they were 'much more liable to fall into the paths of error'.

Although Muslim law made divorce 'at the will of the husband', this was only reasonable given that 'all the laborious work falls to their lot, such as carrying heavy burdens, going to war, repulsing enemies & co.'. Women meanwhile 'spend their lives in repose and quiet'. Nevertheless, it was possible, unlike in Britain, for an Indian woman to get a criminal conviction against her husband. Good grounds, for example, might be 'an unfair distribution of his time among his wives'. In these circumstances 'she can obtain a divorce in spite of him'. It was true that an Indian law court's standard of proof was the evidence of two men or four women. But no one would think this unfair since women had so 'little experience and knowledge' and were, by the nature of their sex, fickle.

Abu Taleb thought it a great shame that men and women in Britain were forced to live together. He understood this was a regrettable but inevitable consequence of high property prices and the steep costs of good servants. Nevertheless, it forced the married couple together excessively. He was surprised to discover, 'both husband and wife eat their food… in one place, sleep together in the same chamber, and cannot avoid being always in each other's company'. The customs of Asia were so much more civilized. In particular, they gave Indian women the freedom to turn their husbands away for days on end.

The Indian wife was fortunate in many other respects. She had far greater power and influence than her husband over both the children and the family's business affairs. Indian husbands generally entrusted their wealth to their wife. The children automatically adopted her religion and she tended to have the greater say in choosing their marriage partners. A particular advantage was polygamy, which spared her the need always to be obliged to her husband. Instead she could enjoy time to herself without him suffering. Abu Taleb felt very sorry for British husbands: 'this privilege not being allowed by the English law, is indeed a great hardship upon the English husbands: whereas the Asiatic law, permitting polygamy, does the husband justice, and wrongs not the wife'. Nevertheless, Abu Taleb candidly admitted, 'it is easier to live with two tigresses than two wives.'

———————

It would be a mistake to draw expansive conclusions from the story of Abu Taleb or the other evidence of British and Indian mutual cultural exploration in the late eighteenth century. Its significance as much as anything, is that it happened at all. A more blinkered age was about to dawn, in which the blinds and barriers were gradually run up. Open minds increasingly closed and racist stereotypes inhibited the possibility of real relationships.

Sezincote and Brighton, Hindoostanee Airs and shampooing – these were all instances of a significant fashion, but not a seismic cultural shift. 'John Homespun' would have been relieved to know that chicken tikka masala would take another 200 years to become the British national dish. Meanwhile in India, the British rulers did not follow the example of the Mughals and turn, generation by generation, from foreigners into Indians.

Still, since the preconditions were so strong, it's worth asking: why not?

In India as Governor-General, Warren Hastings had acted as godfather to the 'Indian love affair'. In Britain in long retirement, he had grown his Daylesford chillies, continuing symbol and patron of a better sort of British–Indian relations. But paradoxically, Warren Hastings's own stewardship of British India both spawned a more tolerant, hybrid, multicultural vision and sowed the seeds of its destruction. Hastings's conduct in India became a national obsession, and the focus of a tumultuous nine-year investigation. Over this period of his rule and impeachment, changes in British society, in Company politics, in world affairs and in the realities on the ground in India were already pushing things in an entirely new direction. This was the opposite of what Hastings intended. Ironically, however, the man who said, 'I love India a little more than my own country', found himself inexorably sucked into a more troubled and aggressive relationship with Indian regional powers. This was still accidental. There was still no master plan. For much of the time, far from expanding, the Company's hold on India looked like weakening. But as time went on the empire was taking root. And with it would come imperial attitudes worlds apart from Warren Hastings's vision of mutual respect.

CHAPTER SEVEN

FIRST AMONG EQUALS

I t is almost impossible to wander around the sleepy South Indian village of Srirangapatnam and imagine it in its late-eighteenth-century heyday as one of the world's major seats of power. Today it is a typically ramshackle, nondescript settlement, with most of the action focused on the tea-stalls and tyre-workshops catering for the truckers who noisily plough the main road from Mysore to Bangalore. Even the Kaveri River, which splits here to define the small, low island of Srirangapatnam, fails to impress, though it is serene and charming, especially at sunset when the village women go to the river-banks to collect water and bash their laundry into submission. Ox carts and the occasional auto-rickshaw jolt down dusty lanes off the main road. And it's there, amid the scrub and overgrown wasteland, that you catch your first glimpses of ruined ramparts and fortifications, a hint that this place was once firmly on the map.

At last, in the north-east of the island, an elegant late Mughal summer palace reassures visitors that they haven't come to the wrong village. An imposing, domed gatehouse

IN CELEBRATION OF HIS VICTORY OVER THE BRITISH, TIPU SULTAN COMMISSIONED THIS MURAL TO COMMEMORATE HIS TRIUMPH AT THE BATTLE OF POLILUR.

opens on to a formal Mughal garden where a tree-lined water course leads up to an open pavilion. Inside, the veranda walls are decorated floor-to-ceiling with murals chronicling the courtly and martial glories of the palace's former owner, Tipu Sultan, 'the Tiger of Mysore'.

The most striking mural celebrates Tipu's spectacular defeat of the British at the Battle of Polilur in 1780 (see page 154). Tipu and his father Haidar Ali are mounted on richly decorated elephants as they survey their troops' attack. In a nice touch, despite the heat of battle Haidar Ali imperturbably sniffs a rose, which in Mughal iconography points up the sheer class and effortless refinement of a man who was, in fact, an illiterate usurper. On the other side of the battlefield, General Laly, commanding Haidar and Tipu's allies the French, also watches events unfold with the aid of an impressive telescope. The fiercest action involves the tight British square, within which the British commanding officer, Colonel Baillie, sits in a palanquin, nervously biting his finger. The British troops wear red-coats, white breeches and tall hats and have their muskets drawn. They are barely holding the line against close assault from the Indians and their French allies. The artist has chosen to capture the decisive moment when the tumbrel carrying the British ammunition has taken a direct hit from French cannon. A massive explosion indicates their impending doom, as a pair of worried British officers on horseback clearly appreciate. The day belongs to Tipu and to France. Britain's presence in South India was looking increasingly precarious.

Few people that day in 1780 would have bet on the emergence of the British Raj. Indeed, a single India under any regime still looked deeply implausible in the late eighteenth century. Instead, developed regional powers seemed likely to take the subcontinent in the opposite direction. This was not just because of one military setback, however severe. What was far more telling was that from Srirangapatnam, Haidar Ali and his son and successor Tipu Sultan ruled a prosperous, technologically advanced and independent nation with all the trappings of modern statehood. Elsewhere in India, other regional powers like the Maratha Confederacy, the State of Hyderabad and the emerging Sikh kingdom in the Punjab were also growing in strength, identity and confidence.

Later, at the height of the British Raj, the imperial straitjacket produced something close to a single India, which after independence evolved into a unitary nation state (or rather three – India, Pakistan and Bangladesh). But the fissures and tensions in the subcontinent today hark back to the strong regional identities that dominated India 200 years earlier. This is how India was, might have been and might just be again – a network of powerful regions, possibly linked by a loose confederacy. Then the British in Bengal were just one of several contenders in the subcontinent. Today, the very distinct regional histories and identities of British Asians are finally dawning on a wider audience. Indeed, many of Britain's two million Asians are less likely to self-identify as Indian or Pakistani by origin, than as Punjabis, Sikhs, Bengalis, Gujaratis, Pathans or Tamils.

None of this was necessarily anathema to the British at the time. Warren Hastings's mission remained to protect the Company's existing interests, influence and territories, not to expand them further. To do this, he used all necessary means, which usually meant a combination of economic clout, force of arms and intrigue. But he viewed India's other rulers as equal players in the game. As we have seen, his honest conviction in 1779 was that British dominion over India was 'an event which I may not mention without adding that it is what I never wish to see'.

In any case, the issue of British dominion was largely academic. Hastings's achievement, in itself remarkable, was to hold the whole British show together and prevent the East India Company's position in India from utterly collapsing. One doubts many others could have succeeded. Not that that would prove enough to silence his critics.

———————————————

For Warren Hastings, the underlying problem was money. Throughout his Governor-Generalship (1774–85) the Company's coffers were bare. Yet it owed the British Government £1 million for bailing it out after the post-famine share price collapse. Moreover, under the 1773 Regulating Act it was committed to an annual contribution to the Exchequer of £400,000. Above all, military costs continued to spiral, not least because the Bombay and Madras Presidencies made a point of acting unilaterally, even though officially they were now subject to the authority of Hastings in Bengal. Thanks to spectacularly inept diplomacy, they succeeded in provoking and alienating their powerful neighbours, the Marathas and the Mysore Sultanate. Soon the Company found itself at war on both these fronts, with the very real risk that Bombay and, following the defeat at Polilur, Madras might be overwhelmed. These were not wars of Warren Hastings's choosing. But he had little choice other than to ensure they were not lost.

Looking to London for extra forces or resources was out of the question. The Americans had risen up against the British, and Lord North, the Prime Minister, could think of little else other than helping the King to hang on to his colonies. Indeed, some of Hastings's lengthy and carefully wrought dispatches to Lord North would turn up years later, still unopened. One vital document was finally traced to the Prime Ministerial lavatory. Hastings would have to sort out his own problems. So he was continually forced to scour the subcontinent for money, especially in order to send reinforcements to the rescue in the west and south. Ironically, that drew him into yet more conflict as he felt the need to prosecute highly dubious wars purely for cash. As John Keay succinctly puts it: 'Seldom can a ruler so averse to war and so avowedly indifferent to conquest have been engaged on so many different fronts.' Many of these campaigns would later become key issues at his impeachment.

Hastings's first controversial engagement had been a shabby alliance in 1774 with the Nawab of Oudh against the Afghan Rohillas, a war-like clan based to the north of Oudh, which was primarily intended to net him nine million rupees (£900,000). It did land him more than half of that, but at the cost of getting involved in what Colonel Pearse, a close friend and colleague, described as an 'un-British war'. The allied forces killed many Rohillas in battle and expelled almost all the survivors, an action we would now deem 'ethnic cleansing'. The Rohilla War would later return to haunt him because it seemed clearly to violate the London Directors' standing orders that they 'utterly disapprove and condemn offensive wars, distinguishing, however, between offensive measures unnecessarily undertaken with a view to pecuniary advantages and those which the preservation of our honour, or the protection of safety of our possessions, may render absolutely necessary'.

It is just possible to argue that, unless checked, the Rohillas would have made common cause with the Marathas and thus endangered the Company's allies in Oudh. But for once the hyperbole of Hastings's enemy Edmund Burke rings true. At his trial, Burke charged Hastings 'with gross injustice, cruelty, and treachery against the faith of nations, in hiring British soldiers for the purpose of extirpating the innocent and helpless people who inhabit the Rohillas'. Perhaps, however, 'innocent and helpless' is an odd way to describe a clan of 50,000 Muslim Pathans who had recently taken advantage of the disintegrating Mughal Empire to invade Rohilkhand and lord it over the native population of two million Hindus.

Hastings's equally high-handed treatment of the Raja of Benares, Chait Singh, also looked to the prosecutors who later impeached him like the un-British action of an Oriental despot. As we saw in Chapter 4, Hastings went to the holy city in 1781 to 'encourage' its ruler to pay a rapidly escalating 'war tax' and provide a thousand troops at Benares' expense for the Company's over-stretched armies. The fact that Hastings took a token force and the landscape artist William Hodges suggests he did not envisage trouble. But when Chait Singh failed to cough up sufficient funds, Hastings ordered his arrest. Military cock-ups are quite as typical for this period as brilliant and courageous actions. And on this occasion, no one thought to supply the small force of officers and sepoys who were arresting Chait Singh with any ammunition. They were almost all massacred, with special mutilations being reserved for the British officers. As the city of Benares rose in rebellion parading British heads on sticks, Hastings made a hasty and undignified exit, only just saving his own head. Hodges, by some minor miracle, saved his drawings. To this day, an Indian seeking to describe total panic and confusion may use the Hindi saying, 'Howdah on the horse, saddle on the elephant, that's how Warren Hastings fled'. It took two months to quash the uprising and depose Chait Singh. By then almost all of the money that had inspired Hastings in the first place had vanished.

THE VIEW FROM THE VERANDA OF TIPU'S SUMMER PALACE AT SRIRANGAPATNAM WHICH HE CALLED DARIA DAULAT BAGH (SPLENDOUR OF THE SEA).

To add to this complex and tawdry catalogue of what came to be seen as Hastings's 'high crimes and misdemeanours' was the notorious affair of the Begums of Oudh. In fact. within a few years there can't have been a drawing-room in London that didn't echo with phoney sympathy for these supposedly denuded widows and their ill-treated eunuchs. Once again, the issue was money.

To put it mildly, Asaf-ud-Daula, the Nawab of Oudh, did not get on with his mother and grandmother. In fact, granny so hated her grandson she would personally smash to pieces any chair he had sat upon. The Nawab especially resented the fact that the Begums had inherited from his father, the previous Nawab, a jewel hoard valued at £2 million, while he had been saddled with his father's debts to the Company. A plot was hatched between Hastings and Asaf-ud-Daula to cover the one by confiscating the other. Hastings's grounds were thin but legitimate, in that the Begums had aided Chait Singh in the recent rebellion.

In 1782 the troops were sent in and captured the Begums' palace. Despite the overblown rhetoric later deployed by Burke and the playwright Richard Brinsley Sheridan, who literally swooned at the climax of his speech at the trial describing the indignities the Begums suffered, there is no evidence that either matriarch was in any way abused. On the contrary, the troops did not do anything so offensive as entering the *zenana*, thus helping the Begums to salt away most of their fortune. No such chivalry was afforded the eunuchs who, it was rightly suspected, knew where the Begums had hidden their treasure. The Resident in Oudh, Nathaniel Middleton, reassured Hastings by letter that 'when force could be employed it was not spared'. Eventually one of them succumbed to the pressure. But only five and a half million rupees were uncovered. The eunuchs were clapped back into irons for another year in the hope of shedding light on the missing millions. If they knew anything more, they weren't saying. Warren Hastings pathetically concluded on his return to Calcutta that 'I return to an empty treasury which I left empty.' The younger Begum lived another thirty years. Shortly before her death she was still worth seven million rupees. The campaign had clearly not just been squalid. It had also largely failed.

If the Company was no more than first among equals in India, Hastings's problem was that he personally was no more than that among his colleagues. Moreover, there was little doubt that Hastings's enemies on Calcutta's four-man governing Council were a far deadlier threat to him than any raja or nawab. In a debilitating war of attrition lasting years, governance became almost impossible because the highest-ranking officials were at each other's throats – sometimes, as in the case of Hastings and his arch-rival Philip Francis, literally.

A small vestry in St John's Church in Calcutta contains an unprepossessing hexagonal table whose size and green baize top make it look like a card table. This was Calcutta's council table, deliberately shaped that way to underscore Hastings's dependence on his colleagues. It is almost impossible to imagine the torrents of vitriol that flooded across this small table.

The 1773 Regulating Act had created the post of Governor-General. But it had also introduced the Council and a provision that all decisions were to be taken by a majority vote. Only if there was deadlock in Council did Hastings get the casting vote. It condemned him to torrid battles over almost every decision. Often it forced him to pursue initiatives that were the direct opposite of those he advocated. For much of his period in office, three members of the Council continually opposed him. They did this deliberately and automatically, not on policy grounds but purely because of personal enmity and classic eighteenth-century politicking. Luckily, though countless books have been written on the subject, the tedious details of these debilitating disputes need not detain us much because they had little to do with how best to govern India and everything to do with vanity, envy and sheer bloody-mindedness.

The trouble had started even before the first ever Council session. Under the Regulating Act, the Prime Minister Lord North had appointed the Council members without consulting the Company's Directors, let alone Hastings. There is little evidence that the distracted North deliberately set out to undermine Hastings. It is far more likely that he made the appointments casually, manipulating his patronage in the time-honoured way to reward those who lobbied hardest or were awaiting a decent post. The three newly appointed Council members who set out from London spent much of the voyage plotting. When they were greeted at Calcutta in October 1774 by a mere seventeen-gun salute instead of the twenty-one-gun salvo they felt was their due, the die was already cast. Spoiling for a fight, they deemed it a terrible insult that Warren Hastings greeted them in an unruffled shirt. The first formal Council meeting was devoted to these gross breaches of protocol. Hastings, no doubt predicting all too clearly the troubles ahead, considered resigning. He decided instead to tough it out, calculating that the Bengal climate might, with luck, kill off some of the newcomers and leave seats vacant for more favourable appointees.

Two of the three did indeed die, though not half as quickly as Hastings would have liked. But Hastings's greatest foe, Philip Francis, showed great stamina, drinking, gambling and womanizing in notorious excess but remaining in rude health, sustained no doubt by the constant animus of his loathing for Hastings. Since Francis showed no signs of dying, Hastings would eventually determine to kill him.

Before his appointment, Philip Francis had spent a year in London unemployed, though he had previously served as a medium-ranking civil servant. Even members of his own family could not understand how he had landed such a highly paid and powerful job. He had no knowledge or experience of India. Once there, he developed no interest, let alone fondness, for the place. It would not be unfair to claim he had just one policy – to replace Hastings as Governor-General. His tactic was to lose no opportunity to bad-mouth his rival to London or within India.

At one stage in 1777 Calcutta came close to civil war, with Francis's faction claiming Hastings had resigned and mounting an unsuccessful coup d'état. The plot failed when the Company's troops stayed loyal to Hastings. Then the dispute moved to the courts which unanimously found in favour of Hastings. But as Hastings related in a dispatch to Lord North, it had been a close run thing.

> [The other faction] took possession of the council chamber, demanded from me the keys of the fort and treasuries... and I presume would have proceeded to the last extremities of violence... This, my Lord, is an epitome of the transactions of this Government during a convulsion of four days, which might have shaken the very foundation of the national power and interests in India; nor is it yet safe. The spark of sedition, though latent, will break out, and with a blaze, which the same prudence, the same vigilance, and moderation may prove ineffectual to extinguish.

Matters reached a head again in the high summer of 1780. By then Hastings found Francis's continuing obstructionism was seriously compromising his ability to send any troops outside Bengal to assist the other Presidencies, then beleaguered by the Marathas and Haidar Ali. Hastings took the decision to submit a deliberately provocative formal minute to the next Council session. In part it claimed that:

> [Francis's] sole purpose and wish are to embarrass and defeat every measure which I may undertake, or which may tend even to promote the public interests, if my credit is connected with them. Such has been the tendency and such the manifest spirit of all his actions from the beginning... I judge of his public conduct by my experience of his private, which I have found to be void of truth and honour. This is a severe charge, but temperately and deliberately made from the firm persuasion that I owe this justice to the public and to myself, as the only redress to both, for artifices of which I have been a victim, and which threaten to involve their interests, with disgrace and ruin. The only redress for a fraud for which the law has made no provisions is the exposure of it.

Francis had no choice but to rise to the bait. As the Council meeting broke up, Francis got up from the table and challenged Hastings to a duel.

Soon after dawn on the morning of 17 August 1780, the two parties and their respective seconds met near Hastings's house in Alipur. The affair was fairly farcical from the start. Though honour had to be satisfied, neither man knew the first thing about duelling. In fact Francis had never even handled a pistol, while Hastings had never fired one in anger. They squabbled about the duelling ground (the first place chosen was too busy, the next too dark), about the time (they could not synchronize their watches, which apparently one had to do) and about the distance (with no one seeming to be aware quite how many paces they were meant to stand apart). They couldn't even see eye to eye about whether they were meant to stand behind, on, or in front of the lines drawn in the dirt to mark their positions. When the preliminaries were eventually completed, Francis discovered that his pistol could not be primed because its powder was damp. Incredibly, neither he nor his second had thought to bring spare powder. Hastings's second kindly offered Francis some of the Governor-General's own supply. At last, both parties were ready to get down to business. Francis fired first, and missed. Hastings counted to three and, as his second, Colonel Pearce, recounted, 'his shot took place. Mr Francis staggered, and in attempting to sit down, he fell and said he was a dead man. Mr Hastings hearing this cried out, "Good God! I hope not," and immediately went up to him.' There is no way of knowing whether he was really pleased that Francis's wound turned out to be slight.

The duel was nevertheless decisive. Not long afterwards, Francis resigned from the Council. Its arithmetic was now against him and he rightly calculated that he could do far more harm to Hastings in London than by continuing to slug it out in Calcutta. He would beaver away for the next fifteen years in conspiring with Hastings's enemies to impeach his hated rival. Not wishing to lose a moment, Francis dispatched a letter to Edmund Burke which arrived in London shortly before its author. He claimed 'the British Empire in India is tottering to its foundation… in spite of everything I could do to save it.' Though his second assertion is laughable, Francis's first statement was indeed close to the truth.

While he and Hastings had been busying themselves with pistols, Haidar Ali and Tipu Sultan took control of the entire plain of Karnataka. Their pretext for declaring war had been that their ships had lost access to Mahé, a French Compagnie port that the British Company had recently seized (in retaliation for France's alliance with the American colonies on the other side of the world). But the real reason for the war was simple opportunity. The Company were hard pressed in the west by the Marathas and were very thinly stretched. Within weeks Tipu had defeated the British at Polilur. A French officer who fought with Laly and Tipu that day was not exaggerating when he wrote, 'There is not in India an example of a similar defeat.' In a single morning almost the entire Madras army was wiped out – over 2,000 European and sepoy troops and sixty of the eighty-six British officers. Colonel Baillie and the other survivors were taken in triumph back to Srirangapatnam as prisoners. They may well have swiftly envied their dead comrades.

You can still visit the dungeons where the senior British captives were held for three and a half years. A freelance guide will attach himself to your group and assist in conjuring up the full horror of the place by acting out all the parts. With great relish he'll show you how the prisoners were chained in a sort of crucifixion position between stone piers for twenty-two hours a day. He'll then lead you to the darkest corner of the dungeon and point out how they administered extra punishment when it was needed. An ingenious series of sluice gates allowed the guards to flood the entire cell with water straight from the Kaveri River. The level rose remorselessly and for hours or even days at a time the prisoners could barely hold their chins above water. Of the twenty-four prisoners confined to this cell, only eleven survived the experience. When a treaty finally secured their release and a temporary end to the conflict, they naturally lost little time in recounting just how awful it had been. Captain Henry Oakes became the new John Zephaniah Holwell.

These indignities and outrages scandalized British society even more than the Black Hole of Calcutta. For the first time since then, an individual enemy became the focus of popular attention. Siraj-ud-Daula had been a tyrant, but his actions were considered a threat to Calcutta, not the British way of life. Now, a generation later, Tipu began his journey into

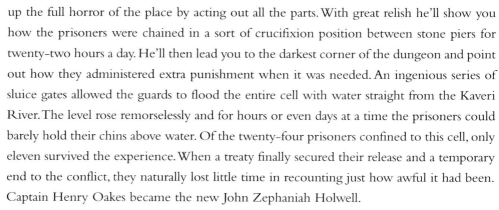

demonology. By the mid 1790s he had become the original 'black bogeyman' who might gobble up English children in their beds in the English shires. The pernicious cocktail of fear, racism and nationalism that created this transformation is considered in the next chapter.

Grim as the prisoners' treatment had been, it is worth comparing it to how Tipu's men might have fared had the situation been reversed. Remarkably, this was just the question posed by the publisher of Oakes's gruesome account in 1785. He included in the same volume an appendix by a Lieutenant John Charles Shean who had fought in the south over the same period. Shean described how he had participated in a successful campaign to take the fort at Anantapur. 'Orders were issued for a storm and no quarter, which was immediately put into execution, and every man put to the sword… A most dreadful sight then presented itself: above four hundred beautiful women either killed or wounded with the bayonet, expiring in one another's arms, while the private soldiers were committing every kind of outrage, and plundering them of their jewels, the officers not being able to restrain them.'

This was not some regrettable, freak outrage, staining Britain's military honour every bit as much as the horrors of Mai Lai shamed America during Vietnam. The 'rules of war' to which

the British then subscribed certainly permitted the cold-blooded slaughter of enemy combatants if it was deemed that their surrender had come too late. Moreover, though wholesale rape, plunder and slaughter of women was never officially condoned, it is remarkable how many commanding officers during this period felt the need to offer a routine, feeble apology for being quite unable to hold back their men in the moment of victory.

Balancing the horrors committed by each side, the publisher of Oakes's and Shean's accounts had the commendable sense to reach a conclusion which must have been hard for many of his readers to stomach: 'His [Tipu's] Conduct was evidently founded upon Principles of Retaliation: and Candor must acknowledge that the Conduct of the Company's Army goes a considerable Way in Justification of that of the enemy.' Two centuries later, the Indian historian Professor Irfan Habib wryly concludes, 'The fault of Tipu then, was that he gave quarter and took prisoners alive. The English gave no quarter, and so they had few prisoners with them to ill-treat.'

It suited the British to dwell more than anything on Tipu Sultan's supposed barbarity. Yet their growing fear of the kingdom of Mysore was actually a tribute to the modernization and formidable resistance that it came to represent. Even Tipu's enemies acknowledged 'his country was the best cultivated and its population the most flourishing in India'. It boasted a developed economy, an efficient administration, a well-equipped army and even the makings of a navy that could challenge British maritime supremacy. Tipu's merchant fleet was capable of trading with Arabia and the Ottoman Empire. He even had plans to send the first Indian trading vessels to Europe. Meanwhile, his ambassadors were winning influential friends in Constantinople and Louis XVI's court at Versailles.

If Tipu's majesty was renowned in Europe, it was adored at home. He awakened the potent spirit of Islamic militancy to inspire his Muslim subjects to serve God in serving him. His wars were holy wars and the enemy were infidels. But at the same time, he maintained warm relations with his Hindu subjects and though his origins were entirely foreign, he used the local vernacular Kannada rather than courtly Persian to symbolize his closeness to all the people. Like the great Akbar, another Muslim monarch ruling a majority Hindu population, he employed Hindus at the highest levels of his administration, became a benefactor of temples as well as mosques, and took care to offer up prayers through brahmin priests as well as his mullahs. So his population and army were united, almost uniquely for the period, in feeling some patriotic allegiance to his tiger-stripe flag and the other ubiquitous tiger-motif symbols of his kingship. There is of course no question but that he was a despot. But the evidence is clear that he was a very enlightened one. This then was a far more sophisticated adversary for the British than their previous Indian opponents. What is extraordinary is that the House of Haidar Ali had achieved all this in less than a generation.

Haidar Ali was an ordinary soldier who had seized effective power in Mysore from the ruling Hindu maharajas as recently as 1761, primarily because he had mastered the new methods of warfare brought to the subcontinent by the Europeans. He developed a large standing army that used the superior flintlock muskets rather than the customary matchlocks. It adopted European codes of military discipline and even drilled in English. He learnt from the French the ability to cast cannon every bit as effective as those made in Europe. Regardless of his lack of formal education, he was an astute student of politics. In one letter he perceptively commented, 'The English first try to secure a footing in other territories by outward professions of friendship and then gradually they bring them under their full sway.' His preferred response was to face up to the Company by building alliances with other Indian powers. In the First Mysore War (1767–9), he joined with the Marathas and the Nizam of Hyderabad and took his fight all the way to Madras, greatly enhancing his prestige when the British were forced to sue for peace on his terms. In 1780, at the start of the Second Mysore War, the British were again simultaneously threatened by the same alliance, this time supported by the French (who as allies of the Americans were once again at war with Britain). As the magnificent victory at Polilur indicated, his strategy very nearly paid off.

Tipu inherited a modernized army from his father, who died in 1782. The son's achievement was to work with remarkable energy over the next seventeen years to introduce equally radical change to the state and the economy. His fertile territories depended on agriculture. So he introduced public works to improve irrigation and drainage and individual loans to peasants to strengthen agricultural investment. Moreover, tax collection was adjusted to ensure a steady revenue stream rather than the oppressive levies that risked driving the farmers off their land. An industrial economy was nurtured, with the introduction of silk production and sugar refinement. Artisans were brought in from France to spread their technological know-how. Soon the kingdom was producing paper, watches, knives and needles. But a French surgeon was dismissed because Tipu claimed he knew nothing about medicine that was not already common knowledge in Srirangapatnam. Later, Tipu returned an order of 500 French muskets because they were inferior to his own production.

Perhaps, however, Tipu's most startling project was to take the first steps towards turning his state into a rival international trading enterprise to the East India Company. By developing his navy and his merchant fleet, Tipu signalled his ambitions to establish a commercial presence in the West that was the equal and opposite of Europe's in the East. Why, he seemed to realize, should the Europeans rather than Mysore enjoy the huge profits on sending pepper, sandalwood, textiles and cinnamon westwards? By 1785 he had even founded a factory and foreign settlement in Muskat and Oman, just like the British had done in Calcutta a century earlier. Then in 1787 he sent an embassy to Constantinople to try and persuade the Ottoman Emperor to sell him the equivalent of a *firman* for the port of Basra in Iraq. This mission ultimately failed, as did an even bolder plan to open up a trading route straight to France.

Tipu's eventual overthrow in 1799 means we will never know what might have been achieved had he had more time. Nevertheless, the Company official William Kirkpatrick, who edited the *Select Letters of Tippoo Sultan* after his death, gives an interesting indication of just how much the British were rattled: 'It may, indeed, be reasonably doubted, whether either the resources of the country, or his genius, were equal to the realization of so bold a plan, but it is as well perhaps, that he was not allowed time for the experiment.'

Yet for all Tipu's schemes and the Company's interests, the fate of the two need not perhaps have been a permanent collision course. Back in 1784, Warren Hastings, ever the pragmatist, had ended the Second Mysore War by signing a formal treaty with Tipu Sultan which acknowledged a kind of stalemate and led to the return of captured territories by each side. But in 1785 Hastings headed back to England after thirteen years of service in the top post in Calcutta – his wife had returned the previous year through ill-health and they were both desperate to be reunited. It would have taken exceptional diplomacy on both sides for

Hastings's vision – that the Company and Mysore could be strong, independent powers without becoming deadly enemies once again – to survive. Hastings's successors entirely lacked this vision and his agility. There would be a Third and a Fourth Mysore War.

———————————

Warren Hastings arrived in Plymouth on 13 June 1785. While Tipu Sultan was reaching the height of his powers and exulting in the acclaim of his people, Hastings was rewarded for his efforts with ten years of what amounted to slow, painful and public crucifixion. Days after his ship landed, Edmund Burke told the House of Commons he 'would at a future day make a motion respecting the conduct of a gentleman just returned from India'. The process had begun.

In the spring of 1786, Burke laid before the House no fewer than twenty-two charges against Hastings. They ran to nearly 400 pages, all meticulously prepared by Philip Francis. Not surprisingly, the former Governor-General, who had been naively expecting honour, acclaim and perhaps a peerage, took a while to realize just what was happening to him. He made the cardinal mistake, common to those who know they are right, of spurning lawyers, refusing to lobby those who would decide his fate and relying on the truth unmediated by any oratory. His own abilities as a parliamentary speaker were very limited. In essence his simple case, tediously laid out over two days, was that he had been in India since he was a schoolboy and throughout his thirty-six years' service had always tried to do his best. This involved responding to 'the emergencies of the times' with 'the resources of his own mind'.

This defence was not just limp, it was counter-productive. The world had changed during those thirty-six years and many now turned their noses up at the pragmatism and brinkmanship which had been his genius and was the natural modus operandi in India. Respecting Indian ways and mastering Indian politics, intrigues and all, may have been the key to his success and the Company's survival in the subcontinent. But to many in Britain this reeked of Oriental despotism and 'un-British' nabobery.

Over the course of more than a year's deliberations, the Commons voted to impeach Hastings on several of the charges, among them the Chait Singh affair and the treatment of the Begums of Oudh. The oratorical skills of Francis, Burke, Sheridan and Charles James Fox helped swing the balance. British factional politics did the rest. For the first time in sixty years, Parliament had decided there was a sufficient prima facie case to stage an impeachment – a criminal trial, prosecuted by selected representatives of the Commons before a jury of the House of Lords and theoretically punishable by death. On 21 May 1787, Warren Hastings was arrested and brought to the Lords where he was made to kneel as he was formally charged with 'high crimes and misdemeanours'.

With hindsight, what is nauseating about the parliamentary assault on Hastings is the hypocritical attempt of his accusers to claim that every Indian was on their side. Hastings's prosecutors might deserve our sympathy had they been advocating, even in theory, a retreat from Calcutta to follow Britain's recent eviction from the American colonies. But of course they argued no such thing. They were, practically to a man, ignorant and uninterested in the subcontinent except as a theoretical playground for their arguments about political philosophy (though they were very keen on trimming the independence of the Company). Almost all the tears flamboyantly shed for India during the 'trial of the century' were crocodile tears. Thus, star playwright Richard Brinsley Sheridan held the House spellbound for five hours as he milked the plight of the Begums of Oudh. His peroration, of course, failed to mention they were sour, scheming and still very rich:

> You cannot behold the workings of the heart, the quivering lips, the trickling tears, the loud and yet tremulous joys of the millions whom your vote this night will forever save from the cruelty of corrupted power. But though you cannot directly see the effect, is not the true enjoyment of your benevolence increased by the blessing being conferred unseen? Would not the omnipotence of Britain be demonstrated to the wonder of nations by stretching its mighty arm across the deep, and saving by its fiat distant millions from destruction? And would the blessings of the people thus saved dissipate in empty air? No! if I may dare to use the figure – we shall constitute Heaven itself our proxy, to receive for us the blessings of their pious gratitude, and the prayers of their thanksgiving. – It is with confidence, therefore, that I move you on this charge, 'that Warren Hastings be impeached'.

With that kind of warm-up, it's not surprising that when the trial itself got under way in Westminster Hall in February 1788, it was the hottest ticket in town. From the Queen downward, everyone who was anyone tried to be there. The queues started early in the morning and stretched halfway round the block. When the day's order of play seemed promising, and one of the star orators was scheduled to take his turn at humiliating the prisoner, it was difficult to get hold of a ticket without parting with fifty guineas. Once inside Westminster Hall, the large establishment crowd above all wanted entertainment. They sat in boxes, waved across at their friends, and chattered, ate and drank their way through the boring bits. It was just like the opera, only much more fun. There, centre stage, in a simple pen or dock, sat the accused. Though he rarely even had a speaking part, he was emphatically the main attraction. What ultimately compelled people to turn up was the awesome magnitude of a man so reduced. As the Whig MP William Windham put it to the diarist Fanny Burney, 'What a sight is that! To see that man, that small portion of human clay, that

KNAVE OF DIAMONDS.

Publish'd as the Act directs 11th July. 1786. by J. Burke.

Day passes to the Gallery at Westminster Hall for Warren Hastings's impeachment were sold by touts for over £50.

poor feeble machine of earth, enclosed now in that little space, brought to that Bar, a prisoner in a spot six foot square – and to reflect his late power! Nations at his command! Princes prostrate at his feet! – What a change! How he must feel it!'

At this distance, what seems paradoxical is that Parliament chose Hastings as their victim. In comparison to so many of his predecessors, his sins were trifling. There is no evidence that he accepted bribes, profited from the ubiquitous culture of 'presents', or used his station to his own advantage. He came back from India with a far more modest fortune than many of his contemporaries. What is more, he had largely fulfilled his brief to stamp out the wholesale abuses of the nabob era. Even the endlessly paraded scandals of Chait Singh and the Begums of Oudh, though unedifying, were unremarkable for India or their times. On the contrary, Hastings was respected and liked by most of the Indian rulers and subjects he encountered. His successor Lord Cornwallis, a man with little time for Indians, acknowledged he was 'beloved by the people'. More than any British administrator before or since, he developed an understanding and respect for the country under his charge, learning its languages, exploring its culture, considering its own qualities in guiding his policies and actions. Most of his successors were too arrogant and too blinded by their imperial mission to consider the intrinsic worth of Indian civilization. Perhaps indeed this 'overfondness for Indians' was his weakness in many Britons' eyes. Yet these same critics might have observed that, in deeply troubled times, he had nevertheless preserved and enhanced the Company's authority, on many occasions marshalling depleted resources to pull British India back from the brink. It was the American colonies that had recently been lost, not Britain's new empire in India. As Hastings later protested with great passion: 'I enlarged, and gave shape and consistency to the dominion you hold there… I maintained the wars which were of your formation, or that of others, not of mine… I gave you all, and you have rewarded me with confiscation, disgrace, and a life of impeachment.'

Edmund Burke, who opened the case for the prosecution with a masterful four-day oration, helps us explain this paradox. What he made very clear from the outset was that the trial was not about justice, it was about ideology. He explicitly asked the jurors to reach their verdict 'not upon the niceties of a narrow jurisprudence, but upon enlarged and solid principles of state morality'. In other words, if he is innocent of the charges, convict him all the same for not measuring up to your Lordships current national self-image. What really appalled Burke was that Hastings might claim that one had to do things differently in India, what Burke called 'geographical morality':

This geographical morality we do protest against; Mr Hastings shall not screen himself under it; and on this point I hope and trust many words will not be necessary to satisfy your Lordships. But we think it necessary, in justification of ourselves, to declare that the laws of morality are the same everywhere, and that there is no action which would pass for an act of extortion, of peculation, of bribery, and oppression in England, that is not an act of extortion, of peculation, of bribery, and oppression in Europe, Asia, Africa, and the world over.

This idealism seems noble enough, until one realizes that what Burke is automatically advocating is not universal morality, however this might be derived, but the global application of British morality. Naturally, he did not appreciate that this was also an example of the very 'geographical morality' which he claimed to find abhorrent:

'I trust and hope your Lordships will not judge by laws and institutions which you do not know, against those laws and institutions which you do know, and under whose power and authority Mr Hastings went out to India.' As Hastings's recent biographer Jeremy Bernstein comments, 'Burke seemed to be saying there was only one set of laws and one standard of behaviour – those of England.'

Later in the trial, Burke gave a good example of the perils of being too convinced that one's own moral code is universal. One of the incidents that came up from time to time in the trial was a large sum of money that the wealthy *banian* Nobkissen had made available to Warren Hastings at a time when the Company was so broke that it could not even pay the Governor-General's wages. The prosecutors argued this sum was a personal gift or bribe, and that it therefore violated the rules against 'presents'. But Hastings maintained that to guard against any question of impropriety he had placed the sum, though offered to him personally, straight into the Company's account. The details, in any case, are far less interesting than the underlying reasons for Burke's deep-seated horror at the commercial relationship: 'This Nobkissen was a Banyan; and if there was anything more flinty, more gripy, more thrifty, or more careful to improve the value of money than a Jew, it was a Gentoo Banyan, or Money Broker.'

There was clearly little future in Hastings's programme of ruling, Akbar-style, in accordance with the customs and laws of Indian civilization. So what had changed? Britain in the late eighteenth century was undoubtedly forging a sense of her own providential destiny. The Industrial Revolution was in its infancy and growing wealth and confidence reinforced Britain's traditional self-belief, strongly rooted in her ancient liberties. But the conservative backlash against 'alien' ideas was more a product of panic than of confidence. The loss of America had traumatized the British ruling classes. It was largely responsible for encouraging them to insist the British state take a much more

OVERLEAF:
THIS AQUATINT
COMMEMORATES
THE FIRST DAY OF
WARREN HASTINGS'
IMPEACHMENT IN
A PACKED
WESTMINSTER HALL.

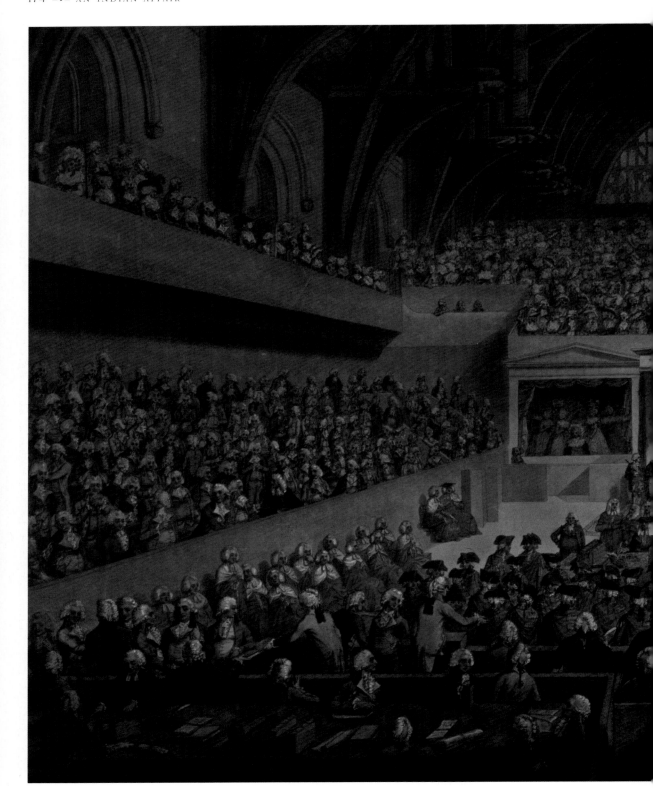

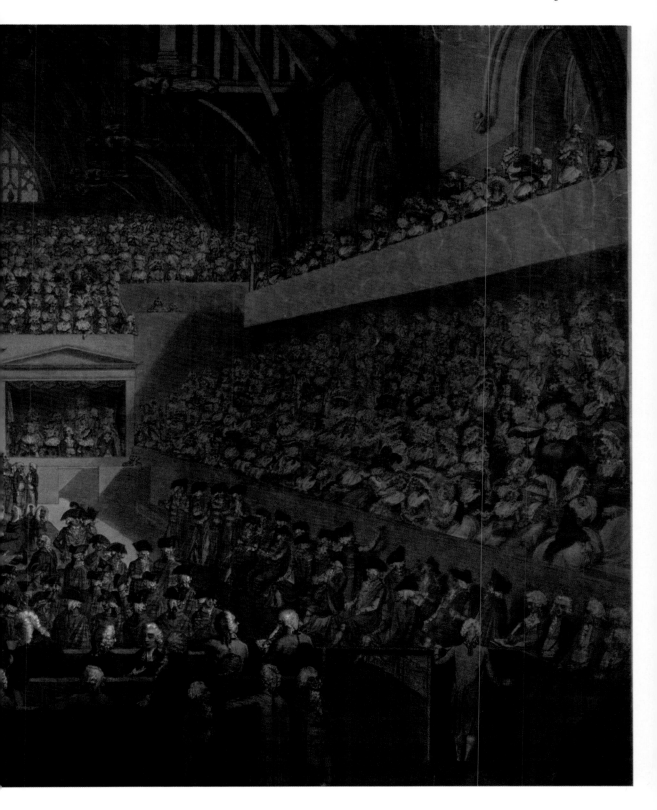

direct role in India. By now, aristocratic opinion was affronted that a private trading company muddled along in India, motivated by profit rather than the 'nobler' ideal of spreading the beneficent British mantle over India's millions. Not, of course, that Burke or the others were offering British liberties to the Indian population. The Americans had been driven to revolution because they resented taxation without representation. There was no way the Indians were about to get representative democracy or a voice at Westminster.

The trial went on and on and on. This was partly because the great orators seemed hard put to make their point in less than a week – Sheridan rehashed his Begums of Oudh number for another four mesmerizing days of almost wholly fictitious rhetoric, and Burke's closing address was a marathon nine-day wonder. But Hastings's inordinate ordeal was just as much due to the parliamentary schedule. Other business, not least real, pressing affairs of state, meant that only a few days of each session could be devoted to the trial, after which the House adjourned for the recess. On one occasion Parliament actually dissolved, which led to protracted arguments about whether they would have to start all over again with the new Parliament.

After four years, Hastings's patience snapped and he begged the Lords to accelerate the trial's conclusion. The prosecution had taken so long that the case for the defence had not even started:

> It is not pleasant for me, from week to week, from month to month, from year to year, to hear myself accused of crimes, many of them of the most atrocious die, and all represented in the most shocking colours, and to feel that I never shall be allowed to answer them. In my time of life – in the life of a man already approaching very near to its close, four years of which his reputation is to be traduced, and branded to the world is too much.

Burke objected to any change of procedure and the snail's pace continued.

Eventually, in 1792, the defence began. But no one was as interested in it as in the prosecution. The trial had dragged on so long that the galleries were thin and even the majority of jurors, the Lords, did not bother to attend. Some days there was not even a sufficient quorum of Lords to proceed at all. The crowds did return in June 1794 for Burke's concluding statement, which was also his swansong from Westminster. As the trial closed, argument seems to have been entirely sacrificed to insult:

> He is a captain general of iniquity – thief – tyrant – robber – cheat – sharper – swindler. We call him all these names, and are sorry that the English language does not afford terms adequate to the enormity of his offences… Revenge is a sort of wild

justice — it is the test of heroic virtue — we will continue to the end to persecute. I vow that we bear immortal hatred against this scum, filth and pollution of Indian guilt; if the Commons do not, I take it all to myself.

Of course, when it came to deliberating on the verdict, it turned out there was not much of a case for Hastings to answer. After seven years of trial, just twenty-nine peers felt they had attended with sufficient regularity to be entitled to a vote. These jurors did decide to judge the case on the law, not Burke's standard of morality. In less than a month, one by one, they threw each charge out. On 23 April 1795, Warren Hastings was finally acquitted on all counts. The trial clerk concludes, 'Mr Hastings bowed respectfully and retired.'

Warren Hastings lived another twenty-three years, much of it tending his Indian plants in happy retirement at Daylesford. But both in India and Britain, the tendencies towards tolerance and fusion that he had embodied were losing out to a new and strident spirit. Quite aside from the trial, these had been tumultuous years. No sooner had the British aristocracy recovered from the shame of losing America than they had to face up to the shock of the French Revolution. Some even feared liberty, equality and fraternity might sprout in India. Even worse, Tipu might turn into another Bonaparte. Over the course of little more than a decade, the British in India would replace humility with arrogance and lose the plot. British imperialism was born of a kind of counter-revolution — a conservative backlash that had emerged through fear but became destiny in the self-congratulatory afterglow of Waterloo. From then onwards, the British knew best and had a mission. Superiority and ideology make potent companions.

CHAPTER EIGHT

THE NEW ROME

Government House in Calcutta is far from accidental. It's as deliberate a statement of full-blooded imperialism as a building can be. The elect approach through triumphal arched gateways surmounted by monumental lions and sphinxes. A sweeping formal staircase draws them majestically up to a grand Ionic portico. Once inside, the state apartments include a Doric marble hall, an Ionic ballroom and a chamber that was dubbed the Throne Room long before British Governor-Generals actually became Viceroys and were entitled, at least by proxy, to demand regal seating. Just in case the visitor still doesn't get the message, there are a dozen Roman emperors on plinths – wise icons like Augustus Caesar, and even mad, bad ones like Caligula and Nero. Today Government House, once Britain's top address in India, has been renamed Raj Bhavan and makes an odd home for the Governor of Communist-run West Bengal. Its construction at the turn of the nineteenth century marked the moment when Empire became the purpose of the British presence in India, not the unanticipated, even undesired, consequence.

DETERMINED THAT INDIA 'SHOULD BE RULED FROM A PALACE, NOT A COUNTING HOUSE', RICHARD WELLESLEY MADE HIS IMPERIAL STATEMENT IN STONE.

When Richard Wellesley, an ambitious Irish aristocrat out of Eton and Christ Church, arrived in India in 1798 to take up his post as Governor-General, the demeaning living arrangements had horrified him. They may have suited Warren Hastings, who had served his lengthy apprenticeship in up-country Bengal marking out cotton piece goods. But they definitely would not do for the imperious Wellesley, a man no doubt proud that he did not know his chintz from his calico. Within a month of his arrival, Wellesley ordered the construction of Government House, adopting the off-the-shelf solution of modelling its design directly on Robert Adam's Kedleston Hall in Derbyshire, the most admired new neo-classical house in England. Modesty was not one of Richard Wellesley, the Earl of Mornington's, virtues, yet this was not just an act of personal aggrandisement. It was also a monumental political assertion. As Wellesley's friend, Lord Valentia, explained, India 'should be ruled from a palace, not a mean counting-house… with the ideas of a Prince, not those of a retail-trader in muslins and indigo'.

Regardless of the realities of power, in Hastings's day the etiquette had been for him to go out and pay his respects to Mughal ambassadors and Indian royalty. Wellesley insisted that in future Indian princes come to Government House and pay obeisance to him. For all their differences, one thing British and Indian culture of the time had in common was an obsession with protocol. To neither was this change insignificant. Once again, Lord Valentia was ready with the explanation: 'The Head of a Mighty Empire ought to conform himself to the prejudices of the country he rules over.' No doubt it was true that Indian princes were thrilled the British chief prince had at last moved into suitably palatial headquarters. But it suited Richard Wellesley's prejudices too. At night, he used to wander alone among his imperial busts, no doubt replaying in his head his grand plan yet one more time. There would be an expanded empire, a triumphant homecoming, a better title and real power along with the laurel wreaths from a grateful nation. When the Company's Directors received a bill for £179,000 for Government House they were outraged. It was a sign of the times that the Governor-General had not even bothered to consult his supposed employers before building it. Throughout his Indian career, he showed almost nothing but contempt for the Directors, whom he dubbed 'the cheese-mongers of Leadenhall Street'. Though the cheese-mongers' shareholders continued to pay his wages, by now a new Board of Control, appointed by Parliament, set the Company's political directions. These now had little to do with quiet trade.

British India would remain, at least in name, the Company Raj for more than fifty years. But from the turn of the nineteenth century, India was seen far less as a trading concession than as a dominion. The point of ruling large swathes of India was to rule large swathes of India. Of course there were still economic motives: India as an arena for British enterprise, as a source of commodities and, it was still vainly hoped, revenue, and increasingly, as the Industrial Revolution transformed Britain, as a market for British manufactured goods. There were also valid strategic arguments for Empire. According to the prevailing British assessment of nineteenth-century geo-politics, if Britain didn't dominate India then it risked falling into the hands of the French. Later, their role as Evil Empire was conveniently taken over by the Russians. But above all, Britain's Indian Empire was a matter of national pride and glory – Empire was what big European countries did. Spreading British values could do nothing but benefit subject peoples as well as the mother country. After all, there had surely never been a more perfect civilization, coupled with a more prudent and judicious political culture, than Britain's. Not, at least, since the great days of Ancient Rome.

Once again it would not have happened without the French. When the Bastille fell in 1789, the British establishment had tended to welcome the prospect of French absolutism evolving into British-style constitutional monarchy. Edmund Burke was a far-sighted exception, warning as early as 1790 that these events may have been sublime but they were also terrible. To overthrow an old, established system before fully articulating its replacement courted dreadful danger. Sales of Burke's *Reflections on the French Revolution* took off in earnest early in 1793, when the French emphatically abandoned the British model and lopped the King's head off. Britain was thrown into total panic. Soon afterwards, Robespierre's Terror followed Burke's script and the guillotine basket began to overflow with aristocratic heads. By then Britain and France were at war. A young Corsican revolutionary general, Napoleon Bonaparte, seemed well nigh invincible in mainland Europe. This was a world war, and Britain and Austria alone seemed, for the moment, to be capable of withstanding the advance of universal tyranny. By the time Richard Wellesley arrived in India, Napoleon had overthrown his employers, the revolutionary government of the Directory. Though he did not crown himself Emperor until 1804, he was already ruling an empire in all but name.

Richard Wellesley had an almost pathological loathing of the French, despite, or perhaps partly because, he was stormily married to a French woman. Rationally, Britain in India had almost nothing to fear from France. Clive had permanently removed any military threat from Pondicherry or Chandernagore back in the 1760s. Tipu's powers had been substantially pegged back after a Third Mysore War between 1790 and 1792, which negated any real threat from his continuing fondness for the French. Moreover in 1798, as we have seen, James Achilles Kirkpatrick in Hyderabad managed to neutralize what might have developed into a real threat from a French sepoy army without a shot being fired.

Reason, however, had little to do with the Great Fear that spread with Wellesley from Britain to India. Not for the first or last time in history, what people did worry about is far more important than what they should have worried about. In 1950s America at the height

Storming the breach —
the final assault on
Srirangapatnam became
one of the most famous
subjects in British
historical paintings.

of McCarthyism, perfectly intelligent New Yorkers fretted that the Russians might start popping up through the manholes on Fifth Avenue. Likewise in 1798 and 1799, the British Government were convinced that Napoleon might move forward from Egypt overland to India. Belittling the legendary achievements of Hannibal and even Alexander the Great, this feat would have involved marching a vast European army with their beasts of burden across the deserts of Arabia, the plains of Persia and the mountains of Afghanistan. In India, the scenario continued, the French would make common cause with Tipu's blood-crazed zealots, and drive the British into oblivion. Since in August 1798 Nelson's defeat of the French navy at Aboukir left the French army not masters of the Levant but desperately stranded there, the hysteria was entirely unwarranted.

It is difficult to know whether Wellesley really feared the French or just used them as an excuse to go for glory. Whichever was the case, he cited the French threat as the reason for a total reversal in Company policy in India. The historian Percival Spear went so far as to call it a revolution. In little more than seven years, the map of India was transformed. State after Indian state faced the same invidious choice. Either stand up to the Company and succumb to almost inevitable military defeat, or kowtow to the Company by signing up to a subsidiary treaty that effectively denied the state its autonomy while guaranteeing it, at vast expense, 'protection'. These protectors were, of course, a garrison of the Company's own forces, the very power who had in effect removed the Indian state's independence and was henceforth permanently stationed in its capital, heartily discouraging any back-sliding.

Officially, this policy, which came to be called the Forward Policy, was still anathema to the Company and to the Government. Moreover, it was almost certainly illegal. Pitt's India Act had in 1784 removed the last vestiges of the Company's political independence and subordinated its policy-making to the oversight of the Board of Control. The Act clearly stated that 'to pursue schemes of conquest and extension of dominion in India are measures repugnant to the wish, the honour and policy of this nation'. Warren Hastings's successors Lord Cornwallis and Sir John Shore had, in the main, adhered strictly to this non-intervention policy.

Pitt's Act naturally included a get-out clause permitting defensive wars against enemies threatening British India. So thanks to the French, Wellesley felt liberated to abandon non-intervention and vigorously to pursue the Forward Policy. Not that he ever asked for, or received, licence from London for his unilateral actions in India. Like the McCarthy era's reds under the beds, Wellesley saw, or pretended to see, Frenchmen everywhere. Unchecked, they would spread 'the most virulent and notorious principles of Jacobinism'. And if one looked and didn't find them, that only went to prove how dastardly they were and how well they were hiding. Moreover to Wellesley, like to the post-war superpowers carving up the Third World into rival spheres of influence, it was not really necessary to prove the existence of a clear and present danger from the enemy. Indian states were volatile, which was, in the circumstances, too much of a risk. At some future time, the French might be able to take advantage of Indian instability to inveigle themselves into the subcontinent. What was needed was a British pre-emptive strike. Thus Wellesley set about securing British supremacy throughout India, the very opposite of the multi-state vision of Hastings, while simultaneously claiming it was a defensive policy.

Almost as soon as Wellesley arrived in India, he set his sights on toppling the Tiger of Mysore. If anything, Tipu's undoing was to overestimate the reach of the French every bit as much as Wellesley did. Revolutionary France had been far too preoccupied with its own internal turmoil at the beginning of the 1790s to come to Tipu's aid in the Third Mysore War. From 1793 onwards, even though France was at war with Britain while Mysore was officially neutral, Tipu seemed far keener than the French to take on the British in India. He made secret diplomatic overtures to France in 1796, promising joint action against their common enemy if she landed 10,000 troops in southern India. France, of course, neither had the troops to spare nor any practical means to get them there. This disappointment only encouraged Tipu to court France more openly. First, a Jacobin Club was opened at Srirangapatnam. Then in May 1797, at a remarkable (and remarkably provocative) ceremony there, 'Citoyen Tipu', as he styled himself for the occasion, raised the Tricoleur and planted a Tree of Liberty, honouring the Revolution with a salvo from 2,300 guns. You can well imagine how all this reverberated in Madras, Calcutta and even London. In the end, Tipu encouraged fewer than a hundred Frenchmen from Mauritius to join his cause. Worse, news of this recruiting swiftly reached the newly arrived Wellesley. It was just the casus belli he was looking for.

In March 1799, three armies simultaneously entered Mysore territory. The Company's Bombay army invaded from the west. Meanwhile its Madras army crossed the border from the east. Alongside it marched the Nizam of Hyderabad's army, which was now at the service of the Company (thanks to Kirkpatrick's deft diplomacy, no doubt aided by his secret personal treaty with the Nizam, his circumcision and his beautiful Muslim wife). Such were the powers of nepotism that this last army was under the joint command of Meer Alum, thought to be the Nizam's illegitimate son, and Arthur Wellesley, undoubtedly the Governor-General's younger brother, though more than a decade away from becoming the Duke of Wellington and defeating Napoleon at Waterloo.

Not surprisingly, history has tended to award the battle honours at the Siege of Sriringapatnam to the future Iron Duke, who was experiencing his first major campaign. In fact, Arthur Wellesley did not even enter the city until all the fighting was over. The fiercest action he saw had occurred a few weeks earlier – a bungled night-time attack on Sultanpetah Tope, an outlying wood near Tipu's capital. In one of the most inauspicious starts to any military career, Arthur Wellesley succeeded in getting detached from the troops under his command and hopelessly lost himself. Firing raged from all sides in the pitch dark among the trees. Not surprisingly, of the twenty-five British casualties that night, a significant number were shot by their own side. Perhaps that is why, when it came to deciding who should mount the final British assault into Srirangapatnam, a Colonel Dunlop got the left column, a Colonel Sherbrooke got the right column and Colonel Wellesley got to watch it all from a distance as commander of the reserve forces on the other side of the river.

The combined forces facing the walls of Sriringapatnam in late April 1799 were fighting the calendar as much as Tipu. If the fortifications could withstand artillery bombardment for a few more days, the monsoon would break and the Kaveri River would swell with the rains and become unfordable. On 3 May a small breach was finally achieved at the north of the island near where the two branches of the river met. There was now thought to be just enough of a gap in the French-engineered defences for men to pass through single file with musket and fixed bayonet. The assault was set for 1 p.m. the next day – the plan being for the two columns to ford the river and climb the incline towards the breach together, then fight their way in and split in two, taking control of the entire circuit of the city's walls before moving on to seize the city. The two columns were led, in both senses of the word, by General Baird, a forty-one-year-old Highlander who had endured nearly four years of horror in Tipu's dungeons after the Battle of Polilur. No doubt this experience suitably stiffened Baird's sinews and summoned up his blood to terminate the actions of the Tiger.

The plan worked perfectly and within a few hours all resistance was snuffed out and the city was taken. That afternoon and evening, General Baird must have fully sated his lust for

OVERLEAF: TIPU SULTAN WAS BURIED IN THE BEAUTIFUL GUMBAZ OR DOMED CHAMBER WHICH HE HAD BUILT FOR THE TOMB OF HIS FATHER, HAIDAR ALI.

revenge. True to their 'rules of war', no quarter was given. They later buried 9,000 of Tipu's soldiers. The victors suffered just 389 casualties, killed or wounded (343 European, 46 sepoy). Arthur Wellesley entered the city in the late afternoon and was led by a guide to the city's Water Gate, where, under a heap of bodies, women as well as men, the party discovered the corpse of a short, fat officer with a musket wound through his forehead. The body of Tipu Sultan was borne back to his palace in his own palanquin. Arthur Wellesley retired back across the river to his tent to catch up on his sleep. That night, Baird's troops had free rein to murder, rape and plunder. Only next morning was Wellesley given the order to relieve Baird. He later wrote, 'I came in to take command on the morning of the 5th, and by hanging, flogging etc restored order among the troops. I hope I have gained the confidence of the people.'

That same day Tipu Sultan was buried with full British military honours at the magnificent mausoleum Tipu had built for his father Haidar Ali. An eyewitness reported that many of his former subjects lined the smouldering streets to watch his funeral procession. While their houses continued to be plundered, they 'prostrated themselves before the body and expressed their grief by loud lamentation'.

The mountains of booty seized that day from Tipu's palaces included one particularly intriguing curiosity. A brightly painted life-size wooden tiger savages a Company officer, its jaws agape to deliver the coup de grâce. One can imagine that day the delight of the soldier who first discovered the tiger and turned the crank handle at its side. A series of screeches and howls mimic the roar of the animal and the scream of the Englishman. The bowels of the beast contain a hidden bellows and simple organ keyboard.

Tippoo's tiger was shipped home to the Company's museum in its headquarters at Leadenhall Street. It quickly became one of the most potent icons of imperialism. In itself it symbolized the savagery and monstrosity of Britannia's native enemies. Yet at the same time its emasculation in a museum cabinet in London demonstrated British invincibility. By the same token, the Campaign Medal awarded to the victorious troops at Srirangapatnam was utterly appropriate. A rampant British Lion destroys a tiger. Tipu's real tigers, of which he kept several as pets, were all shot.

The news of victory at Srirangapatnam caused untold rejoicing in Britain. In terms of popular consciousness, this was probably the biggest good news story out of India since Plassey. This over-reaction had everything to do with the notoriety acquired by Tipu the bogeyman since Polilur, but little to do with the actual threat posed by Tipu to British interests. Nonetheless, with Napoleon on the rampage in mainland Europe, it is understandable that people chose to elevate and celebrate their famous victory over the 'Napoleon of the East'.

The elder brother, Richard Wellesley, however, saw Tipu's overthrow as just the beginning. He embarked on an energetic and decisive diplomatic and military sweep across the continent that eminently deserves the adjective Napoleonic. Less than six months after Srirangapatnam, he wrote to Henry Dundas, the President of the Board of Control in London, a breath-taking letter of brutal candour: 'If you will have a little patience, the death of the Nizam [of Hyderabad] will probably enable me to gratify your voracious appetite for lands and fortresses. Seringapatam ought, I think, to stay your stomach awhile; not to mention Tanjore and the Poligar countries. Perhaps, I may be able to give you a supper of Oudh and the Carnatic, if you should still be hungry.' He was as good as his word, though it is doubtful Dundas ever ordered such a feast. Over the next five years, these territories and much besides were either directly annexed by the British or fell under Britain's indirect rule. What's more, Richard Wellesley, aided and abetted by young Arthur, succeeded for the first time in humiliating and dividing their only real potential foe, the Marathas, unsurprisingly dubbed 'the Frenchmen of Asia'. Dundas's dessert was unexpected and magnificent. In 1803, British forces captured Agra and Delhi, exactly what Clive and Hastings, for all their differences, agreed should never happen. Henceforth the Mughal Emperor Shah Alam was a British puppet rather than a pawn of the Marathas.

The gargantuan meal came at a hefty price. To Wellesley this hardly mattered. He cared little for the 'mercantile interests, prejudices, and profits' of the Company. There was almost no commercial logic to spending vast sums on conquering territories that could never pay their way. The Forward Policy had taken advantage of what in India was a largely nonexistent French threat to deliver British supremacy in India. But it also condemned the Company and Britain to a continually mounting bill for the government and defence of India. Every war required large new loans raised on the London markets. Starved of cash in Bengal, the Company was forced to borrow yet more money in India just to buy the cargoes which were supposed to be their bread-and-butter business. With fifty million Indians and dozens of displaced princes now under British subjugation, it was difficult to imagine any future strategy that might cut costs or raise income. Only massive and permanent militarization was likely to deter future war or rebellion. In their moment of undesired triumph, the Company was doomed.

Though the damage had been done, even the British Premier William Pitt eventually realized Wellesley 'could not be suffered to remain in the government'. A successor was appointed and instructed that it was 'not in the opinion only of ministers, or of a party, but of all reflecting men of every description' that there was no purpose to a British Empire in India which remitted 'little other profit except brilliant gazettes'. This was 1805, a few months before Trafalgar, a moment when the French threat to Britain was chillingly real and 'brilliant gazettes' thin on the ground. Just a few months earlier, Napoleon had been in Boulogne boasting 'should we be able to control the English Channel for six hours, we will be the masters of the world'.

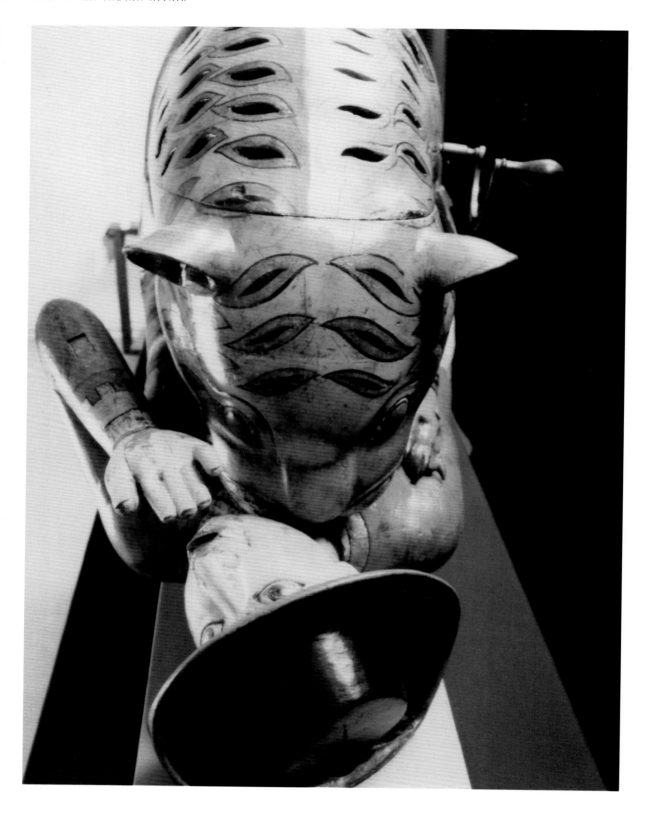

If any Governor-General deserved impeachment it was Richard Wellesley. The charge list was convincing enough – breaking treaties, wasting money, utterly ignoring the Directors' orders, riding roughshod over his Council, behaving, in short, like a despot. But an attempt at impeachment fell at its first hurdle. After the Hastings marathon, few people in Britain had the stomach for another grand parliamentary trial. Moreover, though it was no more than a decade since Hastings's ordeal had finally ended, British values had dramatically shifted in the interim as a reaction to events in Europe. Hastings's Whig prosecutors had rooted around for every conceivable piece of evidence that the accused could possibly be deemed to have been corrupt or acted illegally. By that measure, Wellesley had cheated and illegitimately overthrown a dozen Chait Singhs or Begums of Oudh – though not, it must be added, for money. But the Conservative backlash in the wake of the French Revolution was born of a popular assumption that British ends justified all possible means. Few people now much cared to argue that glorious British India had been won ingloriously, still less that it shouldn't have been won at all. Richard Wellesley went on to become Foreign Secretary and later became Viceroy of Ireland. It was said that had he not been so addicted to prostitutes he might have gone all the way to 10 Downing Street.

To many people today, Wellesley's actions will seem wholly illegitimate. But a cornerstone of the imperial mindset then fast evolving was the conviction that British supremacy was in India's best interests. By that yardstick, Britain had not conquered India so much as secured deliverance for its subject peoples. As Wellesley put it in 1800, the British ruled 'the most opulent, flourishing part of India, in which property, life, civil order and liberty are more secure, and the people enjoy a larger proportion of good government than any other country in this quarter of the globe'. Thus, Wellesley was the opposite of some Machiavellian monster thrilled with the wickedness of his every scheming triumph. He thought of himself as a Roman proconsul, enduring privations and dangers so that he could selflessly spread civilization to the barbarians. Though this may seem like a monstrous delusion, the Raj was not just built on personal ambition or the pursuit of national glory. Only a far higher moral purpose could have delivered and sustained it. The rarefied cadre of imperial administrators who ruled India for the next 150 years were high-minded and principled, utterly devoted to public service. They worked tirelessly in what they saw as the cause of peace, justice, enlightenment and progress, for a fraction of the reward of their eighteenth-century predecessors. The tragedy was that their lofty bearing and moral certainty made them increasingly distant and contemptuous of India itself.

The political revolution had been accompanied by a no less profound cultural shift in relations between Britons and Indians. Broadly speaking, the onset of the imperial age brought an end to the phase of more equal communication and mutual respect. Particularly at the more senior levels of Company service, open fraternization with

DISCOVERED AFTER THE FALL OF SRIRANGA-PATNAM, TIPU'S LIFE-SIZE MECHANICAL TOY BECAME A SYMBOL OF BOTH INDIAN SAVAGERY AND BRITISH SUPREMACY.

Indians was now frowned upon unless it was a diplomatic duty. From around 1800 onwards, men started keeping their *bibis* as guilty secrets rather than open blessings. Their Anglo-Indian children were increasingly likely to be disowned rather than adored. Moreover, now that private trade was banned to Company servants, there was little occasion to form close relationships with *banians* or get out and among the people, talking to producers and suppliers. To do so risked undermining what with monstrous arrogance came to be seen as British moral superiority. This depended on keeping a haughty distance from Asiatic corruption and vice. There were too many clear and shameful examples of earlier generations of Britons who had been depraved by India to continue to tolerate the Company's lax old ways.

In time, the separation between the races came to be seen as a crucial cornerstone of the Raj. For example, a Lieutenant-Colonel H. B. Henderson, writing in 1829 after two decades of experience in India, recorded the convictions of his colleagues: 'No native, however high his rank, ought to approach within a yard of an Englishman; and every time an Englishman shakes hands with a *Babu* he shakes the basis on which our ascendancy in this country stands.' Deploying the same twisted logic that was later used to justify apartheid, the new breed of official felt that this hauteur was critical if the natives were to respect the *sahibs* (masters). Thus, as with apartheid, it was possible to believe that it was actually in the interests of the natives as well as the whites that the two races were living apart and never meeting on equal terms, that the British were now disdainful of Indian culture, and that new legislation prohibited Indians from the more senior ranks of every profession in their own country.

Akbar and Hastings had resolved to rule India by turning themselves from outsiders into insiders. Even the Romans had tended to take up local gods to add to their pantheon. Moreover, Romanized barbarians achieved the highest ranks within the imperial service, some making it all the way to Rome as emperor. But for much of the nineteenth century the British could not conceive of Indian self-rule, or Indians attaining high rank within the wider British Empire – not, at least, for generations to come. Nevertheless, it was argued with honest conviction that this was all in their best interests: the subject peoples were enjoying every blessing of British civilization to which they were suited. Like women, it was obviously not appropriate for them to vote or serve in high office. But that could hardly be adduced as an argument that they did not enjoy the full measure of Great British liberty to which they were fit.

Charting a precise history of racial attitudes is notoriously hazardous. What people think is often different from what they say and do. Changes in official policy may reflect or run ahead of wider social opinion. There are numerous examples of racism and bigotry towards Indians before 1800. Equally, as we have seen, many remarkable individuals in the nineteenth century continued to defy convention and 'go native' themselves as well as to speak out, like Hindu Stuart, against the increasingly racist mindset of their colleagues. Nevertheless, there is a dramatic difference between the prevailing British attitudes to Indians in the tolerant Hastings' era and those a generation later in an age of overt, institutionalized racism, underpinned by an ideology that viewed native culture as irredeemably debased and corrupt.

In 1813 Warren Hastings wrote to Lord Moira (later the Marquess of Hastings, but no relation), who had just been appointed Governor-General and was about to set off to take up his new post. The eighty-one-year-old Hastings had some important advice for the younger man: 'Among the natives of India, there are men of as strong intellect, as sound integrity, and as honourable feelings as any of this Kingdom… by your example make it the fashion among our countrymen to treat them with courtesy and as participators in the same equal rights of society with themselves.'

Yet soon after Lord Moira arrived in Calcutta he confided to his journal his first reactions to the subcontinent: 'The Hindu appears a being nearly limited to mere animal functions, and even in them indifferent.' Despite Warren Hastings's heartfelt counsel, Moira concluded Indians seemed to possess 'no higher intellect than a dog, an elephant or a monkey'. Hastings had gone out to India as a teenager and served a near twenty-year apprenticeship before taking on the top job. Moira, by contrast, was quite typical of later patterns in being expected to rule India as Governor-General the very first day he set foot on the subcontinent.

Back in 1786, Warren Hastings's immediate successor as Governor-General, Lord Cornwallis, had been the first top Company official in India not to have a track-record there. It is perhaps not coincidental that Cornwallis was also the first to legislate against Indians and to make blood a factor in the administration and armed forces. Cornwallis was an aristocratic soldier who had arrived in India fresh from surrendering to George Washington at Yorktown in the last encounter of the American War of Independence. In Geoffrey Moorhouse's opinion, 'He was by breeding and application a lofty man, who came to India in the conviction that every native was irreversibly corrupt; that most of his fellow-countrymen were almost as defective, better only insofar as they might be civilized if one tried hard enough to propel them along the straight and narrow.' Almost overnight, Cornwallis overthrew the Hastings model that had been rooted in partnership between Company servants and Indian officials working together in the tried-and-trusted ways that had evolved from Mughal systems. Every single Indian official (bar one judge) was removed from high office.

A similar fate awaited Anglo-Indians, tainted as they were by Indian blood. These were the very group of people whom the Company had previously encouraged and who had served its interests with such distinction. Now a series of acts and edicts barred new Anglo-

Indian recruits from the covenanted ranks of the civil service and from every rank of military service (except, bizarrely, that of bandsmen, fifers, drummers and farriers). What made this all the more contemptible was that when there was a war to fight and a pressing need for soldiers, Anglo-Indians suddenly found their background no impediment to military service. But no sooner had the fighting stopped than they were ejected from their regiments.

Living allowances for soldiers' wives were twice as high for European women as for Anglo-Indians, on the grounds that the latter were 'born in India and habituated to live chiefly on rice [so that] the wants and wishes of the Half Caste are much more confined than those of a European woman'. Indian wives and their dependent children were banned from accompanying their husbands back home to Britain. 'Natural' children, even if they had been sent to the best schools in England, were prohibited from serving the Company in any capacity purely on grounds of race. In 1791, for example, the Company's Directors were asked to consider the case of one John Turing, living in Britain, who had been nominated to a cadetship in Madras but was discovered to have had an Indian mother. The Directors ruled 'that no Person, the son of a Native Indian, shall henceforth be appointed by the Court to employment in the Civil, Military or Marine Service of the Company'. This was the same Company who a century earlier had been subsidizing mixed-race marriages in India as an investment in future generations of potential employees.

There could be no clearer sign that the fetishes of ideology had trumped decent common sense than this treatment of Anglo-Indians. At the time, a pretext for excluding them was that recent mulatto revolts in the Caribbean against Spanish and French rule demonstrated the potential disloyalty of mixed-race people. As the egregious Lord Valentia put it, 'In every country where this intermediate caste has been permitted to rise, it has ultimately tended to the ruin of that country.' Such fears in the Indian context were absurd. Anglo-Indians invariably gravitated towards European culture, not least because it was their misfortune to be rejected by traditional Hindu and Muslim society. Now they would be increasingly cut off from both sides of the family, caught in a no-man's land where they were deemed European by Indians and Indian by the Europeans, and destined to be despised by both.

The real reasons for this discrimination lie far more in prejudice than in fear of disloyalty. As the nineteenth century progresses, the word 'nigger' becomes more and more commonplace. Fathers with fairer-skinned 'natural' children express relief and imply that their prospects will be better than those of their darker-skinned siblings. With luck, they might even pass off as white, the daughters marrying a gentleman, the sons gaining an honourable position. But it is salutary to recognize that the prejudice that led to discrimination against Anglo-Indians probably came as much from Indian as British society. The Company's Directors confessed to a Parliamentary Committee in 1830 that excluding Anglo-Indians was essential to preserving the prestige of the British in the eyes of their

Indian subjects. This is not simply a lame British excuse. In a caste-oriented society, birth status and family origins mattered. Anglo-Indians were despised by high-caste Indians because their mothers were invariably outcast or low-caste in origin. How, the Directors wondered, would Indians continue to look up to their imperial masters, if these fabled ranks included half-castes?

Despite their second-class status, Anglo-Indians continued to be vital functionaries of the empire, later becoming a dominant force in the newly emerging private merchant houses and making the postal and railway services their own. But even the most courageous and talented were tainted by their origins. The legendary James Skinner, the son of a Scottish captain and a Rajput princess, was a natural military leader whose origins forced him to build his career as a mercenary commander in the service of the Marathas. After their defeat, he was allowed to serve the Company, but only through his own irregular cavalry force, Skinner's Horse, distinguished by their yellow coats and their fearless reputation on the battlefield. Colonel Skinner's familiarity with the terrain and military tactics of North West India, and the fierce loyalty he inspired in the traditional Mughal military families from which he recruited, were invaluable in the early-nineteenth-century campaigns to pacify these notoriously restive regions. Skinner was equally renowned for his personal aura. He was known to his men as Sikander Sahib, the Indian title for no less a hero than Alexander the Great. He held elaborate durbars at which his personal authority over newly acquired territories was cemented using traditional Mughal ceremony. He was famous not least for having seven wives of diverse religions and being devoted to his eighty children. He built a mosque for one wife, a Hindu temple for another, and St James's Church in Delhi for himself.

Skinner was widely recognized as unique and revelled in several lifetimes' worth of experiences and achievements. Yet his writings occasionally betray glimpses of real tragedy on account of his mixed origins. In his memoirs, originally written in Persian, he explains that, although his mother was devoted to his father, she 'could not endure that her two younger daughters should be forced from her and sent to school. She conceived that by their being taken away from her protection, the sanctity of the purdah was violated, and the Rajput honour destroyed; and, apprehensive of their disgracing themselves, from being removed from the care of all their female relatives, contrary to the custom of the Rajputs, she put herself to death.' It is not clear whether Skinner's mother would have been relieved or distraught that her three daughters in fact all made successful marriages 'to gentlemen in the Company service'.

Many years later, Skinner, who was by then a famous war hero, chose to send some of his own children to school in Scotland. There, he hoped and expected, they would receive a warm welcome from his great friend the artist James Fraser, brother of Skinner's closest friend and associate William Fraser (Fraser Sahib), the 'White Moghul' Assistant Resident at Delhi. On more than one occasion Skinner had even saved William's life. This was definitely a case of the bonds that tie... But to James Fraser's distress and embarrassment, his new Scottish wife was clearly bridling at the prospect of having her house overrun by half-castes. In his final letter to Fraser, Skinner gracefully withdrew the request for hospitality. He explains that he would not wish to burden the Fraser family with 'his poor black children', knowing Mrs Fraser had 'a great aversion to children of that description'. His letter pathetically concludes that he will trust his children to 'Him who gave them birth, where I hope black or white will not make much difference before His presence'.

The prejudices of Jane Fraser are reminiscent of Lord Moira's first reactions to the Indians he met on arriving in Calcutta. They suggest that British revulsion against Indians, far from being a consequence of long acquaintance with natives on the subcontinent, may actually have been imported from Britain. Certainly the earlier generations, with long experience of working alongside Indians, were far less likely to possess instinctive prejudices than those who had never met any or whose experience of Indians was limited, whether by direct contact or reputation, to the tiny and troubled Asian community in Britain.

From the 1780s onwards, Britain began to feel it had a 'black problem'. This was largely a result of its 14,000 former slaves of African origin, their numbers recently swelled by those who had won their freedom serving in the British forces in the American War. Britain's smaller Indian population became part of the same 'problem' in the eyes of philanthropists, officials and hostile Londoners alike. It was all too common for Indian servants, mistresses or sailors to find themselves abandoned and destitute in London. Others were so ill-treated aboard ship or by their English employers or lovers, that they preferred to take their chances on their own. Labour shortages made lascar numbers rise steadily throughout the Napoleonic Wars, and between 1808 and 1813 over a thousand Indian sailors were arriving in London each year. The 'problem' seemed more extreme because it was highly localized, with most tending to gravitate to London's East End. Since the only acceptable solution was thought to be repatriation rather than assimilation, let alone multicultural enthusiasm for a separate Indian community in Britain, the indigent Indians had little or no control over their destinies. Penniless, cold and wretched, the majority were concentrated in homes for ayahs or lascars, entirely dependent on charity or the reluctant support of the Company. They were denied opportunities in Britain and were forced, sometimes for years, to await the chance of working a passage home. Disease, overcrowding, criminality and widespread begging exacerbated the fear and distaste many Londoners began to feel for these aliens. If they took jobs, the cry went up that this undercut or deprived English or Irish workers. If they relied on charity or turned to crime, this only antagonized British popular opinion further, confirming that they were lazy, stupid or corrupt.

Mrs Fraser cannot have been too troubled on her occasional trips to Inverness by the fear that Britain was turning into a foreign land. Her concern was the more conventional one, that it would be an offence against propriety to show familiarity to Skinner's children. Historians have tended to give women more than their fair share of the blame for the growing racism and the deterioration in relations between Britons and Indians. The case against the memsahibs is that they came out to India in greater numbers in the nineteenth century and not surprisingly brought with them a moral backlash against the lax, familiar and godless ways of the prevailing bachelor society.

Changes in sexual behaviour increased the gulf between the races. Now that the ladies were present, openly keeping a *bibi* was of course increasingly unacceptable. If men had to have mistresses (and many wives continued to tolerate or silently suffer their husbands' promiscuity) then it was essential they brought no shame on society by indulging openly. Calcutta estate agents were no longer likely to boast about a well-situated bungalow with en suite *bibi-khana*. Of course, there was still plenty of inter-racial sex. A sixteen-year-old cadet, Edward Sellon, wrote of his arrival in India in 1834, 'I now commenced a regular course of fucking with native women.' Clearly, however, this lacks something of the romance, companionship, respect and love that had characterized so many earlier relationships. The British–Indian sexual encounter was truly reduced to basics.

The memsahibs have been charged with far more than seeing off their Indian rivals. They were more than likely to try to banish India from their lives altogether during the many unpleasant years they were condemned to stay there. Deprived of any other role in British India, they devoted their energies to turning their homes into perfect cocoons of reassuring Britishness, falling upon the most rigid conventions in order to keep the hearth unpolluted by incomprehensible, scary and degenerate India. Having built a perfect microcosm of the Raj in their own home, they devoted their remaining energy to high-minded moral and religious campaigns. At best, these were condescending and paternalistic. At worst, they were incontrovertibly racist. Victorian values would flourish in India in ways inconceivable a generation or two earlier.

Yet it really will not do to lay most of the blame on the memsahibs. For a start, their nineteenth-century role was hardly their own creation. The idealized specimen of Victorian womanhood was a part largely scripted for them by men. But at a more basic level, as we have seen, the changes in mindset, which drove the two cultures further apart, predate by several decades the arrival in British India of significant numbers of women.

Instead, relations worsened primarily because of the type of people who now dominated India, which in turn reflected the fundamental shift away from trade and into administration. Of course the Company was still commercially driven. But trade was now 'beneath' most of its senior Indian personnel, public servants whose duties to the nation overrode their responsibilities to their paymasters. The former generation of traders and pragmatists, mostly drawn from the minor gentry, had been replaced by aristocratic ideologues, the type no doubt stung most painfully by Napoleon's acute jibe that England was a nation of shopkeepers. At the level of Governor-General, old Indian hands gave way to career soldiers and diplomats who turned up to rule India with their ideas fully fledged, based upon their experiences in Westminster, America, Ireland – pretty much anywhere except India. At all other ranks, recruitment remained confined to people who had pledged themselves to Company service while still scarcely more than children. But regardless of their

birth, the exclusive education they now received indoctrinated them into believing themselves a race apart. Perhaps even a master race.

RICHARD WELLESLEY WAS THE FIRST BRITISH RULER IN INDIA WHOSE PRIORITIES WERE EMPIRE AND CONQUEST, NOT TRADE AND ADMINISTRATION.

Warren Hastings had been a typical product of the old system – a quick course in basic book-keeping in England followed by two years of brain-numbing ledger-work as a writer, then close to a decade up-country mastering the finer details of the silk and cotton trade. When Richard Wellesley first swept into India, he could not imagine a worse apprenticeship for empire-builders. It was no wonder, he reasoned, they fell into the clutches of nautch girls, card-sharps and grasping banians.

Wellesley determined instead to mould these tender teenagers into the upright young men the Empire needed. In 1800 he established Fort William College in Calcutta, specifically to isolate its pupils from the 'habitual dissipation and corruption of the people of

India'. As well as protecting his charges from India, the College would 'fix and establish sound and correct principles of religion and government in their minds at an early period of life'. In 1805, Haileybury College in Hertfordshire was founded by the Company to complement Fort William College. Now the process could start even before the imperial fast-stream first encountered 'the climate and the vices of the people of India'. A boy went into Haileybury at fifteen and emerged from Fort William College at twenty quite convinced he was ready to rule the world.

For all its arrogance, there is no doubt that this system, the prototype model for turning out members of the august Indian Civil Service, was among the finest and most influential achievements of the Imperial Age. Generation after generation of young men graduated with the extraordinary mix of knowledge, confidence, duty and sense of purpose to go straight on to govern regions the size of European countries pretty much singlehandedly.

Paradoxically, too, a system designed to keep the real India at bay nonetheless initially continued to give pupils a thorough grounding in Indian civilization. The curriculum at Fort William College naturally featured Greek, Latin, European modern languages, English law, natural history, botany, chemistry and astronomy. But despite Wellesley's horror at the 'depravity of the people of India' he nonetheless insisted its special emphasis was on Oriental languages and culture. Though boys would have made a start on these at Haileybury, it was in Calcutta that they were expected to get to grips with Arabic, Persian, Sanskrit, Hindi, Bengali, Telugu, Mahrathi, Kannada, Tamil, Islamic law, Hindu law and 'the history and antiquities of Hindoostan and the Deccan'. The college was the forcing-house of Britain's imperial mission, yet it became the leading centre of Oriental scholarship in the world, publishing hundreds of works in Oriental languages and amassing the world's finest Oriental library. To Wellesley, there was no contradiction. The core strategy underpinning this emphasis on Orientalism was very different from the free-thinking intellectual curiosity and moral relativism that had inspired children of the Enlightenment like Warren Hastings and Sir William Jones. Wellesley's patronage of Oriental studies was rooted in its utility to the imperial project. Its purpose was to ensure that the new generation of Indian judges, administrators and diplomats could avoid the corrupt clutches of all those *dubashes* and *banians, pundits* and *maulvis.* Master the language and you could dispense with malign influences.

Regardless of Wellesley's original motives, the college's enthusiastic pursuit of Oriental studies must have acted for a while as a positive force, exposing future imperial agents to Indian culture and, just as significantly, to first-class Indian teachers. William Fraser, for example, was a graduate of Fort William College who may have emerged with a sense of his own imperial destiny, but clearly had none of Wellesley's contempt for the natives.

But almost as soon as the college was founded, influential thinkers began aggressively to question the basis of Orientalism, and the wider predisposition towards respect and tolerance that it tended to encourage. What is the point, some began to ask, of devoting such energy to Indian studies when English civilization is manifestly superior? Pursuing this argument to its logical conclusion, these liberals and utilitarians then asserted that Britain's moral duty was to promote progress in India, maximizing the happiness of its subjects. This could only be achieved if Britain encouraged India to turn its back on its past and its values. They argued that a new westernized Indian elite should be nurtured who would boldly embrace the task ahead beyond Year Zero. Together, this fraternity of like-minded pioneers, Indian and British, would fashion a new society, cementing the imperial bond between mother-country and dominion.

Simultaneously, another equally progressive and influential group began to mount a similarly coherent and enticing case. Since, they maintained, Indian religions were so self-evidently misguided, sinful and corrupting, was it not Britain's duty to prepare the ground for the conversion of India to the one true faith of Christianity? To do so, argued the evangelicals, one must confront rather than condone Hinduism's barbarous and idolatrous practices. Preaching the Truth and denigrating Error should therefore go hand in hand. With millions upon millions of Indian souls, both those alive and countless generations as yet unborn, the stakes could not be greater. Surely this must have been the higher purpose of Providence in granting Britain her stewardship over India in the first place? Not to embark on this great project would be a grotesque neglect of India's best interests.

Both the utilitarians and the evangelicals mounted visionary cases with great energy and zeal. Both reached their point of view out of what they saw as commitment to India and to progress. Both were to achieve a measure of success. But of course both utterly ignored the real sensibilities and convictions of India.

The Company's hold over India had been fragile enough when a few thousand members of a self-regarding master race ruled millions of Indians while respecting and safeguarding the subcontinent's customs and values. But a master race that was convinced it knew far better than India what was best for it, and that what India needed was to overthrow not only its institutions but its core beliefs and culture, was a slow-cooking recipe for disaster.

CHAPTER NINE

BROWN ENGLISHMEN

It's the first day of the new school year at La Martiniere in Calcutta, the city's oldest and arguably finest school. Forty-five twelve-year-olds are being given a pep talk by their new form teacher, Mrs Indu Gandhi. 'You are at an age where you have to be independent,' she says firmly. 'You are big boys now and I always want to see good and neat work, evidence of a clean and tidy approach.' She asks the class whether they like reading. Every hand shoots up. 'That's good.' she nods. 'I had a student once who wasn't keen on reading. He found it a big bore. And when the exams came, he only got 45 per cent'. Literature primers are handed round the class. This term there's some Wordsworth, Kipling, Tennyson's 'The Charge of the Light Brigade' and an account of the death of Nelson. Though most of these boys have probably never seen 'a host of golden daffodils', they are to tackle Wordsworth's poem first.

The principal, Paul Flynn, later says that 'you have to move with the times'. So in recent years they have held the occasional Bengali cultural evening and now boast an eastern music band as well as their renowned string

A FIRST-CLASS ENGLISH EDUCATION — TWELVE-YEAR-OLD AMAN BAWEJA STARTS THE NEW SCHOOL YEAR AT LA MARTINIERE SCHOOL IN CALCUTTA.

orchestra and a pipes and drums corps. Until a few years ago, boys could be punished for talking in Indian languages in the playground, let alone the classroom. Now Mr Flynn says he has to encourage English over Indian languages 'in a more roundabout way'. The boys choose to study Hindi or Bengali as a second language. Mr Flynn even says they might one day introduce Sanskrit, though he doubts there will be much call for it, despite the vast majority of the school's 1,800 boys being Hindu. Mr Flynn himself is a Christian, the great-grandson of an orphan given the name and taken under the wing of a Protestant Irish pastor.

La Martiniere, too, naturally retains the Christian character and values of a Victorian English public school, which of course it emphatically still is. Its august nineteenth-century surroundings – the soaring Ionic columns of its portico, the Round Chapel hung with gilt-lettered plaques honouring those boys judged 'Best All-Rounder', the domed library impressively stocked with classics – do not seem any kind of anachronism. Instead, they continue to embody the contemporary values of the school. La Martiniere's pupils compete, seemingly with genuine enthusiasm unsullied by metropolitan or adolescent cynicism, for inter-house competitions in boxing, debating, cricket, elocution and 'smartest turnout'.

The houses, needless to say, commemorate giants of the Company Raj, with not an Indian saluted among them. Hastings House currently reigns supreme. That does not diminish the loyalty expressed by boys for the other houses. The captain of Charnock House (named after Job Charnock, Calcutta's seventeenth-century founder) claims in the school magazine that 'our house has instilled in us those qualities that truly make boys into men'. The head of Martin House, honouring Claude Martin, notes Martinians 'have never been short of sporting spirit no matter what the outcome'. Meanwhile, Macaulay boys, like the great man of English letters himself, 'stand out... for our attitude', accepting reward gracefully before moving on to new challenges.

Of course, for all these claims to separate identity, the essential ethos of each house is identical. This is deeply ironic, since the opposite is true of those after whom they are named. Just one generation separates Claude Martin and Thomas Babington Macaulay, the first the school's founder and benefactor, the second the school's real guiding spirit. It is no exaggeration to say that, for better or worse, the world might look totally different today if British India – and La Martiniere – had chosen the path advocated by Claude Martin rather than that advocated by Macaulay.

These boys know they are masters of the universe. By the time they leave La Martiniere they are armed with a Protestant work ethic, a top-class western liberal arts education, and the manners and effortless self-confidence of the well-rounded Victorian gentleman. In today's globalized economy, dominated by Anglo-Saxon civilization, these remain the most priceless commodities on the world people-market. Their parents will try to marshal the means to send their sons on to American colleges. Once they are clutching MBAs, the world will truly be their oyster. Many will leave India for good. Few will regret having studied more English than Indian poetry.

The principal readily acknowledges that there is a seismic gulf between the values and prospects of La Martiniere boys and those of the rest of the city and country. The English-speaking elite inhabit an entirely different world to the still frequently illiterate masses. With both pride and an edge of concern, Mr Flynn puts his finger on the culture gap that still affects India, more than fifty years after Independence: his boys, he says, 'speak the King's English and stick their noses in the air'. Without knowing it, he was virtually paraphrasing Macaulay's great vision, 170 years earlier, that Britain should create 'a class of persons, Indian in blood and colour, but English in taste, in opinions, in morals and in intellect'.

They came to be known as Brown Englishmen. They were the result of nothing less than a cultural revolution.

As we saw in Chapter 5, General Claude Martin, the open-minded, loose-living White Moghul based in Lucknow, died in 1800 leaving substantial sums in his will to benefit 'the children… of India' via the establishment of schools in Calcutta and Lucknow. In Calcutta, the authorities spent so much time arguing about the character of the maverick benefactor and trying to nuance his intentions into an acceptable form that La Martiniere College did not open for another thirty-six years. In essence, it took them all that time to get hold of Martin's cash without signing up to his tolerant, multicultural vision.

Martin's will, though a vague and rambling tract, had explicitly instructed that children should receive instruction in both Persian and English and should be taught by Christian priests and Muslim mullahs. The only indication that the schools should have any kind of Christian character was one request in the will that its pupils should attend an annual sermon. Not that there was any question in the minds of Calcutta's squabbling Christian denominations but that the school must be Christian. The only issue was according to whose rites. Search the will, and there were precious few clues. The Anglican Bishop of Calcutta complained that the will embodied 'the wildest modern theories of a religious education, repudiating the church altogether, and but just admitting Christianity as its basis'. What, he continued, could you expect when 'General Martin was an immoral man' whose 'adherence to the Christian faith was so slight as to be scarcely discernible' and who was notorious for 'his entertaining, as should appear, four or five wives, whom he called "girls" after the manner of Mussulmans'?

Remarkably enough, agreement was eventually reached that the school should eschew sectarianism, the Established Church being in a weak position to insist Martin had been devoted to the Church of England. So La Martiniere welcomed Roman Catholics alongside

Anglicans, together with members of the Scottish Kirk and the Armenian and Greek Orthodox Churches. But to the relief of all these sects, and almost certainly in defiance of the benefactor's wishes, the lawyers ensured that Martin's gift to 'the children of India' should be exclusively Christian, its boys all European or Anglo-Indian. No one else was admitted until 1935. Certainly not Bengalis, of whom Macaulay once sweepingly commented: 'What the horns are to the buffalo, what the paw is to the tiger, what the sting is to the bee… deceit is to the Bengalee. Large promises, smooth excuses, elaborate tissues of circumstantial falsehood, chicanery, perjury, forgery, are the weapons, offensive and defensive, of the people of the Lower Ganges.' One wonders whether members of today's Macaulay House know he said that.

The thirty-six-year story of La Martiniere's establishment is a near perfect microcosm of the cultural revolution that transformed British India over the same period. In 1800, Europeans were still going native as White Moghuls or soaking up Indian culture and languages with wide-eyed enthusiasm as Orientalists. By 1836, native lifestyles were generally considered utterly degenerate while the totality of Indian knowledge and culture was officially dubbed worthless, even evil. Indians did have a bright future ahead of them – but only by setting their sights on becoming Brown Englishmen.

One reason for the big change was that British India, like the mother-country, was turning increasingly to religion. In matters of faith, the typical eighteenth-century gentleman had been a deist or agnostic, a late child of the Enlightenment living his life as much by Voltaire as the Bible. Now he was far more likely to share the evangelical fervour of London's influential Clapham Sect, a group of Anglican members of the ruling class based just south of the river. The Claphamites were intent on launching a moral crusade within and beyond the Church of England to match and rival the vibrant new appeal of Methodism, which had finally severed its links with the Established Church in 1795. Although an important part of the evangelical message was sobriety and moral rearmament back home, India was always high on their agenda.

The most prominent evangelical champion was William Wilberforce, the tireless social campaigner who had fought long, hard and successfully against the slave trade. To Wilberforce, the conversion of India was an even nobler goal. He pronounced it 'the greatest of all causes, for I really place it before Abolition'. This conviction was partly the result of a simple calculation. The battle for Indian souls affected 'the temporal and eternal happiness of millions; literally millions on millions yet unborn'. But to Wilberforce and other evangelicals, the imperative of spreading the Protestant message to India was as much about Christian and national duty (the moral improvement it brought to the messengers) as about results (a simple reckoning of saved souls).

This modern perspective on Britain's imperial, religious and moral purpose in India was utterly at odds with the limited, commercial and pragmatic outlook traditional within

THE PORTICO OF THE
ROUND CHAPEL AT LA
MARTINIERE SCHOOL,
WHOSE CURRICULUM AND
CHARACTER REMAINS
AS ENGLISH AS
ITS ARCHITECTURE.

the Company. Under the influence of widespread religious revival, Britain's Protestant character became integral to its national and imperial identity. As Claudius Buchanan, an evangelical now influentially placed as chaplain to the East India Company, put it, 'Great Britain unquestionably holds the place now which Rome formerly held, in regard to the power and means of promoting Christian knowledge.' Britain, in other words, truly was God's country, saved by Providence from the 'general wreck of nations' for His purpose. Lawrence James neatly characterizes this outlook: 'Enlightened Protestantism was the essential ingredient in Britain's greatness; it provided the cement which held the nation together and released the genius and industry of its people. It was the partner of all human progress. According to the Evangelical vision, the conversion of India would bring unlimited benefits, for it would liberate the Indian mind and make it receptive to all the fruits of human reason.'

For many years, the message from Clapham was firmly resisted by Calcutta and most of Leadenhall Street. The Company had always prohibited missionary activity in British India, rightly fearing it would antagonize Indians and make its own job unnecessarily difficult and dangerous. Indeed, the Company had always partly attributed its success, in comparison to the French or the Portuguese, to its lack of religious zealotry. Under Hastings, and for a surprisingly long time thereafter, the Company considered it a core responsibility for senior officials to attend Hindu or Muslim ceremonies, act as temple trustees, administer the collection of Hindu pilgrims' tithes, and lend ceremonial guards to add further lustre and spectacle to important festivals. All of this, of course, outraged the evangelicals, confirming the Company's apparent godlessness. When in 1793 the Company's Charter came up for renewal in Parliament, as it routinely did every twenty years, the pragmatists and the Orientalists successfully defeated Wilberforce and a strong evangelical challenge. But by 1813 the evangelical tide would prove irresistible.

What happened on 2 July 1806 at Vellore, a garrison city 100 miles inland from Madras, should have sounded alarm bells all over India and drowned out the continuing evangelical clamour. In what proved to be a small-scale dummy-run of the Indian Mutiny fifty years later, three battalions of sepoys rose up in the middle of the night and murdered over a hundred British officers and men as they slept. The mutineers had been distraught at a new set of crass orders from their commanding officer, who was convinced his men would look smarter if they shaved off their beards, removed their caste marks and earrings and all wore a new model of turban with a leather cockade. Hindu and Muslim sepoys were united in horror at these multiple offences to their religious sensibilities. When they complained, two NCOs were singled out for exemplary punishment and given 900 lashes. No doubt the British officers were convinced they had satisfactorily dealt with what they considered a simple breach of discipline. The night uprising will have persuaded those who survived

MISSIONARIES LIKE THE BAPTIST PREACHER WILLIAM WARD USED THE DANISH STATION AT SERAMPORE NEAR CALCUTTA TO EVADE THE COMPANY'S BAN.

just how serious the religious insult really was. Worse, it quickly became apparent that rumours were flying around among the sepoys that the new uniform was simply a prelude to forcible conversion to Christianity.

If such fears could spread when the Company vigorously fended off all missionary activity, the consequences of making the subcontinent a free-for-all, in which pastors and preachers could set up shop in every marketplace, appalled most old India hands. For all their differences, the veterans Warren Hastings and Richard Wellesley joined forces in Parliament to try to stem the evangelical tide. Thomas Twining, a leading Company shareholder, presciently and succinctly put the case 'Against Missionaries' in a pamphlet of 1807 in which he expressed 'extreme apprehension of the fatal consequences to ourselves, from any interference in their religious opinions':

> I will venture to say, that there is not, in the world, a people more jealous and tenacious of their religious opinions and ceremonies, than the native inhabitants of the East. Sir, the people of India are not a political, but a religious people. In this respect, they differ, I fear, from the inhabitants of this country. *They* think as much of their Religion, as *we* of our Constitution. *They* venerate their Shastah [Hindu sacred writings] and Koran, with as much enthusiasm as *we* our Magna Carta... If ever the fatal day shall arrive, when religious innovation shall set her foot in that country, indignation will spread from one end of Hindostan to the other; and the arms of fifty million people will drive us from that portion of the globe, with as much ease as the sand of the desert is scattered by the wind.

Such mundane concerns could not deter the soldiers of Christ. Wilberforce brilliantly remobilized the wide coalition who had risen up in popular outrage against slavery to this new, greater cause. When the matter came before Parliament in 1813, Wilberforce could brandish no fewer than half a million signatures in support of missionaries, contained in 837 petitions raised around the country. Both the petitions and the debate chose to highlight the Evil of Hinduism alongside the Good News. Petitioners, for example, spoke 'as men, as Britons, and as Christians' in regarding 'with anguish and with horror, the moral depression and religious ignorance of very many millions of immortal beings, who people the plains of India, subject to British power... Their "hearts are pained" at the fearful penances, licentious rites, female degradation, human sacrifices, and horrible infanticide, which there prevail.' In Parliament, Wilberforce put the case with brutal simplicity: 'Our religion is sublime, pure and beneficent. Theirs is mean, licentious and cruel.' Warming to his task, he concluded the Hindu gods were 'absolute monsters of lust, injustice, wickedness and cruelty. In short, their religion is one grand abomination.'

The House agreed, and from 1813 missionaries of all Christian denominations were permitted into India, so long as they held a licence from the Company or, if the application was rejected, on appeal from the Board of Control. When the matter came up again in 1833, the need for a licence was dropped. The evangelicals now had what they had always wanted: a free marketplace for souls.

Though many evangelicals had predicted the wholesale conversion of India to Christianity, missionaries were to find Indians almost totally resistant to Christian salvation. The Wesleyan Elijah Hoole admitted in 1844 that, after thirty years' evangelism, he and his Wesleyan brothers had mustered 342 full conversions and no more than 4,000 Indian congregants in the whole of India. The Anglican Church Missionary Society, a far larger organization, claimed only 1,639 communicants, the vast majority Untouchables whose lot under the Hindu caste system was inescapably wretched.

It was this failure that above all tempered evangelical zeal. But prudence, theology, respect and racism also played their part. Most Anglicans advocated a cautious approach, with education and example considered a stepping-stone to future conversion. Theological debate focused on whether the Hindu could, as historian Chris Bayly puts it, make 'a quantum leap to Grace through an intuitive grasp of the meaning of the Gospel', or whether 'Man could only come to Christ through the exercise of an awakened Reason'. In other words, the crux of the matter was whether Indians were, or were not, too primitive to receive the Gospels. Most thought they were. On the other hand, some churchmen reached India to preach enlightenment and ended up receiving it. Some even came to adopt almost Orientalist enthusiasm for Hindu learning, once they had met real Hindu scholars and holy men and attempted to penetrate Hinduism's spiritual heart, heavily disguised as it was by the horrors of idolatry, superstition and ritual. There were, however, many who discouraged enthusiastic evangelism for entirely different reasons. To them the Church of England was a national church. They did not relish the future prospect of sharing pews with Indians, let alone confront the greater risk, which would come with mass conversion, that their sons and daughters might take one up the aisle. To their mind, there were far too many half-castes already.

So for all these reasons, the Great Crusade never really happened as those fired with the project had hoped in 1813. The Anglicans decided their priority was to recreate the Church of England in India, complete with a cathedral in Calcutta, and the import of what Lord Valentia hoped would be 'the splendour of episcopal worship… in the highest degree our Church allows'. Rather than evangelize directly, this would impress the 'natives… accustomed to ceremonial pomp'. Gradually, the theory went, sung evensong and bishops' mitres would win them round. In the meantime, the Church should concentrate on the uphill task of getting the British in India, a notoriously irreligious set, into their pews.

Moreover, there was plenty of inter-denominational rivalry to preoccupy everyone. For years, for example, Calcutta's bishop protested that the Scotch Kirk should not be permitted a spire, these somehow being an Anglican prerogative. But the Kirk Session held firm and built St Andrew's Church with the tallest spire in Calcutta, topping it off with a cockerel on a weather-vane, set there, so it was said, to crow on all other sects.

Bickering priests and rival temples were aspects of religious life with which most Indians would have been entirely familiar and comfortable. The problem was that religious and secular Britons alike were now far from content to turn in on themselves and leave India to its age-old ways. At the end of the eighteenth century, Hastings and Burke had disagreed about almost everything. But they had shared a deep-rooted conservative respect for tradition; one that liberals now came to believe was a misplaced fetish. In the first decades of the nineteenth century, energetic and high-minded reform would transform almost every aspect of Indian society. Utilitarianism became the near universal creed. India would have Progress, whether she wanted it or not. Most of traditional, conservative India was fairly sure it did not.

The utilitarian bible was James Mill's six-volume *History of British India*, published in 1818. In its way it had just as much influence on British policymakers as the gospels. Reading it today, mindful of the ignorance, half-truth, prejudice and national glorification that contributed to the most potent and murderous ideologies of the twentieth century, it is rather difficult to view Mill's tract as progressive. Mill was an impoverished journalist with a philosophical bent who decided to demolish the claims of Sir William Jones and the other Orientalists about Indian civilization. Mill's tactic was to turn his ignorance to his advantage. Without ever having been to India, acquired any Indian languages or conducted any research into any Oriental subject, Mill collated his massive tome from the simple premise that western civilization was unique while Indian barbarism was generic. It was unfortunate that the book was a best-seller, in part because it was the only general history of British India available, thus serving a large market of readers who actually took up the book out of curiosity or enthusiasm for the subject.

One or two examples will suffice to get a sense of Mill's general tone. No society has 'drawn a more gross and disgusting picture of the universe than what is presented in the writings of the Hindus'. 'Our ancestors… though rough, were sincere, but, under the… exterior of the Hindu, lies a general disposition to deceit and perfidy.' Meanwhile, Muslims innately possess 'the same insincerity and perfidy; the same indifference to the feeling of others, the same prostitution and venality'. And so, for page after prejudiced page, the general-izations accumulate, each with a welter of memorable adjectives. Indians are 'indolent', 'slothful' and yet 'avaricious'. They have 'a weak and timid mind' but a 'cunning and deceitful temper'. They are 'a rude people' and much resemble the Chinese. Both races are tainted with 'the vices of insincerity', are 'dissembling, treacherous, mendacious... cowardly and unfeeling... Both are in a physical sense, disgustingly unclean in their persons and houses.'

It is a mark of how comprehensively British thinking was conquered by this supposedly 'liberal' approach that far from rebutting Mill's views, the East India Company in London coveted his expertise and offered him a job. With a handy salary and undemanding duties, Mill was able to turn most of his attentions towards philosophy and economics, subjects that interested him far more than India. Meanwhile, the pupils at Haileybury were prescribed Mill's volumes as a set text.

Sixteen years later Thomas Babington Macaulay, a man steeped in Mill and utilitarianism to his very core, disembarked in India. Within months of his arrival in 1834 he had published his famous 'Minute on Indian Education', frequently dubbed the most influential text in Indian cultural history, and one which still excites fierce, often unpredictable, debate 170 years later.

Everyone agrees that Macaulay rivals Sir William Jones in brilliance and output. He was to channel his genius down similar avenues but in an entirely opposite direction. His mother was a Quaker from Bristol, his father a tenacious evangelical from the Hebrides who had crusaded against slavery and had served for a time as the Governor of Sierra Leone. Young Thomas, the eldest of their nine children, had written a compendium of universal history and a lengthy romantic narrative poem (in the style of Sir Walter Scott) by the time he was nine years old. So no one was much surprised that by the time he was thirty he was renowned as a brilliant don, a penetrating essayist, a prolific poet, a supple barrister, a talented civil servant and, most recently, the brightest of young reformist MPs with an instinctive flair for parliamentary oratory that older members said reminded them of Burke.

Bright, dynamic utilitarians naturally gravitated towards Indian affairs because the subcontinent was the world's finest crucible for social experimentation. From the start, Macaulay's shining vision was for Britain to lead a servile and degraded people towards a promised land in which reason and morality, both western monopolies, would flourish. Speaking in the 1833 Parliamentary debate on the renewal of the Charter, he asked a rapt House to try to imagine 'the proudest day in English history':

To have found a great people sunk in the lowest depths of slavery and superstition, to have so ruled them as to have made them desirous and capable of all the privileges of citizens, would indeed be a title to glory all our own... there are triumphs which are followed by no reverse. There is an empire exempt from all natural causes of decay. Those triumphs are the pacific triumphs of reason over barbarism; that empire *is the imperishable empire of our arts and our morals, our literature and our laws.* [author's italics]

This then was precisely the reverse vision to Sir William Jones. The great Orientalist had concluded that India needed no lessons from the West in civilization. Macaulay thought civilization existed only in Europe but that it could and must be disseminated to India, which, after a suitable period of westernization, might be ready for something approaching self-rule. One hundred years later, when India still had apparently not yet achieved this state of grace, Mahatma Gandhi was asked on a visit to Britain what he thought of western civilization. He famously replied, 'I think it would be a good idea.'

Visions came easier to Macaulay than reality. When he was offered a post in Calcutta on India's new Supreme Council, he viewed it as an irksome move from Westminster. Nevertheless, he felt impelled to accept because the job offered 10,000 a year, promising him the financial security that was indispensable to any aspiring nineteenth-century politician. Unlike Jones, who went in similar circumstances, repeatedly extended his stay and would die in India, Macaulay headed home with his cash at the earliest possible moment. In the meantime, although he had an open and hungry mind about almost everything else, Macaulay remained remarkably unstirred by India. He made no efforts to learn any Indian languages or study its antiquities. Instead, throughout the Indian years he described as his 'exile', Macaulay buried himself in the consoling comforts of the classics. By the time he returned to Britain he had virtually completed his epic, historical ballad series *The Lays of Ancient Rome.* Not that he could be accused of skiving off the day job.

Macaulay was plunged almost immediately into the great debate between the Orientalists and the Anglicists as to the best method for transmitting knowledge in India. At one level, India's Governor-General, Lord William Bentinck, was simply asking Macaulay to sit on a divided committee and adjudicate between rival claims for a small portion of state funds set aside in the 1813 Charter for education. But everyone recognized that this was a cultural watershed, in which the merit of oriental and western scholarship was being determined once and for all. In his Minute on Indian Education, Macaulay surprised no one in rejecting Sanskrit and Arabic and championing the cause of English. What was astonishing was the tone and intensity of his verdict. Macaulay claimed that he had not met one Orientalist 'who could deny that a single shelf of a good European library was worth the whole native literature of India and Arabia'. Moreover, 'It is, I believe, no exaggeration to say, that all the historical information which has been collected from all the books written in the Sanscrit language is less valuable than what may be found in the most paltry abridgments used at preparatory schools in England.'

Jones the relativist had found wisdom in Indian custom, folklore and allegory, and underlying truth in Indian philosophy, poetry and scripture. Macaulay the rationalist looked only for scientific truth and derided the rest as utter nonsense. His key assertion was to question:

[whether] when we can teach European science, we shall teach systems which, by universal confession, whenever they differ from those of Europe, differ for the worse; and... when we can patronize sound Philosophy and true History, we shall countenance, at the public expense, medical doctrines, which would disgrace an English farrier, Astronomy, which would move laughter in girls at an English boarding school, History, abounding with kings thirty feet high, and reigns thirty thousand years long, and Geography, made up of seas of treacle and seas of butter.'

THOMAS BABINGTON MACAULAY'S CHAMPIONING OF ENGLISH DEALT A FATAL BLOW TO THE ORIENTALISTS AND SEALED THE CULTURAL TRIUMPH OF THE WEST.

With ruthless logic, Macaulay pressed home his case:

What we spend on the Arabic and Sanscrit colleges is not merely a dead loss to the cause of truth; it is bounty-money paid to raise up champions of error. It goes to form a nest, not merely of helpless place-hunters, but of bigots prompted alike by passion and by interest to raise a cry against every useful scheme of education... We are a Board for wasting public money, for printing books which are of less value than the paper on which they are printed was while it was blank; for giving artificial encouragement to absurd history, absurd metaphysics, absurd physics, absurd theology; for raising up a breed of scholars who find their scholarship an encumbrance and a blemish, who live on the public while they are receiving their education, and whose education is so utterly useless to them that when they have received it they must either starve or live on the public all the rest of their lives. Entertaining these opinions, I am naturally desirous to decline all share in the responsibility of a body, which unless it alters its whole mode of proceeding, I must consider not merely as useless, but as positively noxious.

As you read this orotund peroration, you can almost see him putting down his pen with immense satisfaction and granting himself the reward of a welcome hour or two with Livy.

The Minute served its purpose. Bentinck switched all government support for education into English overnight. Oriental scholarship never really recovered. Nor did Sir William Jones's great vision that East and West were culturally linked and of equal worth. From then onwards the brightest Indian and European minds read and thought in English and looked to Europe and America. 'History' now meant western history. 'Civilization' by definition implied western civilization. This, then, far more than Plassey or Sriringapatnam, was the moment that permanently delivered the Triumph of the West. The East, by contrast, was considered by many virtually worthless. According to some sources, Bentinck even hatched a plan to demolish the Taj Mahal and ship its marble to England for sale and re-use. It is said this plan was only shelved at the eleventh hour when the London auction-price for marble suddenly and fortuitously collapsed.

What makes Macaulay's Minute a painful and controversial issue to this day is that many westernized, progressive and secular Indians have come to the brutal conclusion that, for all his insufferable arrogance, Macaulay was right. By the 1830s the world was rushing headlong into the Industrial Revolution, democracy and human rights were beginning to take root in the West, and science was beginning to mount its epic challenge to scripture. Middle-class Indians were also voting with their feet, clamouring to learn English while they spurned official encouragement and financial inducements to absorb themselves in Sanskrit. Of course, in part their appetite for English was a pragmatic calculation of personal advantage and better employment prospects. But an at least equal incentive to learn English was a simple thirst for knowledge. These were precisely the 'class of persons, Indian in blood and colour, but English in taste, in opinions, in morals and in intellect', by whom Macaulay set such store. It may be a bitter pill to swallow, but it is undeniable that Indian nationalism emerged in the nineteenth century from just such a class of people, promoting a secular, liberal agenda which can be directly linked to Macaulay. There is no doubt but that Macaulay would have approved. He had, after all, described this moment of future Indian independence as 'the proudest day in English history'. So in honouring Macaulay, La Martiniere School pays tribute to someone who may have been bigoted and prejudiced, but who also helped India embrace modernity and articulate its identity in one common, and rather useful, tongue.

The great debate was especially pungent because some of the fiercest critics of Sanskrit and advocates of English were Bengali. Calcutta in the early nineteenth century had become the focus for a group of young, liberal Indian intellectuals who have subsequently been collectively honoured as the Bengali Renaissance. They had been inspired, in part by the Orientalists, towards a sense of national pride in India's history and literature. They were enthused, in part by the Utilitarians, with a sense of moral responsibility to reform and modernize society, to question tradition or adapt it rather than blindly follow it. And partly thanks to contact with the more open-minded, non-doctrinaire clergymen and theologians, they had begun to explore underlying monotheistic tendencies within Hinduism, to criticize orthodox practices like *suttee* (widow-burning) and child-marriage, and to prepare the ground for a Hindu Reformation.

The leading figure within this small but highly influential circle was Rammohan Roy, whose family, religious and educational background could not have been more traditional. Roy had been brought up as an orthodox brahmin within a *zamindari* (land-owning gentry) family who had for several generations served the Bengali nawabs. He studied Persian and Arabic at Patna and Sanskrit at Benares, before his family were suddenly evicted from their land and plunged into poverty because they were unable to meet the Company's new fixed land-tax demands. So it was out of financial necessity, but with no likely sympathy for British reformism, that in 1805 Roy had first found himself a minor functionary within the administrative service of the Company. He had quickly found intellectual soul-mates among the Orientalists of Fort William College, mastered English (and later Hebrew and Greek), and was exposed to the latest western science and thought. For the rest of his life, he applied its tools of enquiry, not to reject traditional Hindu society but to campaign to reform it, validating those reforms through resort to long-lost, 'pure' aspects of India's own thought, law and literature.

Bengali education until the early nineteenth century had been unchanged for centuries. Rather as Macaulay would later caricature it, pupils learnt that India sat in an ocean of curd, that the earth was flat and that an eclipse of the moon occurred when it was

eaten by the demon Rahu. Traditional Hindus prohibited sea-travel for fear of caste contamination. Women were kept in purdah and rarely permitted an education. Many children were given away in marriage when they were scarcely old enough to walk. Widow remarriage was quite out of the question, condemning the women, many of whom were still children, to a lifetime of poverty and hopelessness. By contrast, the act of suttee was said to turn those widows who chose to throw themselves on to their husbands' funeral pyres into goddesses. Between 1815 and 1817, 983 women chose suttee, or were encouraged into choosing it, in Calcutta alone. This was also a society in which slavery was common and child human sacrifice far from rare. Calcutta's favourite goddess Kali was normally satisfied, as she is to this day, by daily animal sacrifices. But occasionally, some people thought, the spine-chilling, three-eyed wife of Siva the Destroyer, who wears a necklace of skulls and permanently sticks her tongue out in demand for blood, could be propitiated only with human blood. It was said that in the early nineteenth century a child a week was secretly offered to the goddess in Calcutta. On other occasions it was the custom to feed children to the sharks at the mouth of the Ganges.

In the Hastings era, it had been a core article of faith to the Company that it had no right or responsibility to interfere with religious custom or practice. In the early nineteenth century, utilitarians and reform-minded Bengalis were both convinced that to do so was their moral duty. Although he was a notable Sanskritist, Rammohan Roy became convinced that this modernization could come only with a wholesale shift to English education. A full twenty years before Macaulay settled the issue, Roy began petitioning against government support for Sanskrit and became involved in the establishment of Hindu College, a joint British–Bengali project founded in 1817 whose students were taught mechanics and astronomy, Voltaire and Shakespeare as well as Oriental studies. Later, when Madhususan Gupta, the first Bengali western medical student, dissected a human body as part of his training at the Medical College of Bengal, he was ostracized by his own community but granted a five-gun salute by the British at Fort William.

From Roy and his circle came a torrent of brilliantly argued and tenaciously pursued campaigns for social and religious reform. There were repeated calls to outlaw suttee and child marriage and to encourage widow remarriage. There was the foundation of the Brahmo Samaj, a religious movement dedicated to a purified Hinduism freed from superstition, opposed to caste distinctions and closer to its monotheistic spiritual roots. Roy lobbied vigorously against press censorship and in favour of constitutional, civil and human rights for Indians, encouraging the Indianization of public services and protesting against the discriminatory justice system where juries differed according to the race of the accused.

THE FIERCEST OF THE GODS, KALI GAVE CALCUTTA ITS NAME AND IS THE CITY'S MOST REVERED, AND FEARED, DEITY.

For all these reasons, Rammohan Roy is often dubbed the 'Father of Modern India' and it is true that as early as 1828 he seemed to envisage that India would one day be free, anticipating Macaulay by forecasting that an enlightened, western-educated Indian middle class was the necessary precursor to emancipation. What is less often pointed out is that Roy was a great admirer of the British and was himself regarded as a dangerous outcast by orthodox society. Of the British, Roy wrote: 'Finding them generally more intelligent, more steady and moderate in their conduct, I gave up my prejudices against them and became inclined in their favour, feeling persuaded that their rule, though a foreign yoke, would lead most speedily and surely to the amelioration of the native inhabitants.'

Indeed, at times Roy's enthusiasm for the foreign yoke seems positively breathless:

> Thanks to the Supreme Disposer of events in this universe, for having unexpectedly delivered this country from the long-continuing tyranny of its former rulers and placed it under the government of the English – a nation who are not only blessed with the enjoyment of civil and national liberty, but also interest themselves in promoting liberty and social happiness... among those nations to which their influence extends.

However, it was precisely those measures 'promoting liberty and social happiness' so applauded by Roy that were increasingly alienating traditional Hindus of all classes. Students at Hindu College were castigated as beef-eating, alcohol-drinking, leather-shoe-wearing atheists. Members of the Brahmo Samaj were cornered by mobs who smeared them with treacle and set swarms of wasps at them. It was hardly surprising that orthodox Hindus saw little difference between a tiny minority of Bengali intellectuals offering a liberal critique of Hinduism and tub-thumping missionaries who were now losing few opportunities to rubbish Indian religions with every insult they could muster. As Thomas Twining had predicted in his plea to maintain the ban on missionaries, Indian society would tolerate any amount of interference in its politics and government, but would become outraged at interference in its religion.

Of course, since religion permeated every aspect of life in India, almost every change could be seen to have religious implications. And from the late 1820s onwards, the pace of this change was relentless. When the Board of Control appointed Lord William Bentinck to the Governor-Generalship in 1828, they had told him, 'We have a great moral duty to perform in India.' They had hardly needed to remind him. Before he sailed for Calcutta, Bentinck went to see his guru, James Mill: 'I am going to British India, but I shall not be Governor-General. It is you that will be Governor-General,' he is said to have told the utilitarian philosopher and famous Indian 'historian'.

As soon as Bentinck landed in India, he set to work. His first initiative was to take up the long-standing cause of both Rammohan Roy and the missionaries and outlaw suttee. In doing so, Bentinck was careful to point out he was acting 'as a legislator for the Hindus, and as I believe many enlightened Hindus feel and think'. But the traditionalists were horrified that alien law-makers were legislating against what they saw as a saintly and time-honoured practice. What business, they argued, was it of the British to intervene against a voluntary and heroic action that automatically secured the deification of the woman involved? The vociferous protests all failed. A carefully argued appeal to the Privy Council in London was also dismissed. A few years later a group of brahmin priests complained to the famous British General Sir Charles Napier that suttee was their national custom. 'My nation also has a custom,' Napier supposedly replied. 'When men burn women alive, we hang them... Let us all act according to national customs.'

Over the next three decades of rapid change, traditional society was similarly affronted by reform after reform, each of them high-minded and well-meaning on the part of the zealous modernizers. Forty thousand Britons and perhaps an equal number of members of the new English-educated Indian middle classes approved wholeheartedly of the changes. That left a mere 150 million Indians who were likely to be wary, or at least bewildered, by the pace of change.

Traditional patriarchal society, for example, was traumatized by the first programmes to promote female education and to improve the wretched lot of widows. Efforts to break the solid and ancient taboo against widow remarriage seemed hopeless until 1,000-rupee cash inducements were offered to any man prepared to marry a widow, even if she was ten years old. Despite the financial incentives, the campaign largely failed. There was similar resistance to changes to the property laws to end the prohibition on converts to Christianity inheriting homes and possessions. Surely, some worried, not for the first or last time, these dramatic assaults on the very timeless fabric of society must be a prelude to all India's enforced conversion to Christianity?

In the 1830s the first steam-boats began to ply the Ganges between Calcutta and Allahabad, 800 miles away. At the same time, construction began on the first major tarmac road, the Grand Trunk Road, which would eventually stretch all the way from Calcutta to Delhi. Later, in the 1850s, the first railways began to operate from Bombay and Calcutta. India's vast distances were being conquered for the first time, a stupendous feat of engineering which in a very real sense gave India its first opportunity to become one country. Yet both Europeans and Indians appreciated there was something truly revolutionary about throwing people of all religions and castes together in a railway compartment, or encouraging them to jostle side-by-side on-board a ship's deck. As Charles Trevelyan, one of the most enthusiastic Company modernizers, told a Commons Committee in 1853,

Ram Mohun Roy.

'Railways will… be the great destroyer of caste, and the greatest missionary of all.' Perhaps that explains why, at the height of the Indian Mutiny four years later, enraged rebels took to tearing up railway lines and demolishing engine sheds with their bare hands.

India's grumbles and complaints were scarcely heard, let alone heeded, by the British. Insulated from real Indian feelings by a cocoon of self-righteousness and imperial mission, the new guardians of British India operated with an entirely different rule-book to their predecessors. Though they still nominally governed India on behalf of the East India Company, the truth was that in India the Company was now little more than a procedural ruse. Under the 1813 Charter Act, the Company had lost its historic raison d'être, its monopoly on all British commerce in Asia. Profits had been far too low for far too long for them to hold on to their exclusive franchise. In fact, the only slices of the business they managed to retain were the lucrative tea trade from China and the monopoly within India of opium production (which when exported to China largely paid for the tea). In other respects, the East India Company was now a legal anomaly rather than a commercial entity. Effectively, it only survived as a shelf company through which HMG, preferring still to govern at one step removed, pursued its interests.

In the post-Napoleonic brave new world, Great Britain was repositioning itself as top nation, flying the banner of free trade every bit as vigorously as its heady companions, Empire and Protestantism. But what free trade meant in the Indian context was effectively the moral right to drive Indian handicraft production out of business. A century earlier India had been one of the world's most sophisticated pre-industrial economies. Indeed, exporting its high-quality silk and cotton piece-goods had been the driving-force for the entire Company engagement in the subcontinent. But by the early nineteenth century, the Industrial Revolution in Europe was beginning to transform the entire trading relationship.

On his visit to Britain at the turn of the nineteenth century, Abu Taleb Khan had all but deciphered the writing on the wall. In between the parties and the assignations, the intrepid traveller had taken the opportunity to visit some of the country's new factories and workshops. There alone, Abu Taleb found true wonders that the subcontinent could neither match nor surpass:

> In England, labour is much facilitated by the aid of mechanism; and by its assistance the price of commodities is much reduced: for if, in their great manufactories, they made use of horses, or bullocks, or men, as in other countries, the price of their goods would be enormous… The English are so prejudiced in favour of this science, that they often expend immense sums, and frequently fail two or three times, before they succeed in getting the machinery of any extensive work in order.

RAMMOHAN ROY LED THE BENGAL RENAISSANCE BUT WELCOMED BRITISH RULE AND WAS COMMITTED TO ENGLISH AS A SUPERIOR MEDIUM FOR INDIAN EDUCATION.

THE ARRIVAL OF THE
RAILWAYS IN THE 1850S
SHOCKED INDIA BY
THROWING PEOPLE OF
ALL RELIGIONS AND
CASTES TOGETHER.

Abu Taleb visited iron-foundries, 'the great wheels of which are worked by steam in a very surprising manner'. He pronounced London's hydraulic water supply 'a stupendous work'. And he admitted 'astonishment' when he saw 'a spinning engine' which he goes on to describe in detail to his Indian readers: 'By the turning of one large wheel, a hundred others were put in motion, which spun at the same time some thousand threads, of sufficient fineness to make very good muslin.'

Within fifteen years of Abu Taleb's factory tour, the first British ships were sailing up the Hooghly River into Calcutta carrying cotton textiles made in Lancashire's mills for import into India. For 200 years, India had been the largest exporter of fine textiles in the world. By 1830 it was a net importer of textiles from Britain. By 1850 it was spending £6 million a year on British imports and Bengal's handloom weavers were an endangered species. In effect, Britain had usurped India's position as the workshop of the world, which left India as little more than an enormous market to be flooded with low-cost manufactured goods. Moreover, Indian raw cotton was being exported to Britain to feed Lancashire's mills, from where the finished cloth was shipped all the way back to India. For all their do-gooding, no British Governor-General saw fit to intervene to save India's textile industry. It would take more than a century for India to catch up and then overtake Lancashire again.

In cataloguing the 'defects of the English', Abu Taleb Khan had reached the conclusion that their 'most conspicuous' shortcomings were pride and insolence. He was perceptive enough to realize that these were not just offensive to others, they were a threat to themselves. Just like Louis XVI, who did not face up to the threat of revolution 'till it was too late', the English possessed 'blind confidence, which instead of meeting... danger, and endeavouring to prevent it, waits till the misfortune arrives, and then attempts to remedy it'. Only such blind confidence can explain how the British failed to see the Indian Mutiny coming. As for the attempts to remedy it, they were to respond to an orgy of violence with a blood-bath of retribution. Utilitarianism had supposedly cherished the 'happiness' of the people as its fundamental goal. Like so many ideological convictions pursued in defiance of human feeling, the end result made a mockery of the utopian vision.

AFTERWORD

The great uprising started, seemingly without warning, on 10 May 1857 in Meerut, 30-odd miles from Delhi. Several sepoy regiments of the Bengal army went on the rampage, killing every European man, woman and child they could find, before heading off to Delhi to spread revolt to their comrades. It would be nearly two years before the last embers of rebellion were extinguished.

A century and a half later, the revolt that raged across North India is still a matter of deep controversy. Even what you choose to call it is contentious. The British insisted, as some still do, that it was a mutiny, the product of 'native unreason' distorted by panic, terror and rumour. According to this version, the British fell victim to a spontaneous uprising that spread like wildfire among sepoys who were in the grip of a misplaced and irrational hysteria that a new issue of gun cartridges was greased with pork or beef fat. Meanwhile, today's schoolchildren in India are taught this was the First War of Independence, implying that it amounted to some kind of coherent bid for national liberation. The truth is that it was a major popular rebellion that should neither be diminished as a mutiny nor exalted as a coherent expression of national will. Both definitions fail because there wasn't just one type of rebel or a unifying reason for revolt. Instead, it involved participants from almost every sector of North Indian society, all of whom, for very different reasons, had reached breaking point. There were, as we have seen, countless causes for discontent in India by the mid-nineteenth century. And with hindsight, it is far less surprising that there was a rebellion than that the British in their arrogance did not see it coming.

Warren Hastings had argued passionately that it would be 'wanton tyranny' for the British to do anything more than 'to point the way to rule this people with ease and moderation according to their own ideas, manners and prejudices'. But by the mid-1850s the Hastings vision was long forgotten and, in any case, would have seemed to the Victorian imperialist utterly absurd. By then the British regarded it as axiomatic that their rule was better for native Indians than any other system had ever been or could ever be. Not, of course, that they troubled to ask Indians whether they agreed with this analysis. How on earth could ignorant, infantile Indians be expected to know what was in their best interests?

Lord Dalhousie, the Governor-General of British India on the eve of the revolt, had assiduously pursued the logic of this particular conviction. Since the remaining Indian princely states were so manifestly inferior, he determined to abolish as many as possible 'for the good of the governed'. He conjured up the neatly devised 'Doctrine of Lapse', by which he could annex directly to British India any native state that did not possess a direct male heir on the death of its ruler. This utterly defied Hindu inheritance law, which had for thousands of years allowed a monarch to name the successor he thought most appropriate by the common practice of adopting him as his son. One after the other Satara, Jhansi and Nagpur passed to the British as did, through conquest, the Punjab and Burma. Not since Richard Wellesley had so much territory been acquired so quickly.

In Oudh, where there were heirs aplenty, Dalhousie's new doctrine would not serve his ultimate purpose. Whether from real respect and amity or out of diplomatic courtesy to a legitimate monarch, all Dalhousie's predecessors had made elaborate shows of friendship to the magnificent court of the Kings of Oudh, which had long been utterly loyal to its British allies. For Dalhousie, loyalty was not enough. To him, Oudh seemed irredeemably corrupt, decadent and ill-governed. It would have to go, because 'the British Government would be guilty in the sight of God and man if it were any longer to aid in sustaining by its countenance an administration fraught with suffering to millions'. In February 1856 Dalhousie issued a proclamation ousting King Wajid Ali Shah and annexing the kingdom to British India. His justification speaks volumes: 'With this feeling on my mind and in humble reliance on the blessing of the Almighty (for millions of His creatures will draw freedom and happiness from the change), I approach the execution of this duty gravely and not without solicitude, but calmly and *altogether without doubt*.' Far from being ecstatic at their good fortune, little more than a year later the people of Oudh would rise en masse to become the most fervent and numerous of all the rebels.

The British and the rebels were equally battle-hardened, but the rebellion outdid subcontinental warfare in both its savagery and intimacy. Troops and NCOs cut down their former officers. Household servants who had been working with British families for decades disappeared in the night only to reappear behind rebel lines. Sepoy units and Indian families of all classes were divided, as brothers made different choices over which side to commit to in what was effectively a civil war. Neither side made any distinction between combatants and civilians and used indiscriminate terror and murder as a deliberate tactic. Rage, desperation and a lust for revenge turned men in both camps into beasts. Religious zeal and racial hatred served to dehumanize the enemy so effectively that only opportunity and imagination limited the range of atrocities that were committed.

At Cawnpore (Kanpur), for example, the rebel prince Nana Sahib, an adopted son who had been disinherited from his Maratha throne by Dalhousie's 'Doctrine of Lapse', agreed terms with the British for them to surrender and receive safe passage by river out of the city. Some 600 Europeans, most of them women and children, the bedraggled remnant of a month-long siege, were led peacefully by mutineers towards the Ganges. But as soon as the British boarded the river-boats, they were set upon by musket-fire, grape-shot and artillery. Cavalry-men then rode into the shallow waters and turned on the British with their swords. Eventually, some 200 survivors were brought ashore, whereupon the men were shot and the women and children taken into captivity in the Bibighar, a small house named that way because in happier times a British officer had housed his *bibi* there. Ten days later, with a British relief army pressing towards Cawnpore, Nana Sahib ordered the execution of all the hostages. When the Bibighar's sepoy guards refused to obey this order, local butchers were brought in with their knives from a nearby market. The job took several hours to complete and the women and children were thrown, some still alive, into a well. At the beginning of the siege of Cawnpore there had been around 850 Europeans. Just two survived.

When the British relief force retook Cawnpore, eyewitnesses found the Bibighar pitifully strewn with 'little children's socks and shoes and dresses... all covered with the blood and brains of the innocent'. The British commanding officer, General Neill, ordered that none of this should be cleaned up. Instead, he marched all British troops to the Bibighar on arrival at Cawnpore. The horror had the designed effect. Captain Garnet Wolseley, for example, made the vow that 'most soldiers made there – of vengeance and of having blood for blood, not drop for drop, but barrels and barrels of the filth which flows in these niggers'

OVERLEAF:

AFTER THE MUTINY,

BRITAIN TOOK OVER

DIRECT RULE OF INDIA

FROM THE COMPANY.

THE VICTORIA

MEMORIAL IN

CALCUTTA WAS BUILT

TO RIVAL THE TAJ

MAHAL BUT ENTIRELY

LACKED ITS GRACE.

veins for every drop of blood which marked the floors and walls of that fearful house'. The army's padres even gave religious sanction to Britain's 'avenging angels'. Grotesque revenge attacks fell indiscriminately on the innocent as well as the guilty. The British took to hunting down rebels and giving them a 'Cawnpore dinner', their new term for bayoneting their enemies in the stomach. Captive mutineers were made to lick up bloodied mats before being hanged. Others were deliberately defiled by being coated with pig fat and being force fed pork or beef before being executed. To many British soldiers by this time, all Indians were simply 'niggers'. Even the sepoys who had stayed loyal to the British were considered less than human. As one Lieutenant-Colonel Chardin Johnson put it of the Sikh troops under his own command: 'There is no sympathy between us – we despise niggers, they hate us.'

Whether out of habit or the blackest comedy, the sepoy mutineers sometimes screamed their old battle-cry 'Jai Company Bahadur Ki' (Long Live the Illustrious Company) as they charged their enemy. But in fact the Company scarcely outlived the rebellion itself. As soon as the British regained control of India, the public back home started wondering who to blame. Such a debacle very obviously required a scapegoat. It was highly convenient for the Government to appear to be taking dramatic action by choosing this moment to take over direct rule of India on behalf of the Crown. The East India Company disappeared without trace in 1858, almost entirely unmourned despite its extraordinary 250-year history. The Company Raj was at an end. The British Raj was born. Yet in reality very little changed.

As we have seen, the real revolution had occurred fifty years earlier when the British imperial project took flight in the wake of the Napoleonic Wars and glory and progress began to be prized far more than commerce and good relations. From then onwards, the Company had been an anomaly shorn of its original spirit of enterprise. From then, too, the psychological chasm between Briton and Indian had yawned ever wider. The trauma of the mutiny hardened feelings on both sides, but racism and resentment, disdain and subjection had long perverted the earlier tendencies towards harmony and mutual respect.

Sita Ram Pande signed up for the Company's army in 1812 and spent forty-eight years as a loyal servant of the Raj. In his memoirs he contrasted the attitudes of the British at either end of his long career:

> In those days the sahibs could speak our language much better than they do now, and they mixed more with us… The sahibs often used to give nautches for the regiment, and they attended all the men's games. They also took us with them when they went out hunting, or at least all those of us who wanted to go… Nowadays, they seldom attend nautches because their padre sahibs have told them it is wrong. These padre sahibs have done, and are still doing, many things to estrange the British

officers from the sepoys. When I was a sepoy the captain of my company would have some of the men at his house all day long and he talked with them… I know that many officers nowadays only speak to their men when obliged to do so, and they show that the business is irksome and try to get rid of the sepoys as quickly as possible. One sahib told us that he never knew what to say to us. The sahibs always knew what to say, and how to say it, when I was a young soldier.

There could be no more eloquent illustration of the deterioration in the relationship between the two peoples. At the start of Sita Ram Pande's career, Britons and Indians had still been comrades-in-arms, revelling in each other's company and engaged in a common project. But by 1860 they were clearly a race apart, bound together by habit and unpleasant circumstance which both suffered as best they could.

A century and a half later, both Britain and India are finally shaking off their old identities, influenced so heavily by Empire and its post-colonial aftershocks. The world in the twenty-first century shows some early, encouraging signs of being wary of ideology and dogma, of putting its trust in any rulers who pronounce themselves 'altogether without doubt'. In a smaller world, a global community is a real vision, not just a politician's cliché. Just possibly, this century will jump the rails set for it by the previous two. Old prejudices and fixations fail to flourish in a world of rising living standards, easy communication and self-confident new generations possessing healthy disrespect for their elders. Setbacks and challenges are of course bound to continue. But multiculturalism does seem to be bedding in. For the first time since the eighteenth century, our common humanity seems more significant than all the many ways in which we differ from each other. A better world may be emerging, which respects and values cultural difference and which mixes and interacts to create countless new communities and groupings, based upon choice, not birth or background.

It is all too easy for new trends to be passing fashions. Our age tends to dismiss history and live in what the historian Eric Hobsbawm called 'the permanent present'. Yet the stakes are too high not to recruit history to help ensure that multiculturalism takes root. Reminding ourselves that, though fragile and long neglected, those roots date back over 200 years, might just help the sapling to turn at last into a mighty banyan tree.

SOURCES AND FURTHER READING

GENERAL

Bayly, C.A., *Imperial Meridian: The British Empire and the World 1780–1830* (Longman, London, 1989)

Bayly, C.A. ed., *The Raj: India and the British 1600–1947* (National Portrait Gallery, London, 1990)

Davies, Philip, *Penguin Guide to the Monuments of India* (Volume 2, Viking, London, 1989)

Keay, John, *The Honourable Company: A History of the English East India Company* (Harper Collins, London, 1991)

James, Lawrence, Raj: *The Making and Unmaking of British India* (Little, Brown & co., London, 1997)

Marshall, Peter, *Problems of Empire: Britain and India 1757–1813* (George Allen and Unwin, London, 1968)

ENTRANCE TO THE OLD MISSION CHURCH, CALCUTTA.

Moorhouse, Geoffrey, *India Britannica* (Harvill Press, London, 1983)

Spear, Thomas George Percival, *The Nabobs: A Study of the Social Life of the English in Eighteenth Century India* (Oxford University Press, Oxford, 1963)

Spear, Thomas George Percival, *The Oxford History of Modern India (1740–1947)* (Clarendon Press, Oxford 1965)

1. ROGUE TRADERS AND SPICE GIRLS

Chaudhuri, Nirad C., *Clive of India: A Political and Psychological Essay* (Barrie & Jenkins, London, 1975)

Forster, E.M., ed., *Original Letters from India (1779–1815): Eliza Fay (1817)* (Hogarth, London, 1925)

Ghosh, Durba, *Colonial Companions: Bibis, Begums and Concubines of the British in North India 1760–1830* (Phd dissertation, Berkeley, USA, 2000)

Ghosh, Suresh Chandra, *The Social Condition of the British Community in Bengal 1757–1800* (Leiden, E.J. Brill, 1970)

Gilchrist J. B., *The General East India Guide and Vade Mecum… being a digest of the work of the Late Capt. Williamson* (London, 1825)

Harvey, Robert, Clive, *Life and Death of a British Emperor* (Hodder and Stoughton, London, 1998)

Hyam, Ronald, *Empire and Sexuality: The British Experience* (Manchester University Press, Manchester, 1990)

Ives, E., *A Voyage from England to India in 1754* (printed for Edward and Charles Dilly, London, 1773)

Marshall, Peter, 'Masters and Banians in Eighteenth-Century Calcutta' in *Trade and Conquest: Studies on the rise of British Dominance in India* (Variorum, Aldershot, c1993)

Moorhouse, Geoffrey, *Calcutta* (2nd edition, Phoenix, London, 1998)

Munro, Innes, *A Narrative of the Military Operations on the Coromandel Coast in 1780* (London, 1789)

Nevile, Pran, *Beyond the Veil, Indian Women in the Raj* (Nevile Books, New Delhi, 2000)

Prakash, Om, 'European Commercial Enterprise in Pre-Colonial India' in *New Cambridge History of India II* (Cambridge University Press, Cambridge, 1998)

2. ACCIDENTIAL EMPIRE

Busteed, H E, *Echoes from Old Calcutta: being chiefly reminiscences of the days of Warren Hastings, Francis and Impey* (Thacker, Spink, Calcutta, 1908)

Holwell, John Zephaniah, *A Genuine Narrative of the Deplorable Deaths of the...Black Hole* (London, 1758) reprinted in Macfarlane, Iris *The Black Hole: or, The Makings of a Legend* (Allen & Unwin, London, 1975)

Orme, Robert, *A History of the Military Transactions of the British Nation in Indostan from 1745* (2 Volumes, 1763 & 1778)

3. NABOBS

Edwardes, Michael, *The Nabobs at Home* (Constable, London, 1991)

Edwards-Stuart, Ivor, *The Calcutta of Begum Johnson* (BACSA, London, 1990)

Foote, Samuel, *Plays by Samuel Foote and Arthur Murphy* (Cambridge University Press, Cambridge, 1984)

Ghosh N. N., *Memoirs of Maharaja Nubkissen Bahadur* (Calcutta, 1901)

Spencer, Alfred, ed., *Memoirs of William Hickey* (four volumes, Hurst and Blackett, London, 1913)

OVERLEAF:
THIS OBELISK MARKS
THE SITE OF
THE BREACH
AT SRIRANGAPATNAM
ABOVE THE
KAVERI RIVER.

Holzman James, *The Nabobs in England, a Study of the Returned Anglo Indian 1760–1785* (New York, 1926)

Lawson, Philip and Phillips, Jim, '*Our Execrable Banditti': Perceptions of Nabobs in Mid-Eighteenth Century Britain* in *Albion*, 1988

Macintosh, James, *Travels in Europe, Asia and Africa 1777–81* (London, 1783)

Marshall, Peter, *East India Fortunes – The British in Bengal in the Eighteenth Century* (Oxford, 1976)

Morris, Jan, *Stones of Empire: The Buildings of British India* (Oxford University Press, Oxford, 1983)

4. AN INDIAN LOVE AFFAIR

Bernstein, Jeremy, *Dawning of the Raj: The Life and Trials of Warren Hastings* (Aurum Press, Chicago, 2000)

Cannon, Garland Hampton, *Oriental Jones: A biography of Sir William Jones, 1746–1794* (Asia Publishing House, Bombay & New York, 1964)

Cannon, Garland Hampton, and Brine, Kevin R. ed., *Objects of Enquiry: The Life, Contributions and Influences of Sir William Jones 1746–1794.* Essays by Cannon, Rocher, Kejariwal and Kopf, (New York University Press, New York, 1995)

Feiling, Keith, *Warren Hastings* (Macmillan, London, 1954)

Franklin, Michael J., *Sir William Jones* (University of Wales Press, Cardiff, 1995)

Holwell, John Zephaniah, *Interesting Historical Events Relative to the Provinces of Bengal and the Empire of Indostan … As Also the Mythology and Cosmogony, Fasts and Festivals of the Gentoo's…And A Dissertation on the…Pythagorean Doctrine* (London, 1766)

Kejariwal, O.P., *The Asiatic Society of Bengal and the Discovery of India's Past, 1784–1838* (Oxford University Press, Oxford, 1988)

Marshall, Peter ed., *The British Discovery of Hinduism in the Eighteenth Century* (includes Hastings' Introduction to *Gita*) (Cambridge University Press, Cambridge, 1970)

Murray, Alexander ed., *Sir William Jones, A Commemoration* essay by Thomas Trautmann (Oxford University Press, Oxford, 1998)

Said, Edward W., *Orientalism* (Routledge & Kegan Paul, London, 1978)

5. GOING NATIVE

Archer, Mildred and Falk, Toby, *The Art and Adventures of James and William Fraser 1801–35* (Cassell, London, 1989)

Bayly, C.A., *Empire and Information: Intelligence Gathering and Social Communication in India, 1780–1870* (Cambridge University Press, Cambridge, 1996)

Dalrymple, William, *The White Moghuls: Love, Death and Apostasy in 18th Century India* (Harper Collins, London, 2001)

Dalrymple, William, *City of Djinns: A Year in Delhi* (Harper Collins, London, 1993)

Dalrymple, William, *The Age of Kali* (for sections on Martin and Kirkpatrick) (Harper Collins, London, 1998)

Dalrymple, William, *The White Moghuls* (Sunday Telegraph 20/2/2000)

Llewellyn-Jones, Rosie, *A Very Ingenious Man: Claude Martin in Early Colonial India* (Oxford University Press, Delhi, 1992)

Stuart, Charles "Hindoo"(published anonymously) *Vindication of the Hindoos…The Whole Tending to Evince the EXCELLENCE of the Moral System of the Hindoos and the Danger of Interfering with their Customs or Religion* (London, 1807)

Stuart, Charles "Hindoo" (published anonymously) *The Ladies Monitor Being A Series of Letters First published in Bengal On the Subject of Female Apparel…* (London, 1809)

6. FIRST FUSION

Abu Taleb Khan, *The Travels of Mizra Abu Talib Khan in Asia, Africa and Europe During the Years 1799, 1800, 1801, 1802, 1803,* Written By Himself in the Persian Language – translated by Charles Stewart (London, Longman Hurst Rees and Orme, 1810)

Archer, Mildred, *Early Views of India: The Picturesque Journeys of Thomas and William Danniell 1786–1794: the complete aquatints* (Thames & Hudson, London, 1980)

Edwardes, Michael, *Warren Hastings, King of the Nabobs* (Hart-Davis, London, 1976)

Farrell, Gerry, *Indian Music and the West* (Clarendon Press, Oxford, 1997)

Fisher, Michael, *The First Indian Author in English: Deen Mahomed (1759–1851) in India, Ireland and England* (Oxford University Press, Delhi, 1996)

Head, Raymond, *The Indian Style* (Allen and Unwin, London, 1986)

Mahomet, Sake Dean, *Travels of Dean Mahomet, A Native of Patna in Bengal, through several parts of India, while in the service of the Honourable East India Company* (Cork, 1794)

Mahomet, Sake Dean, *Shampooing, or Benefits Resulting from the Use of the Indian Medicated Vapour Bath* (Brighton, 1822)

Martinelli, Antonio, *India: Yesterday and Today, Thomas Danniell, William Danniell, George Michell* (Swan Hill Press, Shrewsbury, 1998)

Visram, Rozina, *Ayahs, Lascars and Princes: Indians in Britain 1700–1947* (Pluto Press, London, 1986)

Wright, Lawrence, *Clean and Decent: The Fascinating History of the Bathroom and The Water Closet* (Routledge, London, 1960)

7. FIRST AMONG EQUALS

Habib, Irfan, ed., *Confronting Colonialism: Resistance and Modernization under Haidar Ali and Tipu Sultan* (papers presented at Indian History Congress 1999) (Tulika, New Delhi, 1999)

A GRAVE IN THE ABANDONED BRITISH CEMETERY AT SRIRANGAPATNAM.

Oakes, Captain Henry, *An Authentic Narrative of the Treatment of the English Who Were Taken Prisoner…by Tippoo Sahib* (London, 1785)

Sultan, Tipu, *Select letters of Tippoo Sultan* (annotated and translated by William Kirkpatrick) (London, 1811)

8. THE NEW ROME

Butler, Iris, *The Eldest Brother, The Marquess Wellesley, The Duke of Wellington's Eldest Brother* (Hodder and Stoughton, London, 1973)

Carver, Field Marshal, *Lord Wellington and his Brothers* (The First Wellington Lecture, University of Southampton, Southampton, 1989)

Holman, Dennis, *Sikander Sahib: The Life of Colonel James Skinner 1778–1841* (Heinemann, London, 1961)

Teltscher, Kate, *India Inscribed: European and British Writing on India 1600–1800* (Oxford University Press, Delhi, 1995)

Weller, Jac, *Wellington in India* (Greenhill Books, London, 1993)

Woodruff, Philip, *The Men Who Ruled India* (2 vols. Jonathan Cape, London, 1953)

9. BROWN ENGLISHMEN

Furneaux, Robin Smith, *William Wilberforce* (Hamilton, London, 1974)

Mill, James, *The History of British India* (1818, 4th edn, 8 vols, 1840)

Millgate, *Jane, Macaulay* (Routledge, London, 1973)

Mitra, Chandran, *Constant Glory, La Martiniere Saga 1836–1986* (Oxford University Press, India, 1987)

Mitra, Debendra B., *The Cotton Weavers of Bengal 1757–1833* (Firma KLM, Calcutta, 1978)

Rajan, Balachandra, *Under Western Eyes: India from Milton to Macaulay* (Duke University Press, Durham N.C., 1999)

AFTERWORD

Edwardes, Michael, *Red Year* (Hamish Hamilton, London, 1973)

Hibbert, Christopher, *The Great Mutiny: India 1857* (Allen Lane, 1978)

Hunter, Sir William Wilson, *A Brief History of the Indian Peoples* (21st edn, Oxford, 1895)

INDIAN ENGLISH DICTIONARIES

Yule, H. and Burnell, A.C. ed., *Hobson-Jobson: a Glossary of Colloquial Anglo-Indian words and Phrases* (Routledge, London, 1983)

Lewis, Ivor, Sahibs, *Nabobs and Boxwallahs: A Dictionary of the Words of Anglo-India* (Oxford University Press, Oxford, 1991)

ACKNOWLEDGEMENTS

A book like this has one name on the cover, but it is in fact the result of massive collaboration. It is rooted in the inspiration, research, creativity and sheer stamina of my colleagues at Takeaway Media, makers of the Channel 4 Television series *An Indian Affair*, which this book accompanies.

Back in the last century, Tim Gardam, Neil Cameron and I had breakfast and discovered we shared a fascination for Robert Clive and the peculiarly resonant entrepreneurialism of the eighteenth century. Tim and his colleagues at Channel 4 have supported the television project ever since. In its various phases of development and production, we have been grateful for the support and guidance of Pat Younge, Yasmin Anwar, Janey Walker, Narinder Minhas and Mike Flood-Page. Early in this process, Sandy Holton at Channel 4 encouraged us to think hard about a book and I was especially encouraged by her enthusiasm for the early treatments.

My colleagues at Takeaway Media have contributed enormously to this book, over and above the work they have

ALTHOUGH THE PALANQUINS HAVE GONE, HAND-PULLED RICKSHAWS CONTINUE TO SERVE CALCUTTA'S STREETS.

been doing on the series. *The Indian Affair* production team has, of course, fully shared with me the fruits of their research. But they and other members of the Takeaway family have also had to cope with my increasing absences from the office and have done more than I could have hoped to help me devote more time to this book. Warm thanks go to the India team – Jim Burge, Pratap Rughani and Yasmin Hai and also to Takeaway colleagues Jayne Rowe, Stephen Haggard and Tabitha Jackson who, in their different ways, made my life easier at the cost of burdening their own. Special thanks go to Zed Rafique and Lisa Soverall, who qualify in spades in both categories.

Charlie Carman and her team at Channel 4 Books have been supportive and unflappable throughout. Thanks go to Charlie, to designer Jane Coney and to Christine King, who copy-edited the text under great pressure and with great sensitivity. I am especially grateful to my editor Verity Willcocks, not least for her patience, care and good humour.

Over many years travelling in India, I have never ceased to be amazed and humbled by the kindness and hospitality of both friends and strangers. The research trip for this book was greatly assisted by Bob Wright who shared his fifty years' experience of Calcutta with me; the Principal, teachers and pupils of La Martinière College, Calcutta; Dr Pander and colleagues at the Victoria Memorial Hall, Calcutta; the Staff of the Asiatic Society of Bengal; the team at Annalakshmi in Chennai, who managed to reunite a lost wallet with its owner; and the managements and staff of the Tollygunge Club in Calcutta and the Fort View Resort in Srirangapatnam.

In Britain, I am especially grateful to Sir Anthony Bamford for showing me his home at Daylesford Park in Gloucestershire, formerly owned by Warren Hastings. I am similarly grateful to Mrs Peake for showing me Sezincote, the remarkable Mughal-style eighteenth century house in the Cotswolds. My thanks also go to Alan Tritton of the Calcutta Tercentenary Trust; Rupert Featherstone, Conservator at the Royal Collection, Windsor Castle; the British Association for Cemeteries in South Asia; Pat Clough for his photographic advice and assistance; the Staff of the incomparable Oriental and India Office Collection of the British Library; the art-dealer and scholar Charles Greig; and Ian Bremner at the BBC. I am particularly grateful to John Eskenazi, both for his advice for the series on Indian sculpture and, more generally, for his infectious enthusiasm for all things subcontinental.

This type of book owes greatest acknowledgement to other writers and historians, from whose scholarship it is derived. They are listed in the bibliography. Durba Ghosh, O.P. Kejariwal, Peter Marshall, Rajat Ray, and David Washbrook were especially free with their time and advice to the makers of the series. I owe particular thanks to William Dalrymple for generously sharing with me his ideas and insights, some of them as yet unpublished, about those Britons who 'went native', the subject of Chapter 5.

Some of the thanks I offer here are up to twenty years overdue. Lionel Knight first ignited my interest in Indian history at City of London School, where Jonathan Keates, both by example and inspirational teaching, nurtured an ambition to write in so many of his pupils. At Oxford, Tapan Raychaudhuri and Gowher Rizvi taught Indian history so engagingly that, though I moved on to other things, I always knew I would, one day, return to it. I owe equal thanks to Bryan Ward-Perkins, Peter Carey and Ian Archer for communicating the sheer intellectual pleasure of history. I have been travelling to India, on and off, since 1982 and have always been grateful for the hospitality, friendship and advice of Samiran and Mita Nundi in Delhi.

I inherited an obsession for history from my father, Hugh Baron and am enormously grateful that, both by example and encouragement, he made me realize how much it matters. Both to him, and to my mother, Wendy Baron, I owe more than filial gratitude. Though I have failed to emulate either in scholarship, I have, I hope, inherited their dogged determination and serious sense of purpose. This book would not have been possible without the support of Giuseppe and Laura Eskenazi, whose constant and enthusiastic grand-parenting allowed Monica and I to travel to India to research and photograph this book and to devote more time in London to the task than many parents could have managed. I owe special thanks and apologies to my children, whose dad was boringly always in front of the computer screen and who failed to write his book nearly as quickly as Hannah managed her India School Project or Ella her first book.

Finally I want to thank four people who, though they are entirely innocent of any of its errors or inadequacies, will be utterly responsible for any pleasure or insight this book might give.

Helena Braun researched the series with quiet but awesome tenacity and organised that research in such a way that no fool of an author could have gone far wrong. Oxford historian Maria Misra, who is both presenter and historical consultant of *An Indian Affair,* largely shaped its thesis. She has been unfailingly generous to me with her time, encouragement and advice and provided invaluable comments on the typescript. From its inception, the overall architect of *An Indian Affair* has been Neil Cameron, its Series Producer and my partner at Takeaway Media. Over the last two years, this series has drawn upon every ounce of Neil's stamina, editorial insight, creativity and management skills. His calmness, good humour and clear-thinking have been the rock upon which this book and much else besides have been based.

My wife, Monica Eskenazi, took many of the photographs for this book. But her contribution has been immeasurable in so many other ways. Monica's support, enthusiasm and love have sustained what otherwise might have proved a hopeless task. This book is dedicated to her, Hannah and Ella. And so, with all my love, am I.

INDEX

PICTURE ACKNOWLEDGEMENTS